A Sociology of Religious Emotion

A Sociology of Religious Emotion

Ole Riis and Linda Woodhead

OXFORD
UNIVERSITY PRESS

OXFORD
UNIVERSITY PRESS

Great Clarendon Street, Oxford OX2 6DP

Oxford University Press is a department of the University of Oxford.
It furthers the University's objective of excellence in research, scholarship,
and education by publishing worldwide in

Oxford New York

Auckland Cape Town Dar es Salaam Hong Kong Karachi
Kuala Lumpur Madrid Melbourne Mexico City Nairobi
New Delhi Shanghai Taipei Toronto

With offices in

Argentina Austria Brazil Chile Czech Republic France Greece
Guatemala Hungary Italy Japan Poland Portugal Singapore
South Korea Switzerland Thailand Turkey Ukraine Vietnam

Oxford is a registered trade mark of Oxford University Press
in the UK and in certain other countries

Published in the United States
by Oxford University Press Inc., New York

British Library Cataloguing in Publication Data
Data available

Library of Congress Cataloging in Publication Data

Library of Congress Control Number: 2010927169

Typeset by SPI Publisher Services, Pondicherry, India
Printed in Great Britain
on acid-free paper by
MPG Books Group,
Bodmin and King's Lynn

ISBN 978–0–19–956760–7

1 3 5 7 9 10 8 6 4 2

Cover illustration: Professor António Barbosa da Silva stands in front of
Kjell Nupen's stained glass window in the chapel of Ansgar Theological College,
Kristiansand. Photo by Ole Riis.

Contents

Acknowledgements

This book has been planned, written, and revised in a close and equal collaboration between Woodhead and Riis (the order of names is merely an accident of alphabet). Each of us had been working independently on religious emotion, and it was thanks to Kajsa Ahlstrand and a conference organized by the Church of Sweden Research Unit that we learned about our common project, and decided to embark upon it together.

We are grateful to many colleagues who helped us along the way, including Peta Ainsworth, Helen Berger, Rebecca Catto, Douglas Davies, Jan-Olav Henriksen, Kim Knott, Meredith McGuire, Shuruq Naguib, Enzo Pace, Pål Repstad, Le Ron Shutz, Jim Spickard, and Piers Vitebsky. We benefited from feedback when we presented our ideas at: the Association for the Sociology of Religion in Boston, Leeds University, the University of Ottawa, the University of Aarhus, and the University of Durham. Colleagues and students at Agder University in Norway and Lancaster University in the UK assisted us in many ways. Sylvia Walby and Mary-Jo Neitz were kind enough to read and comment on draft chapters. Andrew Sayer read the entire book, and we benefited greatly from his feedback.

The comments from the three anonymous reviewers for OUP helped shape the book at an early stage. Thanks to Tom Perridge at OUP for commissioning it in the first place, and to Elizabeth Rowbottom for helping prepare it for publication. Gro Anita Homme took many of the photographs and we owe a great deal to her skill in capturing appropriate images. The National University of Singapore enabled Woodhead to visit and photograph religious communities in Singapore. Woodhead would also like to record her thanks to The British Academy for a grant that supported research in Asheville, USA, in 2006, and to the Leverhulme Trust for an earlier grant that supported research in Kendal, UK, in 2000–2: these projects helped inform and illustrate the study. On a more personal note, thanks to Sandy for putting up with conversations on Skype and for being endlessly supportive.

Introduction

It may seem banal to claim that religion involves emotion: surely it is obvious that being religious involves *feeling* something? If someone meditates but never experiences a sense of equanimity, takes part in Diwali celebrations without being infected by a sense of joyous playfulness, or participates in a funeral without feeling even a touch of sadness or solemnity, something is clearly amiss. In the contemporary situation religious emotion is more visible than ever. Taking a religious tour of the world at the start of the twenty-first century, the journalists Micklethwait and Woolridge (2009) discover that it is the emotionally 'hot' forms of religion that are doing best, from Brazil to Beijing. Even in the exceptionally secular waters of Europe, it is those forms of religion that speak to heart rather than intellect that are attracting the most converts (Champion and Hervieu-Léger 1990).

Strange, then, how little attention has been paid to the emotional dimension of religion in academic work, relative to the vast amount of work devoted to religious beliefs and practices. The bias is even more surprising given how much interest was paid to religious emotion at the time when the academic study of religion was initiated. In an introduction to Rudolph Otto's *The Idea of the Holy* written in 1923, J. W. Harvey wondered aloud whether the sheer quantity of studies of religious emotion and intuition threatened to swamp the field. Such studies derived not only from theology and philosophy, but from 'Anthropology, Sociology, Psychology, and the history and comparative study of religious forms and institutions'. So completely had 'the almost purely rational and ethical approach' to religion been abandoned, he suggested, that enquiries into the nature of religion had 'tended to overweight the opposite scale'. 'Feeling', he fretted, 'has perhaps more than come into its own' (Otto 1917/1923: pp. x, xi).[1]

Harvey might have had in mind any number of contemporary studies. In anthropology he was probably thinking of the school that Evans-Pritchard (1965) later dubbed 'emotionalist', and whose representative R. R. Marett (1914: p. xxxi) famously claimed that 'savage religion is something not so much thought out as danced out'. In sociology he was referring to Durkheim, whose account of religion emphasized the centrality of religious gatherings and the 'collective effervescence' that they generated. In the psychology of religion, William James had recently published *The Varieties of Religious Experience* (1902), in relation to which James himself said that he was 'almost appalled at the amount of emotionality which I find in it' (James 1902/ 1981: 464–5). In theology, philosophy, and devotional literature there had also been an explosion of interest in religious emotion that went further than Mathew Arnold's milky 'morality touched by emotion' to put instinct and emotion at the very heart of things: Bergson's vitalism in France; studies of mysticism by Evelyn Underhill, Dean Inge, and Baron von Hügel in Britain; Rufus M. Jones's copious writings on the mystical element in the world's religions in America—and, of course, the work of Otto himself.

It is interesting to consider what has happened between then and now to make Harvey's worries about the emotional overburdening of the study of religion look so ill founded. Within sociology an important part of the explanation lies in the supervening influence of positivism, which led to a focus upon those aspects of religion that, like church attendance or neurological activity, can be observed and measured in a way that is dissociated from the personality and social position of the investigator. From this perspective, even belief, in so far as it can be clearly articulated and recorded, seems more solid and significant than feeling. In much empirical sociology of religion a concentration on church religion, and in particular on measurable levels of church attendance and doctrinal belief, reinforced the positivist agenda. Even for sociologists of religion who eschewed positivism,

---

[1] Harvey was not alone among his contemporaries is expressing this concern. To give a single example, Baron Friedrich von Hügel (1909: ii. 309) mused that 'evidences of a predominantly individual, personal, directly experimental kind . . . have hitherto been all but completely overlooked by trained historical investigators . . . now the opposite extreme is tending to predominate, as in Prof. William James's *Varieties of Religious Experience*'.

this bias towards the behavioural and intellectual dimensions of religion was reinforced in the post-war period by theoretical approaches like that of Berger and Luckman (1966), which interpreted religion as the means by which human beings render the world meaningful by imposing cognitive order upon ontological chaos. The 'cultural turn' or 'linguistic turn' in the social sciences from the 1970s reinforced the emphasis on language and rationality, and turned religion and culture into systems of signs that could be decoded apart from their social and affective contexts.

A belief-based approach to religion is now so well established in academic and wider discourse that it is common to find the terms 'religion' and 'belief' being used synonymously; or to read studies that assume that an inability on the part of individuals to articulate their beliefs clearly and systematically implies a dilution or diminution of religion. As its very name implies, the rise of 'rational choice theory' in the sociology of religion is not well placed to challenge this bias. Even in disciplines like anthropology that have stronger defences against positivism, and have done most to keep the study of religious emotion alive, a focus on meaning systems and socio-cognitive structures has led to some neglect of emotional, bodily, and relational factors. A recent shift of attention to the body, practices, and material culture has the potential to serve as a useful corrective; in practice, however, it often dwells on linguistic-mediations and constructions, thereby reinforcing neglect of non- or only quasi-linguistic dimensions of life. A bias towards the study of textually mediated religion has also characterized work in religious studies, though the influence of phenomenology prompted some awareness of the multidimensional nature of religion (thus Ninian Smart's analysis (1998) of the seven dimensions of religion includes at least the 'experiential'). In academic theology the rise of Neo-Orthodoxy has also tended to reverse an interest in emotion by rejecting Liberal theology's concern with the more experiential dimensions of religion.

The study of religious emotion is also inhibited by the natural biases of intellectuals and academia. As William James (1902/1981: 89) trenchantly put it:

The first thing to bear in mind (especially if we ourselves belong to the cleric-academic-scientific type, the officially and conventionally 'correct' type, 'the deadly respectable type', for which to ignore others is a besetting temptation) is that nothing can be more stupid than to bar out phenomena from our notice, merely because we are incapable of taking part in anything like them ourselves.

Scholars of religion have been characteristically interested in religions with texts, doctrines, beliefs, and literate male elites. Forms of religion or 'spirituality' that have more to do with supporting the everyday lives of ordinary people have been neglected by comparison. Yet the intensive study of religious texts remains a privilege of the few, and religions that speak to the emotions have more widespread appeal, including for those with little schooling and extensive experience of material hardship. The neglect of emotion reflects class, ethnic, and gender bias in the study of religion. Emotional labour, particularly care and concern for the feelings and emotional well-being of others, often lies in the hands of the least privileged in society, who are also poorly represented in the academy.

Given the combined weight of these forces ranged against the study of emotion, it is hardly surprising that the brief flowering of interest in the emotional dimension of religion identified by Harvey and his contemporaries was quickly cut down. What is more surprising is that there are some recent signs of regrowth. In the first chapter of this book we consider the recent multidisciplinary revival of interest in emotion in general, and, in the second chapter, the (lesser) revival of interest in religious emotion. Some of the reasons for this revival of interest are compatible with a positivistic ethos: most notably, the discovery of the significance of emotion by cognitive science, partly as a result of improved techniques of neurological investigation. As we will see, some of this work is turning our traditional picture of cognition on its head by suggesting that sensory and emotional experience is prior to conceptual and linguistic classification and abstract reasoning: we do not first conceptually map the universe and then act in it and experience it, but the other way round. Other causes of revival include the sheltering and stimulating influence of disciplines and approaches that have remained more open to the breadth of social experience, including the phenomenological approach, field-based anthropological and sociological studies, feminist approaches, and philosophical and theological work that has stimulated a revival of interest in classical and medieval traditions of reflection that take emotions seriously, including the Aristotelian and Thomistic.

Nevertheless, the study of emotion continues to be held back by the lack of a systematic account of emotion that can integrate relevant disciplinary approaches into a defensibly scientific approach—particularly for the human and social sciences. It is this lack that left previous studies of emotion vulnerable to the positivist challenge, which continues to render the sociological study of emotion marginal to the mainstream of sociological enterprise, and which discourages many scholars of religion who might otherwise be interested from taking emotion seriously. This book is designed to make a contribution in this area by proposing a new conceptual framework that can integrate social, cultural, and humanistic approaches, and counter charges that the study of emotion is impossibly undisciplined and subjective. It takes religious emotion as its focus not only because of its historical and scientific importance, but because it has such obvious power in social and personal life, and because it throws many different dimensions of emotion—the social as well as the cultural, bodily, and material—into high relief. Given this intention, the book is deliberately entitled a study of religious emotion (in the singular) rather than religious emotions (in the plural), because particular species of emotion such as love, joy or fear are of interest here primarily as illustrations of the genus of emotion.

A conceptual framework

In developing a conceptual framework for making sense of religious emotion our own disciplinary commitment—to the sociological study of religion—influences the starting point. What this means is that a widespread popular as well as scientific tendency to reduce emotions to something private, personal and subjective—to inner states accessible only by introspection—is rejected in favour of an analysis of emotion as constructed in the interplay between social agents *and* structures. On this account emotion is 'both–and' rather than 'either/or': both personal and relational; private and social; biological and cultural; active and passive.

To illustrate what is meant by this, imagine a woman employee complaining to her male boss about the fact that her case for promotion has been turned down. In the middle of the interview she feels tears welling up and her voice beginning to quaver. Noticing this, the boss wonders whether he is being manipulated into feeling sorry for her. He reflects that if he were in the same situation he might feel angry, but he would never allow himself to cry. He feels wary. What this example shows is that emotion is never 'just' about some purely personal, 'inner' state of feeling. The woman does indeed experience 'psycho-physical sensations'. She may find it hard to choke back the tears and she may go away and cry in private. But her feelings do not belong to her interiority; they belong to the situation as a whole (the lack of promotion, her position in the company, her relationship with this man). They register this situation, set her stance within it, and propel her to try to change it. In that sense, her tears do indeed have a purpose. In addition, the woman feels upset—rather than angry— because she has been socialized to feel this way in this sort of situation (one of frustrated ambition and/or perceived injustice, one in which a less powerful woman confronts a more powerful man). Innumerable social and cultural influences have been brought to bear over a lifetime to engrain the belief in both participants that sorrow is a more 'normal' and acceptable emotion for women to feel than anger or rage. If she were to become angry she might be categorized as difficult, emotional, or irrational, or even hysterical. Thus her emotions follow the social norm. This does not mean that they are any less real or 'genuine' than the anger of a man in the same situation. It simply shows that emotions express our assessment of a situation and try to influence that situation in the ways that are socially available to us. In other words, emotion is an essential part of the varied socio-cultural contexts that frame our ongoing social encounters and set pathways of opportunity and constraint.

In insisting that emotion is thus social *and* personal, we set one of the cornerstones of our approach. We also distance ourselves from the kind of sociological approach that stresses the importance of social construction or conditioning or structures to such an extent that it neglects the possibility of individual agency altogether. This enables us to recognize the value of both sociological and psychological (as well as some biological and neurological) approaches, and to offer a framework that can hold the two together. To a greater extent than many sociologists of emotion, however, we emphasize the two-sidedness of the relations between emotional agents and structures. Only in a one-sided situation are emotions overwhelmed or determined by society. In other circumstances emotional norms are strong, but not irresistible: agents can resist and change them as well as reproduce them, albeit in conditions that are not of their own choosing.

Despite what some sociologists and psychologists often imply, however, emotions are shaped not just by interpersonal relations but by our ever-changing relations with complexes of cultural symbols and material settings. Read any good novel and you will find that the mood is set not only by descriptions of human beings and their interactions, but by settings and objects. Our emotional life is shaped by encounters not only with living beings, but with dead ones, imagined ones, transcendent ones, and inanimate ones. To consider only self and society is to miss the significance of the culture, material objects, memories, places, and symbols. The study of religion is particularly impoverished by such neglect. Religious emotion has to do not only with social relations in the narrow 'human' sense, but with 'super-social' relations—such as those we may have with sacred sites, landscapes, artefacts, and beings.

In order to capture these aspects of emotion, the scheme we propose pays attention not only to the relations between agent and society, but to those between agent and symbol, and between society and symbol. We speak more of 'symbols' than culture simply because they are so important in religion for mediating between the human and the divine. Sometimes we vary the usage and speak of 'material-symbols' in order to capture the material dimension of a symbol—for example, blood, water, a particular place in the landscape, an artefact, a book, or a building. We also speak of 'culture' or 'material culture' as a general way of designating this whole category of extra-human significance, and of mediating between different academic discourses.

Thus the scheme we propose considers emotion as generated in the interactions between self and society, self and symbol, and symbol and society. As we will see, the relations between society and sacred symbol have received a limited amount of attention, not least in Durkheim's recognition of the importance of the relations between a sacred gathering and a 'totem' (Durkheim 1912/2001) and in Mary Douglas's exploration of relations between different types of social structure and different symbolic systems (Douglas 2003). Such work notes the importance of sacred symbols for collective emotion, and vice versa. Thus a national flag may be a powerful means of generating, focusing, and communicating national sentiment; but when such sentiment wanes the symbol also loses its power. Our scheme emphasizes the two-sidedness of the relation. Collective symbols do not automatically generate, shape, and sustain emotion in the way that is sometimes implied by Durkheim. Certainly a sacred symbol may serve as a powerful stimulus for collective anger, hatred, worship, or joy; but it is also true that social groups and gatherings may fail to be moved by symbols intended to stir them, may reject symbols proposed by an elite, or may turn cold towards places, objects, and rituals that were once the focus of collective sentiment.

The relation between individuals and symbols is more neglected in sociological study. More illumination is provided by psychological approaches such as object-relations theory and dream analysis, and, in relation to religion, by anthropological studies that analyse the emotional significance of selected objects and symbols for individuals as well as groups and societies. Without denying that there is a social dimension to the way in which, say, a migrant brings to a new land gods from his or her old life, we argue that it is also important to pay attention to the element of personal selection, election, and some-times resistance—and the emotional dimension of all these. Individuals carry 'in their hearts', and sometimes on their bodies, symbols that have uniquely personal emotional resonances: an icon, a talisman, a form of dress, a vial of holy water, a lock of hair, images of ancestors, photos, and so on. Such objects may assist personal emotional cultivation that reinforces collective emotion or offers an escape and an alternative, or both. In some cases individuals create new sacred objects: new representations of gods, demons, saints, and so on, and these may eventually be consecrated by a group and become the focus of collective sentiment.

As these examples show, it is often impossible to draw a neat line between personal and social-material symbols. Yet the distinction is important for opening up perspectives that an exclusive concentration on emotion in relation to society and its symbols closes down. Just as we reject the view that emotional structures squeeze out emotional agency, so by separating out the relation between agent and personal symbols we reject the view that cultural and religious traditions are hegemonic disciplines imposed on individuals by whom they are uncritically internalized. Cultural and religious traditions set para-meters and continuities, while allowing room for manœuvre and change through the manipulation of ideas and symbols. Individuals shape and modify symbols in a way that gives purchase over their own lives and personal dramas, while at the same time relating them to wider webs of symbolic and social significance.

The three sets of relations that give shape to our analytic scheme should not be interpreted as separate, self-contained processes. Rather, this way of conceiving of them serves to prise apart processes that are in reality closely bound up with one another. For example, in the actual flow of religious life, feelings are not stirred first in collective ritual, then through contemplation of sacred symbols, and later in the privacy of one's own home. Rather, a Roman Catholic woman may, for example, show personal devotion to Mary, whose statue she venerates in church, whose hymns she sings with joy, whose image decorates the main room of her house, and whose example she tries to embody in a life of care for others. Each element relates to, feeds back on, informs, and reinforces the other. It is also possible to think of examples in which the processes undermine rather than reinforce one another, and we pay as much attention to these 'disconnections' and their emotional significance as to the connections. Our tripartite scheme is a tool that can be used to make sense of the interwoven elements of such exchanges, taking them apart to understand them better, but not neglecting to put them back together and show how they relate, or fail to relate, to one another.

In what follows we speak of these three sets of relations as 'dialectical' relations, because they are interactive, mutually shaping, and often mutually constitutive. As we will argue, perfectly balanced or reciprocal dialectics are probably the exception rather than the rule in emotional life. A dialectical approach helps to clarify instances of one-sided relations and identify not only what is present in an emotional situation, but also what is absent or 'blocked'. Thus our scheme allows us to investigate not only why something does occur, but why it does not. Many social, psychological, material, and cultural factors influence an emotional pattern. An analysis of unbalanced dialectics can ask which forces are absent, what hinders positive feedback, and what leads to a negative feedback or a broken connection. For example, when a religious leadership establishes a new religious symbol in a sacred space, it is as important to be open to the question whether and why it fails to evoke the expected emotional response in the religious community as to whether and why it succeeds. Similarly, if individuals consistently fail to feel what is expected in a particular ritual setting, it is useful to consider whether this is because the emotional standards of the community are undefined or vague, or because individuals have become unwilling to accept the authority of the community, or both.

Emotional regimes

In order to hold together the different dialectical processes involved in emotional situations we propose the concept of an 'emotional regime'. This captures the way that emotions are integral to the structured social and material relations that constitute a particular social unit or setting—whether a business, a family, an Internet-based fan club, or a religious community. Like the wider social ordering with which it is bound up, an emotional regime has an internal coherence and boundedness, though it can enter a state of flux, imbalance, or disintegration. Regimes persist over time, and transcend individuals, shaping what they can feel, how they can feel it, the way they can express their feelings, and hence the forms of social relationship and courses of action that are open to them. In this way they play an important role in shaping and reproducing structures of power. Countering the widespread assumption that emotions are of little public or political significance, we build on the work of authors like Arlie Hochschild (1983, 1998, 2003) and William Reddy (2001), plus a growing number of political theorists, who point out the significance of personal and collective emotion in shaping relations and inequalities of power.

The concept of an emotional regime also allows us to characterize religious emotion in terms of the social and cultural relations that help to constitute it, rather than by reference to a particular type of feeling: whether the awe, thrill, and fascination proposed by Rudolph Otto; the solemn and expansive sentiments singled out by William James; or the sense of peace and calm that has more recently come to be associated with spirituality. On our account, religious emotions are first and foremost those emotions that are integral to religious regimes— and hence to their social and cultural relations. They may include any emotion or combination of emotions: hatred or love, anxiety or calm, grief or joy, terror or equanimity.

Characteristically, an emotional regime holds together a repertoire of different emotions, and specifies their rhythm, significance, mode of expression, and combination. Religious regimes confront the everyday empirical world with an ideal social and material order, and interpret the one in relation to the other. Setting personal and social life in relation to such 'alternate ordering',[2] they place human life in a

---

[2] This term, taken from Quaker theology, is discussed and further explained in Chapter 2.

perspective that stretches before and beyond a finite lifespan. In the process, religious regimes display, regulate, and enforce the standards by which some emotions are exalted and others are abased. They offer a structured emotional repertoire that guides how adherents feel about themselves, one another, and their wider circumstances. They educate and structure sensibility not only in relation to daily tasks and duties, but across the life course, and they help in the navigation of its transitions and crises.

As well as being a significant context for the formation, cultivation, disciplining, and expression of emotion, religion is one of the most important crucibles for emotional change and transformation, even on the part of adults. To join a religion is to experience a new way of feeling about self, others, society, and the world. Religious people learn to sound the emotional notes approved by the religions to which they belong, and to do so in ways that are authorized by their communities of belonging. In doing so, their emotional lives are formed according to an approved pattern of coherence, not through mere conditioning but through active engagement. Though they utilize endlessly different techniques and strive at an equally varied range of outcomes, most religions promise to transfigure emotional lives according to a pattern of order that is embodied and expressed by a religious group, its members, and its sacred symbols, both personal and collective.

We can illustrate many of these points by way of the sacred–secular example of Christmas. It is impossible to understand this festival without taking account of its emotional regime, in which notes of joy, benevolence, family feeling, relaxation, goodwill, humour, hospitality, fond remembrance, forgiveness, and loving warmth are especially stressed. The emotional regime of Christmas is engendered, in part, by established but evolving social relations: parties, family gatherings, family rituals, religious rituals (nativity plays, church services), civic and national rituals (street decorations and lighting; the message of pope, president, or monarch). These are interwoven with cultural and symbolic elements: special television programming, Christmas presents, food, alcohol, spruce trees, scents, lights, and music. The emotionally laden symbols of Christmas include the nativity scene, angels, Father Christmas/St Nicholas, carol-singers, snow, robins, reindeers, and parcels. Together, all these elements conspire to shape 'the Christmas spirit'—the emotional regime of Christmas.

It is called a 'regime' for a good reason. There are inducements to conform, and sanctions for non-compliance. Those who remain indifferent, grumpy, anti-social, or mean-spirited at Christmas time will come under heavy pressure to give a more appropriate emotional performance. Emotional dissidents are sanctioned and castigated as 'Scrooges', 'bah humbugs', and general miseries. The office worker at the Christmas party who refuses to wear a paper hat, sing carols, or smile threatens to lower the emotional tone for others. It would be better if he had stayed at home. Likewise, inappropriate objects must be excluded. Even though this is a Christian festival, no one would display the crucified Christ: the story of the Japanese tea house that displayed a crucified Santa is humorous because it flouts the unwritten rule. There is an emotional logic to the situation that must not be contradicted. It is possible to rebel against the emotional regime of Christmas, but not to escape. Those who 'get into the spirit' find personal and social satisfaction not only in doing so but in conforming to the regime. Those who do not are left to dwell on their feelings of loneliness, irritation, or defiant rebellion.

Dangers of reductionism

There are many dangers to be faced in developing an account of religious emotion, and several of them involve some kind of reductionism. The conceptual scheme proposed here reacts against three common forms in academic treatments of emotion: sociological reductionism, which reduces emotions to social forces and collective sentiments; psychological reductionism, which is interested only in individual psychic states; cultural or symbolic reductionism, which reduces emotions to cultural scripts and symbolic systems. Put more positively, the scheme we develop integrates all three approaches and seeks to broaden them by relating them to one another.

Even if we avoid these dangers, however, there is another to be wary of—namely the tendency to claim an exaggerated role for emotion itself. In a study of religious emotion the temptation is to reduce religion to its emotional aspects—especially when this element has been so neglected in previous work. Although this book attempts to demonstrate the importance of religious emotion, we suggest that the place of emotion in a given form of religion is an issue that should remain open to empirical exploration. There is significant variation in the degree to which different forms of religion are emotionally expressive and emotionally 'explicit'. At one extreme there are those kinds of religion, including most contemporary spirituality, that have as their stated aim emotional amelioration and transformation, and whose teachings, rituals, and so on are explicitly directed to this end. At the opposite extreme are forms of religion that make little reference to the emotions, and that play down and proscribe emotional expression. Some of the latter may be strongly practice based—what matters is doing things rather than feeling things—whereas others are more oriented to scholarly study and interpretation—what matters is knowledge not feeling. These variations are important. While it is hard to think of a religion that makes no reference to emotion (even to love, or peace, or lust), and plausible to suggest that even the most rational forms of religion have their own emotional regimes (which probably exalt equanimity and sanction emotional display), the genuine diversity should not be downplayed.

There is a further danger to be faced in trying to capture feelings in scholarly language. We have noted how the linguistic turn with its emphasis on discourse leads in this direction. Some historians of emotion have proposed an approach that considers not emotions but 'emotionology': a society's articulated and textually accessible emotional teachings and rules. This points to important truths: that emotions are bound up with language, that being able to put emotion into words shapes the emotion itself, and that emotional standards are often set in the texts, teachings, and symbols of an emotional regime. However, it is an intellectual's wishful thinking to imagine that language can ever capture and convey the complexity and ambiguity of emotion. Scholarly language (like this) is clumsy in dealing with feelings compared with the language of fiction, poetry, and drama. Emotion, including religious emotion, is expressed through ritual, music, art, and architecture precisely because rationalized language does not suffice. With this in mind, an academic discussion like this one must frankly acknowledge its limitations. It is easier to study intellectual aspects of religion than emotional ones, because the tools of the academy are honed for the task. But it is unfair to dismiss the study of religious emotions—let alone the emotions themselves—because academic language is unable to unfold the full complexity and profundity of emotional life.

Reason and emotion

We have left a final obstacle to the study of religious emotion to last—but not least. Put simply, this objection holds that all emotions—religious ones included—are irrational disturbances of our 'animal nature', which have more to do with the body and inner sensations than with thought and reason, and which are irrational and unintelligible. As Martha Nussbaum (2003b: 275) summarizes this approach, emotions are nothing but 'thoughtless natural energies'. As such, emotion is assumed to be not only difficult to study, but unworthy of study.

This view has been influential in much positivist and empiricist-derived philosophy and cognitive psychology. Its traces can be discerned in fields as widely spread as law, public policy, economics, and theology. Even influential writers on emotion have shared some of its presuppositions. For philosophical 'emotivists' like A. J. Ayer and R. M. Hare, emotion is an expression of personal inclination or disinclination rather than any kind of rational, descriptive, cognitive engagement with the world. Even for Freud, emotion is something basic and untamed that propels us from within and threatens to well up from inner depths and shake the veneer of civilized life. This view of emotion as a dark and dangerous force—a beast within—was anticipated by social commentators in the revolutionary era who feared the power of crowds, uprisings, and mob rule. The influence of books like Charles McKay's *Extraordinary Popular Delusions and the Madness of Crowds* (1841) has lasted to the present day. Faced by unexpected events like the upsurge of feeling surrounding the death and burial of Princess Diana, it is interesting to see how many people fall back on explanations that involve ideas about irrational foolishness, irresistible mob sentiment, dangerous and uncontrollable populism, and the hysteria of uneducated masses.

At the root of this approach lies a stark opposition between reason and emotion that goes back to the beginning of the modern era and has played an important role in structuring Western thought ever since. For Enlightenment thinkers reason held the key to progress, and unreason was the enemy. In so far as it was riddled with emotive superstition and priestly dogma, religion must be banished or reformed. Although Romantic thinkers opposed this view and attacked the inhuman and destructive potentials of reason, science, and industry, they often perpetuated the idea that reason and emotion stand in opposition to one another.

Such a dichotomous way of thinking was a child of the era of scientific discovery, technological progress, industrialization, bureaucratization, and colonialism. It is alien to other cultures and, indeed, to earlier Western thought. Classical thinkers including Plato, Aristotle and the Stoics had different ways of classifying the parts of the soul and the dynamics of human knowledge, and a greater appreciation of the rationality of emotion (Sorabji 2002; Nussbaum 2003a; Konstan 2005). Christian culture supported a biblical view in which the 'heart' is the seat of knowledge, and the cultivation of sentiment is an essential part of the quest for wisdom and truth. In a long tradition of practical and theological reflection, unruly and uncontrollable 'passions' are seen as the enemy of both knowledge and righteousness, and a right ordering of feeling—particularly of loves—as essential for discernment and discrimination (O'Donovan 1980; Dixon 2003; Rosenwein 2006).

Many of the serious flaws in the modern tendency to divide reason from emotion have been exposed in recent decades, not only by philosophy and a revival of interest in classical thought, but by developments in cognitive science. One of the intriguing findings of neuroscience is that, far from being the enemy of reason, rationality seems to require it. The neurologist Antonio Damasio reports on research that finds that people who suffer damage to part of the prefrontal cortex become unable to make a decision. In *Descartes' Error*, Damasio (1994/ 2005: 193–4) describes the process of trying to make an appointment with a patient suffering such damage:

I suggested two alternative dates, both in the coming month and just a few days apart from each other. The patient pulled out his appointment book and began consulting the calendar. The behaviour that ensued, which was witnessed by several investigators, was remarkable. For the better part of half an hour, the patient enumerated reasons for and against each of the two dates: previous engagements, proximity to other engagements, possible meteorological conditions, virtually anything that one could think about concerning a simple date. [He was] walking us through a simple cost–benefit analysis, an endless outlining and fruitless comparison of options and possible consequences.

Damasio concludes that without feeling we are unable to navigate the world and make sense of it. As the philosopher Ronald de Sousa (2003: 249) puts it, 'emotions are among the mechanisms that control the crucial feature of *salience* amongst what would otherwise be an unmanageable plethora of objects of attention, interpretations, and strategies of inference and conduct'. Even disciplines such as physics and maths seem to involve intuition, 'hunches', inspiration, and 'the recruitment of body-based, image-schematic logic to perform abstract reasoning' (Johnson 2007: 181; see also Lakoff and Núñez 2000). These conclusions are supported by work in the philosophy of emotion, which has undermined the non-cognitivism of the emotivists.[3] For philosophers such as De Sousa (1989), Solomon (1993), and Nussbaum (2003a), both reason and emotion have to do with judgements of truth and value and, as such, are amenable to evidence, and involve choice and responsibility. Like thought, emotions are *about* something. They deliver information about the world, and they may be true or false. Indeed, for Nussbaum (2003a), emotions are simply 'upheavals of thought'.

Why, then, has it seemed so obvious to so many people that reason and emotion are not only different, but opposed? One explanation is that this is an instance where our words lead us astray. They make it easy to imagine that 'emotion' and 'reason' are 'things' that can be located and measured and neatly compartmentalized. But it is a mistake to hypostasize the terms. Like emotion, 'rationality' is merely a collective term that directs attention to a range of processes and phenomena. In the case of reason, these include: 'collecting information, listening attentively, elaborating arguments, comparing usages, testing hypotheses' (Lash 1988: 63). Reason is affected by personal, affective, and experiential factors, just as emotion is affected by rational and linguistic ones.

But it is not only our words that lead us astray. So too do the social institutions and cultural practices that shape and embody our ideas. As poststructuralism has taught us, binary oppositions in language are linked to a hierarchical ordering. This is certainly the case for reason and emotion, where claims to superior rationality are used to justify unequal distributions of power and resources between men and women, adults and children, whites and 'lower races', humans and animals, adults and children, academic elites and 'lay' people, science

---

[3] By cognition we simply mean processes that deliver information about the world (whether reliable or not).

and the arts, and enlightened secularism (or rational religion) and popular superstition. Our knowledge is structured by these 'deep binaries', which often reinforce one another in sets of reinforcing pairs—emotion/reason, body/mind, male/female, and so on (Lupton 1998; Braidotti 2002; Ahmed 2004). This process is institutionally supported by the prestige and wealth of certain communities that claim to represent rationality ('hard' science, economics, the law, secularism) and the relative degradation of others (the arts, caring occupations, 'soft' science, religion).

This is not to deny that we can discern real differences between emotion and reason, nor that these also lend plausibility to a separation between the two. Emotion seems more 'basic' and inescapable than rational thought. It involves bodily sensation as well as mental activity. It can be affected by drugs as well as by external circumstance. Feelings can be powerful and urgent, and may seem to sweep us along in spite of ourselves. They may lead us to do foolish and irrational things, and they may seem beyond our control. In what follows we say more about these differences. Our view is not that they are unimportant, but that they are not as absolute as often assumed. Rather than imagining reason and emotion, mind and body, as ontologically different from one another, we can rephrase the distinction in terms of the emergent reflective and abstract cognitive activities—supported by certain institutional arrangements and disciplines—that we associate with mind and reason, but that are nevertheless grounded in, and shaped by, activities of bodily perception, movement, and feeling. Thus Calhoun (2003: 244) speaks of a 'rational cognitive set'—a set of beliefs that consists of reflectively held, articulable judgements—which constitutes only a small illuminated portion of our cognitive life, and a larger 'unarticulated framework for interpreting our world, which, if articulated, would be an enormous network of claims'. The latter is manifest through feeling and sensibility and action rather than in articulated awareness, but may nonetheless be accurate, reliable, and 'rational' (if articulated and examined). An important corollary is that neither emotions nor thoughts are primarily inner, psychic states—they belong not only to the mind but to *situations* that they help us to perceive, assess, and transform. Thus the study of emotion is complementary to the study of other dimensions of social life and culture, including the rational.

Method, scope, and focus

Since we had neither a theory of religious emotion to deduce from, nor systematic empirical material to induce from, our approach is largely abductive: it develops a probable explication of the varied and contradictory manifestations of religious emotions we see around us.[4] It is theoretically driven to the extent that we attempt to reconcile existing theoretical approaches, and it is empirically driven to the extent that it is informed by a wide range of case studies of religious emotion in contemporary and historic societies, both Western and non-Western.

Some of the data we draw on come from our own research: both empirical work carried out in contemporary Europe and the USA, and work in historical sociology of religion (from early Christianity to nineteenth-century revivals).[5] This is supplemented by many examples of religious emotion drawn from a range of studies and disciplines. While there is no attempt to try to cover religious emotion around the world in a systematic fashion, we have sampled emotion across a range of societies and times. As sociologists, our main interest is in religion in modern Western societies. But we could not ignore the benefits of considering emotion in societies besides our own, benefits that include rendering our own ethnocentric assumptions more visible; throwing into relief modern societies' emotional distinctiveness; demonstrating how the emotional rules we take for granted look as peculiar from the perspective of other times and places as theirs do to us.

Nevertheless, the book culminates in an attempt to make sense of religious emotion in late modern societies. We initially thought of this as a test of the conceptual scheme we develop in the preceding chapters. As we probed the subject, however, we became increasingly aware of its inherent interest. Not only is it fascinating to consider the place of religious emotion in late modern societies, but investigating the difficulties and opportunities it faces is also illuminating of wider features of our societies and emotional lives.

---

[4] Deduction and induction are in any case threadbare ways of understanding how we think, since neither takes the importance of concepts and conceptual and theoretical framing seriously enough. No one ever simply induces, and deductions are only ever as good as their premises. (Thanks to Andrew Sayer for reflection on this point.)

[5] A number of the contemporary examples of religious emotion are drawn from Woodhead's research in Kendal, UK (2000–2), which was carried out as part of a team comprising Paul Heelas (PI), Ben Seel, Bronislaw Szerszynski, and Karin Tusting, and was supported by the Leverhulme Trust; and from Woodhead's research in Asheville (2006), which was carried out in collaboration with Helen Berger, and was supported by a British Academy grant.

To clarify the plan of the book as a whole, it moves from the more general to the more particular. In Chapter 1 we start by presenting our understanding of emotion in general, and in Chapter 2 we do the same for religious emotion. We introduce and amplify our concept of an 'emotional regime', which is then broken down into the separate dialectical processes reviewed above. Chapter 3 considers situations where the three dialectical processes reinforce one another, while Chapter 4 looks at what happens when they become disconnected. Chapter 5 considers power and religious emotions, and analyses how emotions help produce, resist, and reproduce inequalities of power and status, both within religious communities and in other social domains. Having constructed this analytic framework for analysing religious emotion, Chapter 6 puts it to use in trying to make sense of religious emotion in contemporary Western societies. After a brief conclusion, we offer a practical appendix to guide those who wish to take the study of emotion further through their own research.

The time is ripe for a systematic study of religious emotion. Besides the illumination provided by the founders of the academic study of religion, we now have a host of empirical studies of religious emotion to draw on, plus a fresh impetus provided by the recent surge of multidisciplinary interest in emotion. Until recently the sociology of emotion has proceeded without much reference to religion, while sociology of religion has proceeded without much reference to emotion. This book illustrates the benefits of bringing the two fields into relation with one another. For the study of religion these include a more rounded approach to the field, and a correction of a long-standing bias towards intellectual and elite forms of religion. For the study of emotion, the effect is to bring some neglected aspects of emotion into sharp focus, including its role in motivation and orientation, the significance of collective rituals and symbols, and the importance of emotions for social change. For the study of late modern societies, attention to religious emotion highlights neglected themes, including the changing nature of sacred values and symbols. Overall, by offering a systematic scheme for interpreting and studying religious emotion, we hope to overcome the objection that the topic is too subjective to be treated scientifically, and show how much there is to be gained by returning to this fascinating subject.

1

Emotion: A Relational View

The word 'emotion' is helpful in some ways, distorting in others. Alternative terms bring different dimensions to light: 'passions' conveys the power of emotions, 'feeling' their embodied aspect, 'sentiments' the way they relate to character and education, while 'affect' suggests their passive and reactive dimension. 'Emotion' is good at conveying the dynamic, motivating force of 'e-motion', but tends to support an individualistic conception of emotions as inner states.[1] Although each term has its uses, none captures the full complexity of what it articulates, and we use them all in this book, depending on context. What this variety helps us to see is that 'emotion' is just another abstraction—like 'religion' or 'economy'—that focuses attention selectively on particular aspects and constellations of social, personal, and symbolic life. Contrary to the idea that emotion is a 'thing' that can be pinned down by the right conceptual tools or scientific apparatus, there are only more or less adequate ways of approaching the subject.

The aim of this chapter is not to capture the essence of emotion, nor to offer a survey of the extensive literature on the topic, but to lay the foundations for a sociology of religious emotion through conversation with existing work on emotion that we find particularly insightful.[2]

---

[1] This reflects the history of the word 'emotion', which, according to *The Oxford English Dictionary*, first appears in 1597, meaning 'a social agitation', and which gains the meaning of a mental agitation much later, particularly as it is appropriated by modern science. Dixon (2003) traces the development of the emotion talk, showing how 'emotion' has displaced talk about 'sensibilities', 'sentiments', and 'passions' only since the nineteenth century. Dixon's narrative postulates a rupture with earlier, classical and religious, traditions of thought, whereas Rosenwein (2006) finds a greater overlap between ancient and modern terms.

[2] For a useful survey of the sociology of emotion see Stets and Turner (2007).

Building on this work, we propose a relational account that rejects the widespread misconception that feelings are private, interior states, and suggests instead that they are psycho-physical orientations and adjustments within relational contexts. Despite our debt to the sociology of emotions, we extend its characteristic purview by stressing the importance not only of social relations, but of relations with material objects, cultural symbols, and environmental settings. This maximally relational approach is captured in the concept of an 'emotional regime' that consolidates our approach.

A multidimensional starting point

Part of the complexity of 'emotion' lies in just how much the term encompasses, including perception, evaluation, physiological modifications, expression, motivation, and subjective feeling states. Different approaches privilege different aspects. In William James's account (1884), for example, emotions are presented as the bodily modifications—such as a beating heart, sweaty palms, and a blushing face—of which a subject becomes aware. By contrast, the philosopher Robert Solomon (1993) presents emotions as cognitive 'judgements' about the self, the world, and other people; they are rational and accountable to evidence. Instead of treating such accounts as incompatible, a multidimensional approach views them as attentive to different aspects of emotion. For such an approach, words such as 'emotion', 'affect', and 'feeling' refer to different aspects of a complex phenomenon.[3] An emotion may well involve an inner state, but it is also a feeling *about* something or someone, such that the understanding of its object is an intrinsic part of the state. It is intrinsically motivating, and the motivation affects the intentional object and the situation as a whole. For example, one cannot see a sight that is pitiful without judging it pitiful, feeling pity (even though one can see that something is pitiful without feeling pity), and experiencing some motivation to act

---

[3] A multidimensional approach to emotion is now widely accepted in the psychology of emotions, as well as by many philosophical approaches, even though the dimensions are identified in varying ways by different writers. For example, Ekman (1994) and Ekman and Davidson (1994) speak of an 'affect-programme' approach and investigate the coordinated elements that make up an emotional response.

(though the motivation may not actually lead to action because of subjective or objective constraints). The communication of an emotion is also integral to the emotion, since the articulation of emotion affects emotional experience itself. Moreover, the actions associated with a feeling like pity change the relationship with the object of the emotion, and the emotion itself.[4]

Although different individuals often have differing degrees of self-conscious awareness of their feelings, along with varied abilities to articulate and modify how they feel, this does not alter the way in which emotional processes unceasingly communicate, monitor, and adjust our stance in the world. Emotions are essential to our constant, active bodily interventions and responses. In Latin they are called *motus animi*—movements of the soul—and in English we say we are 'moved' when we feel deeply. Thus we can liken emotions to a field of forces that attract or repel and that lead to harmonies, tensions, or eruptions. On this analogy, social life is a force field of emotional energies. Emotions are not confined to the heart, or even the brain, of the individual agent, but are integral to the flux of social and symbolic life. As we negotiate through the world, so we range through different emotional fields, shaping and being shaped by them in the process.

The multidimensional character of emotion is nicely illustrated by the range of practical and clinical techniques employed to modify emotional patterns. Psychoanalytical approaches rely on bringing unconscious emotions and memories to conscious awareness through articulate relationship with a therapist. Holistic and body-based therapies stimulate new patterns of affect by way of touch, movement, and manipulation.[5] Drug-based therapies modify emotional states and

---

[4] This account paves the way for an understanding of the moral significance of emotions. For Aristotle, to feel the appropriate emotions 'at the right time, on the right occasion, towards the right people, for the right purpose and in the right manner, is to feel the best of them, which is the mean amount—and the best amount is of course the mark of virtue' *Nicomachean Ethics* 2.6.10–12 (Aristotle 1932: 93). For contemporary statements of virtue and motivation ethics that learn from Aristotle's account, see Zagzebski (1996) and Nussbaum (2003a, b).

[5] Dog-handlers are well aware of the ways in which bodily modifications may directly affect or generate feelings. When a dog is put on the judging table to look its best, the handler will hold up its head and tail. The effect is to make the dog look and feel confident, proud, fearless, and perky. Similar techniques can be used to train a fearful dog to become more confident—by physically removing its tail from between its legs every time it becomes afraid.

dispositions by altering neuro-chemical balances. Group and family therapies recognize the significance of intimate relationships in ordering, disordering, and reordering emotional life. Spiritual therapies use various techniques to access transcendent sources of emotion-shaping energy (Sointu and Woodhead 2008). Cognitive-behavioural therapies work on emotional knowledge and change patterns of feeling by changing patterns of behaviour: like the Stoics two millennia before, they treat inappropriate emotions as the result of erroneous thinking (Beck 1991; Sorabji 2002).

The multidimensional nature of emotion is also evident in the biases of the different disciplines that study it. Psychological, philosophical, behavioural, and neurological approaches consider emotion chiefly in relation to the cognitive and/or biological individual. Literary, visual, theatre, cultural, and media studies are more interested in the symbolic dimensions of emotion. Social-scientific approaches focus on its social aspects. Any of these accounts can be reductionist if it considers its own perspective exhaustive. In the account we propose here, we try to take more account of a wide range of approaches. Beginning with analyses that consider emotion chiefly at the level of the individual (micro-level), we move on to consider accounts of emotion that pay attention to emotions in bounded social interactions (the meso-level), and then emotions at societal level (the macro-level). We then supplement these with approaches that take seriously the cultural and material dimensions of emotional life. Though our sociological bias will probably be apparent, our aim is to construct a multidisciplinary approach appropriate to the multidimensionality of emotion.

Emotions at micro-level

If Freud and the psychotherapeutic tradition must take the credit for making 'rational man' take emotions more seriously in the twentieth century, in the twenty-first century that honour goes to neurological and cognitive scientists, as well as to the linguists who interact with them. The continuing influence of a Darwinian approach, stemming from Darwin's pioneering study of *The Expression of the Emotions in Man and Animals* (1872/1999), has also been important, not only in behaviourist guises, but in the work of scientists like Paul Ekman who have attempted to demonstrate the ubiquity of a small number of 'basic' emotional reactions and expressions across cultures.

Such approaches to emotion have not always been well received in the humanities and social sciences. Opposition has been trenchantly expressed by anthropologists such as Rosaldo (1980) and Lutz (1988), discursive psychologists like Harré (1986; Harré and Parrott 1996), and sociologists like Gordon (1990), who argue that emotions are not inherited attributes but social constructions that vary across cultures. These critics argue that different societies have different 'emotional vocabularies' that engender quite different emotional experiences. In her study of the Ifaluk of the south-west Pacific, for example, Lutz (1988) discovered an emotional vocabulary significantly different from that of her own American society. In this society, for example, *fago* (something like respectful loving compassion) is the mark of manhood: when an American-educated relative returns to the island, his display of pride causes consternation, confusion, and sorrow.[6] Closer to home, we can make a similar point just by pointing out that words such as *Schadenfreude* and *Heimatlich* in German, *simpático* in Spanish, and *hygge* in Danish enable their users to *feel* differently from English speakers. Different ways of conceptualizing emotion in different societies further intensify the cross-cultural variation: where members of modern Western societies experience emotion as embedded in their psyche, members of other cultures, past and present, may associate emotions with certain bodily organs (such as the heart and the liver) or experience them as external forces, both divine and demonic.[7] Radical social constructivists conclude that we should speak not of emotion but of 'emotion cultures' and 'emotional vocabularies', and treat feelings as cultural and social rather than biological and individual.

There is, however, no need to accept the either–or between scientific and cultural approaches to emotion: in order to criticize biological reductionism it is not necessary to embrace cultural reductionism.[8]

---

[6] The central notes in the Ifaluk emotional scale are *fago, song,* and *metaxu.* Although these can be roughly translated as respect, love/compassion/sadness, justifiable anger, and fear/anxiety respectively, Lutz demonstrates—by describing their contexts of use—how such emotions differ from their Anglo-Saxon analogues. They do not, however, differ quite as much as the social constructionist wishes to suggest—hence the ability to translate them.

[7] See, e.g., Sullivan (1995) on ancient Greek views of emotion.

[8] Burkitt (2002: 152) argues that the discursive approach to emotions has more in common with an individualistic, neurological approach than it might like to admit by virtue of the way in which it discovers not a neural–chemical correlate of emotions in the brain, but a discursive correlate of emotion in emotional vocabularies. In this way it

The cultural should be understood as emergent from but not reducible to the biological, while the biological can be culturally modified. Interdependence does not imply reduction of either, or conflation of the two. To emphasize the role of culture and language at the expense of psychophysical components of emotion is to render many aspects of emotional life invisible or inexplicable: the fact that chemical interventions affect emotion must be ignored, non-human animals must be denied feeling, and there can be no account of how involuntary bodily expressions of emotion often contradict what we say—as our emotions leak out in spite of our words.

It is, in any case, false to assume that all biophysiological and evolutionary approaches, let alone all psychological ones, ignore the social and communicative aspects of emotion. Darwin's work (1872/1999) on emotional expressions acknowledges their social and communicative force. Physiological expressions of emotion are elements in a communication that are evaluated by others, whose reactions then provide feedback to the emotional actor, and thus serve to modify and adjust behaviour. For example, a girl who cries in front of her boyfriend is not only responding to perceived neglect, but actively attempting to modify his behaviour.[9] There is no need to assume, as socio-behaviourists like Homans (1961) tend to do, that emotions are regulated *only* by reactions that are rewarding or punishing, for that is to take an unduly narrow view of the possibilities of social interpretation and action. Even the most reductive behaviourism recognized that emotion is somehow relational rather than purely individual.[10]

---

perpetuates the fallacy of looking for a cause of emotions outside of relationships between self and others.

[9] Gregory Bateson (1963: 233) gives a much more sophisticated example and analysis: 'When I open the refrigerator door, the cat comes and rubs against my leg stating some variant of the proposition "meow". To say that she is asking for milk may be correct, but it is not a literal translation from her language into ours. I suggest that more literally we should translate her message as "be mamma". She is trying to define the contingencies of relationship. She is inviting me to accept those contingencies and to act in accordance with them. She may step down somewhat from this high abstract level by indicating urgency—"be mamma now"; or she may achieve a certain correctness by ostensive communication "be mamma now in regard to that jug": but, in its primary structure, her communication is archaic and highly abstract in the sense that its prime subject matter is always relationship.'

[10] See Griffiths (1997) for a useful philosophical analysis of the sense and nonsense in different evolutionary theories of emotion, including those of Plutchik—which he dismisses—and Darwin and Ekman—which he finds to be more robust, but also much more limited in its claims.

Recent work in cognitive and neurological science and in linguistics and philosophy is helping to undermine a simple either/or account of the 'natural' or 'cultural' nature of emotion. Even scientists whose primary interest is in the workings of the brain are starting to reject a picture of the mind as an immaterial, problem-solving calculating machine or super-computer in favour of an account that looks at the psychophysiological whole: the brain in integral combination with sensory-motor experience and higher cognitive and linguistic processes. Antonio Damasio (2004, 1994/2005), for example, argues against a philosophical separation of mind and body, reason and emotions, and applauds Spinoza's account of human beings as emotional first and rational second. Mark Johnson (1987, 2007) and George Lakoff (Lakoff and Johnson 1980, 1999) go further by integrating neurological findings into a philosophy of meaning that rejects mind–body dualism, correspondence theories of truth, and the privileging of philosophical rationality (see also Vygotsky 1987 and Burkitt 2002). They offer an embodied, activist, pragmatic account of meaning, truth, and language in which emotions and the body have a central place. On this account, we understand the world by navigating our way through it in a visceral, embodied fashion, experiencing it not by abstract mental representations but in active, physical engagement with people and objects that either yield to or resist our interventions. This immediate sensory engagement is mediated by 'image schemata' that are prelinguistic patternings of embodied motor activities that give a meaningful structure to physical experience, and that are felt rather than consciously reflected upon. These ground the metaphorical expressions that are the basis of language, meaning, and understanding. Rational reflection comes last, not first, in the cognitive process, and is dependent on prior sensory-emotional processing, rather than antagonistic to it (though it can modify and provide feedback on it).

In many ways this neuro-linguistic approach validates insights that had earlier been arrived at by philosophers of emotion working within the phenomenological tradition. Phenomenology, which 'interprets from within, as a lived experience' (Denzin 1984: 6), represented emotions as continuous processes of embodied, moral, en-cultured, self-relation to the world. The body is not merely a physical object for empirical scrutiny, but a lived-phenomenological body, enacted for others, and enacted for the self. Each of the different forms of the body provides a distinctly different mode of lived emotion. For Merleau-Ponty (1968), for example, the body is the site of a person's feelings and presence in the 'lifeworld'. The human condition of 'being-in-the-world' is simultaneously embodied, cognitive, and evaluative, and thereby involves emotionality. Physical sensations are interpreted as 'emotions' in interpersonal contexts, and emotion is an essential part of human relations that rests on judgements about the situation. It is also the means by which we reach out to others, give ourselves to one another, and connect intersubjectively (Merleau-Ponty 1973: 45–50). Denzin (1984) carries forward Merleau-Ponty's phenomenology of the body in combination with symbolic interactionism to show how emotions emerge in a circular process resembling the hermeneutical one. Previous experiences, the present situation, and future expectations merge in a self-reflective emotional consciousness. An emotional practice is an embedded and embodied practice that produces an alteration in the streams of experience, a practice that is both practical and interpretative. Emotions are not static, self-contained, or self-validating. They call for justification, and peoples' self-feelings depend upon their emotional accounts, as well as vice versa.

Phenomenological accounts of emotion emphasize the micro-social or 'intersubjective' nature of emotion (Merleau-Ponty 1968: 130–55). Here intersubjectivity refers to the reflective flow of individual emotionality from one person to another and back again. The mechanism is explained as a matter not necessarily of mysterious intuition or some 'sixth sense', but of developed mutual awareness, and skilled interpretation of one another's thoughts, actions, speech, tone, movements, and gestures. Denzin (1984: 129–59) draws useful distinctions between feelings in common, where people understand and share an intentional emotion (like grief over a bereavement); fellow feeling, where someone understands another's feeling and 'feels for' him or her; emotion infection or contagion, where an individual or individuals are unknowingly infected by emotions felt by others, but without genuine fellow feeling or emotions in common; emotional identification, where there is an emotional submersion of the self in another (for example, the relationship between a pop idol and a fan); and emotional embracement, where 'the intentional feelings of two or more persons are drawn together into a common and recurring emotional field, thereby producing the conditions of emotional and relational bonding' (Denzin 1984: 152). This approach recognizes that, in a shared field of emotion, it is often impossible to distinguish what one person is feeling from what others feel, and that attempts to study emotions solely at the level of the individual are bound to distort and simplify the everyday flow of emotional life.

Existentialist variants of the phenomenological approach add to these accounts a sharp appreciation of the active, chosen, meaning-making, and world-shaping nature of emotion. Emotion helps construe and create the worlds we live in: worlds that are quite different for, say, a depressed person and a confident one. We are not mere victims of our passions, but responsible for how we feel and what we make of the world. For Sartre (1948) emotions are active powers that shape our world in a 'magical' fashion. The emotional self cuts the cloth of the world to its own requirements. So a woman who anxiously awaits a friend exists in a world in which time is magically telescoped and she possesses her friend even before she arrives. Similarly, people blind themselves to experiences that would elicit painful emotions: they may faint rather than acknowledge something fearful; blame others rather than accept their own failure and shame; see a gentler person as threatening rather than acknowledge their own fearfulness. We believe certain stories and accept certain myths because they support, justify, and provoke how we feel.

Robert Solomon in *The Passions* (1993) takes this approach in a new direction by stressing not only our responsibility for how we feel, but the rationality of emotions. His argument is that emotions involve judgements that may be true or false.[11] He also proposes that, when philosophers talk about meaning, they are really talking about emotion, for it is our emotional stance that renders life meaningful or meaningless. Our feelings set our relations with the world. Nevertheless, we have rational and voluntary access to these relations, and can thus change or alter them. For example, a fearful person may reassess his unconscious judgement that no one is to be trusted, and alter the way he feels in the process. Solomon's greatest contribution is to

---

[11] Solomon's 'cognitive' account of emotion has antecedents and variations in the philosophy of emotions. Both Aristotle and the Stoics agreed that emotions are judgements—though the Stoics thought they were bad judgements (Sorabji 2002; Konstan 2005). For a critical survey of contemporary philosophical cognitive accounts, see Griffiths (1997). The cognitive account also has much in common with the 'appraisal' account of emotion in the psychology of emotions, an approach pioneered by Magda Arnold (1960) and developed by many others, including Richard Lazarus (1982, 1991). This stresses how emotion involves the appraisal of plans, goals, and schemes, seeing emotions as appraisals of objects or events that disrupt or further 'our best laid schemes' (e.g. Oatley 1992—for whom these goals may be personal or social). See also Martha Nussbaum's account (2003a), which is close to Solomon's in many ways, though more influenced by classical thought. Solomon's reader (2003) on emotions presents many of these texts.

develop a highly sophisticated taxonomy of emotions by classifying them in terms of their relational stance ('inner-directed' or 'outer-directed'), status judgement (of self and other), power implication (whether they empower or disempower), and 'strategy' (the sort of actions they motivate). For example, anger is outer-directed, judges the status of the person with whom one is angry to be equal (compared with scorn, resentment, or contempt, which position the object as inferior), and has variable power effects (sometimes leading to direct and effective action, sometimes not), and its strategy is to project one's values onto the world, condemn those who flout them, and thereby define the world in one's own terms. By contrast, guilt is inner-directed, judges the self inferior to others, is powerful in self-condemnation, is generally impotent to rehabilitate the self, and frequently turns outward in resentment. It has varied strategies, including a self-protective strategy of superiority and hostility towards that which provokes the shame (Solomon 1993).

The 'cognitive' approach to emotions, exemplified by Solomon and, more recently, by Martha Nussbaum (2003a), is a useful corrective to non-cognitive approaches that presented emotions as arational or even irrational. However, it goes too far when it ends up by simply assimilating a belief and an emotion, or a thought and an emotion. The solution lies in recognizing the difference between reflectively held, articulable beliefs—which may be emergent from emotional complexes, but are not reducible to them—and what Calhoun (2003) calls 'cognitive sets', which are pre-reflexively held, originally unarticulated structures of cognition, and which are 'felt' rather than thought. To have a feeling is to see the world in a certain way: through the frame of our cognitive sets (or image schemata, in Johnson's terms). This pre-rational way of navigating the world is how we operate for most of the time, and its unarticulated frameworks may clash with our articulated beliefs (for example, I may hold the belief that women are equal to men, but in practice subordinate myself to men by allowing them more conversational space and general deference). This pre-cognitive set or 'emotional structure' is cognitive, but unarticulated. It shapes a stance, and its implicit judgements can be brought to conscious awareness through education, techniques of 'consciousness raising', an uncomfortable awareness of contradiction between belief and action, and so on. Thus the cognitivists are right to reject a non-cognitive account of emotion, but wrong to go so far in the opposite direction that they elide the differences between belief or judgements and emotion completely. As Calhoun (2003: 247) puts it: 'Ordinarily emotions do go hand in hand with typical beliefs. But this is not because emotions *are* beliefs. It is because ordinarily we believe that things are as they seem.'

Emotions at meso-level

What we take from these accounts of emotion at micro-level is, above all, their recognition that emotions are not passive inner disturbances to be conquered by the power of reason, but active, embodied forces central to relational life—the relation of self both to itself and to others. The authors we have considered so far build up a picture of emotion as something that is not wholly outside our control, nor detached from character, reflection, and judgement. On the contrary, our emotional stance towards the world shapes identity, actions, experience, and thought, and is in turn shaped by them. There are feedback loops between perception, body, brain, and reflective mind that are more extensive and sensitive than had previously been imagined.

Given that they remain tied to the perspective of individual experience, these scientific and philosophical approaches have, however, less to say about the power of collective emotion and generalized arousal, and the ways in which group processes and structures involve emotional differentiation, interrelated emotional roles, and emotional juxtapositions.[12] Such issues are better addressed by studies that consider emotions in social settings, groups, organizations, and communities—a meso-level of analysis that has close ties to sociology in general and the sociology of religion in particular.

Thus it is Durkheim and Simmel who still have most to teach us about emotions at meso-level. For Durkheim, strong emotions lie at the root of all social and religious life. In the account he gives in *The Elementary Forms of Religious Life* (1912/2001), emotions are essentially social, just as society is essentially emotional. Feelings do not arise in the solitude of the human heart, but in collective, ritualized gatherings. When individuals gather together to participate in patterned ritual action, the emotional effect is so intense that it generates the

---

[12] For a helpful psychological study that takes emotions seriously at meso- and macro- as well as at micro-level, see Parkinson et al. (2005).

sense of the sacred. The awareness of sacred presence is nothing other than the overwhelming feeling of 'collective effervescence' generated by a united and harmonious gathering. As for the mechanism, Durkheim suggests that feelings generated by the collective process are amplified by being echoed by others, and that a loop of positive feedback occurs that builds to a crescendo. Such emotion, regularly re-enacted, and recalled in between times, forms the basis of social solidarity. For Durkheim this social experience also has a material and symbolic aspect: the 'totem' is the object with which the collective emotional peak experience is associated. Its importance lies in its ability not only to focus and objectify social emotion, but to communicate passion and become its focus in subsequent gatherings. The symbol serves as the symbolic carrier and stimulus of the sentiments associated with the sacred. Nevertheless, it is the social group itself that provides the main fuel of such collective effervescence; it must gather regularly to refresh the symbolic object's power.

Simmel (1912/1997, 1989/1997) parallels Durkheim in his appreciation of the role of social groups in generating religious emotions, but considers a wider range of social situations than ritualized gatherings, and gives greater weight to symbolic objects in the cultivation of religious emotion. For Simmel (1997: 119) the 'power and depth' of religion are found in its 'persistent ability to draw a given item of religious data into the flow of the emotions, whose movements it must renew constantly, like the perpetually changing drops of water that beget the stable image of the rainbow'. Whether such objectification takes shape in scriptures, dogmas, totemic objects, icons of God, or sacred buildings, it is a vital part of the process by which emotions are captured, stabilized, cultivated, communicated, and reinforced.

Durkheim's analysis has been revivified by Randall Collins (2005), who reads him through the lens of symbolic interactionism and social-exchange theory. At the heart of his account of social action is the idea of 'emotional energy' or 'EE', which he considers the motive force of all social life. For Collins, EE is generated by 'ritual interactions', which can range from sexual relations between lovers to a business meeting, football match, or memorial service. Such interactions always involve some expenditure of EE and other resources, but succeed when they generate more EE than they consume. They are successful when they are experienced as congenial and energizing by participants, and worth sustaining and repeating. For Collins all social life consists of 'chains' of social action, with emotional-rational actors feeling their way from one energy-enhancing interaction to another, while endeavouring to avoid emotionally draining interactions. Since emotional energy is generated only by social engagement, interactions have to be repeated regularly. Symbolic objects are, like batteries, capable of 'storing' energy, but they discharge over time, and have to be recharged by becoming the focus of ritual action once more.

Collins's approach is very effective in drawing attention to the emotional flow of social life: to the way in which we navigate social interactions on the basis of emotion, and to the extent to which society can be likened to an emotional field of negative and positive charges. His theory offers an alternative to rational choice theories, which imagine societies made up of rational actors calculating their individual interests, or behaviourist and psychological accounts, which focus on bounded individual psychophysiological organisms confronted by a range of individual stimuli. For such accounts it is the individual who is substantial; everything else is 'environment' or 'resource', whereas for Collins and Durkheim it is society that produces emotions. As Durkheim puts it, individual sentiments 'present the noteworthy property of existing outside of individual consciousness' (1895/1982: 2), and 'we are the victims of the illusion of having ourselves created that which has actually forced itself from without' (1895/1982: 5).

A different sociological contribution is made by Arlie Hochschild, who, like Collins, is influenced by symbolic interactionism, but combines it with a feminist standpoint, greater attentiveness to the body, and greater attention to relations between emotion and structured imbalances of power. Following Erving Goffman, Hochschild imagines social life as a scripted drama in which social actors play different roles, but extends this approach to take account of the 'feeling rules' and emotional 'display rules' that individuals must follow, and the 'emotional work' or 'emotional management' that they must perform in order to ensure that their personal feelings conform to the emotional scripts of society (Hochschild 1983: pp. ix–x). There are expressive norms for the expected display of feelings, but there are also norms of what we should really be feeling 'deep inside' (Hochschild 1979). A feeling can be experienced as misfitting a situation. We can feel too much or too little, or the feeling can be badly timed or misplaced. There are also rules as to the type, intensity, duration, timing, placing, and display of feelings. Hochschild gives the real-life example of a bride who feels nervous rather than happy on her wedding day.

Her distress is compounded by knowing that this is not how she is meant to feel. She holds an inner conversation: 'This is supposed to be the happiest day of one's life'; 'be happy for the friends, the relatives, the presents'. She looks at her husband waiting for her: and 'from then on, it was beautiful. It was indescribable' (Hochschild 1998: 4–8). Thus the bride successfully engages in emotional 'deep acting'. In surface acting we control our appearance; in 'deep acting' we stir up certain feelings and dampen others.

Hochschild emphasizes how much work is involved in transforming unconventional feelings or emotional displays into conforming ones. Social actors constantly intervene in emotional processes in order to modify them. Emotional life is regulated by how we assess our own feelings and how others assess us. Obedience to emotional scripts allays guilt, deflects disapproval, and sustains a positive self-image. Individuals are emotionally scripted from birth onwards. Children learn to distinguish bodily sensations evoked in particular contexts as emotions. Their feelings are shaped by reinforcements, role modelling, imitation, identification, and instruction until they become skilled emotional performers in social dramas.

Hochschild also shows how feeling rules set standards of what is rightly owed and owing in the currency of feeling. Such rules establish the sense of entitlement or obligation that governs emotional exchanges. In private life, we may have some freedom to question the going rate of exchange, but in the public world of work it is often part of the job to accept uneven exchanges. This leads Hochschild (1983) to introduce the idea of 'emotional labour', and to focus on 'the managed heart', or the commercialization of human feeling. She takes the training of airline hostesses as an example, and finds that they are trained to control their own emotions in order to make customers feel better about themselves. In a social hierarchy, negative emotions tend to be directed downwards and positive emotions upwards (Hochschild 1979). Thus an emotional division of labour reinforces social hierarchy and supports unequal distributions of power, including those related to gender, class, and ethnic difference. Hochschild argues that it is hard to maintain a separation between display and feeling over long periods. She proposes a principle of emotive dissonance, analogous to cognitive dissonance. People try to reduce this strain either by changing what they feel or what they feign (Hochschild 1983: 90).

Although Hochschild goes further than Collins and Durkheim in balancing the individual and social dimensions of emotional life (and in highlighting the theme of power), she has nevertheless been criticized for minimizing the role of individual agency, creativity, and resistance in relation to emotional pressure (Lupton 1998: 169; Bolton and Boyd 2003). Such critics point out the ways in which individuals can refuse to internalize emotional expectations (at least behind elites' backs), experience ritual as 'empty', or fail to be moved by sacred symbols and orchestrated gatherings. As Ehrenreich (2007) points out in her history of collective joy, although large gatherings have a unique power to generate emotions (emotions that cannot otherwise be experienced), the orchestration of collective emotion is extremely difficult. As one of the organizers of the Nazi rallies admitted, even a shower of rain could destroy the mood. Such critiques correct the view that crowds automatically become emotionally charged and that individuals are powerless to resist their emotional contagion, and challenge accounts that place so much stress on the internalization of feeling rules that acts of emotional resistance and non-conformity become inexplicable. Against the flow of some sociology of emotion, they remind us that it is important not to discount individual agents' ability to alter the emotional energy of social interactions.

Emotions at macro-level

Our account of emotion can be rounded out still further by reference to studies of emotions at the macro-level of society. Kemper (1978) offers a sociological theory that relates emotions to social structure. Its starting point is the belief that power and status are universal emotion-elicitors. He maintains that, since all social interactions can be analysed in terms of status and power relations, emotional reactions can be predicted by these two variables: for example, an agent's possession or exercise of excessive power will cause guilt, and of adequate power a feeling of security, while the experience of having inadequate power will cause fear and anxiety. Likewise, an agent's experience of having appropriate status conferred by the other will result in happiness, of having excess status conferred, shame, and of having insufficient acknowledgement of status, depression (Kemper 1978: 50–71). Although Kemper's analysis is effective in drawing attention to the way in which power relations structure emotional life, it has less to say about how emotions shape power relations.

Barbalet (2002a) complements Kemper in this regard by showing how emotions transmit social structure, directly affecting the status and empowerment of different social groups.

Social historians and historical sociologists have also drawn attention to the way in which shifts at societal level have emotional correlates, not by way of a general theory, but by analysing specific instances. In *The Civilizing Process* (1939/2000), for example, Norbert Elias draws on earlier historical studies, including those of Huizinga (1924/1955), which suggest that inhabitants of medieval Europe were not subject to the same emotional restraints as later Europeans. Individuals and groups might express intense emotions, or suddenly change their moods. Their emotional lives might be subject to external sanctions, whether from church or lord, but not to inner restraint. As Europeans became subject to the more centralized power of courts and states, however, their bodies and sensibilities became subject to greater self-discipline. Emotional culture was reoriented towards propriety and the restraint of expressions that revealed a person's innermost self. Populations learned to play their roles on the public stage and hide their feelings behind a mask, and they came to consider the body and its passions as impure and dangerous. By the early modern period, according to Elias, a civilized man was one who regarded himself as a detached, autonomous entity with a high degree of bodily control and emotional restraint.[13]

These macro-level analyses of emotion can also be applied to make sense of how social differences within society affect emotion. Norms of emotional control have never been uniformly distributed throughout society. Elites are usually under the greatest pressure to demonstrate an emotional self-control that confirms their control over the social situation. Those in dependent positions, including women, children, and 'lower' races, are more often expected to demonstrate humility, fear, gratitude, and obedience. They may have more freedom for spontaneous display of emotions, but overt expression of emotions like anger and resentment are rarely tolerated, and collective displays of emotion are systematically controlled and discouraged (Ehrenreich 2007). The

---

[13] Elias's and Huizinga's work has been extensively criticized by historians, both by those who find extensive evidence of norms of emotional self-control in ancient and medieval Europe, and by those who take issue with Elias's account of early modern society and his Freudian meta-narrative of the triumph of social superego over social id. Rosenwein (2006: 5–20) surveys the critical work on Elias.

display of emotions *per se* is identified with low status in some social settings. As Lutz (1986: 292) puts it: 'When the emotional is defined as irrational, all of the occasions and individuals in which emotion is identified can be dismissed; and when the irrational is defined as emotional, it becomes sensible to label emotional those who would be discounted.'

Elias was chiefly concerned with the period from the Renaissance and Reformation through to the Enlightenment. The question of how emotional cultures have changed in modern societies is taken up by a number of social commentators and critics, including David Riesman in *The Lonely Crowd* (1950/1965). Paying close attention to emotional characteristics, Riesman identifies three social types in late modern societies: the traditional, the inner-directed and the other-directed. While the traditional type conforms to emotion norms from the past, the inner-directed type is emotionally self-controlled and directed by an inner moral compass, while the other-directed seeks signals of approval from far and near. Riesman discerns a shift in early modern societies from the traditional to the inner-directed in a way that conforms with Elias's description of the civilizing process. But, according to Riesman, modern society has since undergone a further shift whereby the other-directed type has become dominant. All three types seek recognition and approval, but for the other-directed type this becomes the chief area of sensitivity: life revolves around receiving recognition and social approval, or being curdled with resentment when it is not forthcoming.

Riesman's study is focused on North American culture in the wake of the Second World War. More recent studies of societal patternings of emotion, particularly that of Mestrovic (1997), take into account the impact since then of new technologies of mass communication. Mestrovic's idea of 'postemotionalism' refers to a tendency for emotionally charged collective representations to become abstracted from their cultural contexts and then manipulated in artificially contrived, media-saturated contexts. This turns people into voyeuristic consumers of second-hand, displaced, manufactured, and manipulated emotions. 'Citizens' are caught up in public spectacles staged by opinion-makers and spin doctors who sell their campaigns by engineering synthetic feelings. 'Dead' emotions from nostalgia-infused tradition are purveyed as objects to be consumed. Under these conditions, anger becomes indignation, envy becomes craving, hate becomes malice, loving becomes liking, *caritas* becomes tolerance, and sorrow becomes upset and discomfort. Emotional display is rehearsed with its impact in mind, and emotional reference is made only by way of mediated fictions. The result is a 'postemotional' type who is incapable of reacting spontaneously to the present event. Like Riesman, Mestrovic thinks that late modern emotions are revised to be made fitting for the appropriate interest group.

The underlying narrative supported by the accounts of Elias, Riesman, and Mestrovic—that modernization involves the control, repression, standardization, internal policing, manufacture and manipulation of emotion—is contradicted by another set of analyses that focus not on the emotional suppression but on the 'expressive revolution' of modern times. Like Charles Taylor's *Sources of the Self* (1989), these accounts focus less on the Enlightenment than on Romanticism as the pivotal cultural movement of modern times. Modernization is understood in terms of a 'subjective turn' in which the inner depths of each unique soul become the locus of authority. A number of studies of the recent history of particular emotions and related institutions endorse this account. For example, Cancian and Gordon (1988) document how norms for the expression of emotions within marriage changed after the 1960s in a way that encouraged more spontaneous and 'authentic' expression of emotions such as anger and love, more equal emotional expression between the sexes, and a reinterpretation of love in terms of frank self-expression and mutual fulfilment rather than self-sacrifice. Taking as their stage the whole of American society, the authors of *Habits of the Heart* (Bellah et al. 1985) also drew a contrast between traditional–communal and expressive–individual modes of life and moral commitment, and lamented the growing sway of the latter.[14]

There are ways of resolving the contradiction between these competing narratives of emotional modernization. Lupton (1998) suggests that the intensification of self-control and bodily discipline has, as its corollary, the incitement of pleasures of transgression and expression. Thus modern tourist and entertainment industries sell emotional experiences, and vicarious emotional experience is sought through the mass media and celebrity culture. In other words, late modern pressures for emotional self-control are countered by calls for the

---

[14] A similar tendency has been noted by Champion and Hervieu-Léger (1990), Taylor (2002), and Heelas and Woodhead (2005) in their studies of how traditional forms of religion give way to more 'expressive' forms of spirituality in late modern societies.

'emancipation of emotions' (Wouters 1992). In certain social contexts the feeling rules harden, and in others they lessen and diversify: within a 'heartless' competitive society, for example, the home may become an emotional haven (Berger et al. 1974; Stearns and Stearns 1986). We return to the topic of emotion in late modern societies in Chapter 6. What is important for now is simply to note that emotion can be analysed as effectively at the societal as at the individual level.

Emotions and symbols

Having focused mainly on emotions in social relations, we turn now to the symbolic and material contexts and manifestations of emotional life. Most of the philosophers and sociologists of emotion reviewed so far have a tendency to overlook the importance of artefacts, myths, symbols, memories, landscapes, and material settings for emotion. As we emphasize in the next chapter, attention to religion makes it much harder to ignore this entire realm of culture and materiality, partly because religious emotions are so bound up with sacred places, temples, shrines, and landscapes, and partly because they go beyond ordinary social relations to include relations with gods, goddesses, ancestors, and other symbolically mediated beings. Religious emotion can even less easily be separated out from cultural symbols than other forms of everyday emotion can be detached in analysis from their material and symbolic images, stages, settings, and props.

Clearly Durkheim cannot be accused of ignoring the importance of symbols for collective emotion. Both he and Randall Collins recognize that such symbols can somehow 'store' emotions between ritual gatherings, and act as a shared focus of that emotion within the group setting. They also notice that the capacity of symbolic objects to evoke powerful emotions seems to increase with the size of the group for which the symbol is moving. The most powerful of all are those that symbolize and help constitute an entire society; they can be animate (an animal, a charismatic leader), inanimate (a national flag, a crucifix), or intermediate (a relic of a saint, a memoralized leader).

Inspired by Durkheim, Maurice Halbwachs (1992) took this analysis further by emphasizing the importance of the past kept alive in the present by 'collective memory'. He points out that it is not merely the collective representations of the present that shape social action and emotion, and emphasizes the dialectical relation between present and remembered past: how present-day concerns shape collective memory, and how memories shape the present-day concerns. Anticipating recent cognitive-linguistic work that highlights the importance of concrete images in cognition (discussed above), Halbwachs argues that abstract thought becomes potent only when related to concrete figures, symbols, beings, and stories, particularly those whose past existence is memorialized by rituals and symbols. The older a tradition, and the more people who recognize and revere it, the more powerful the emotions it can evoke, and the stronger its social impact.[15]

It is possible to accept the insights of such Durkheimean analysis of the power of collective symbols for collective sentiment, while going beyond it by giving more acknowledgement to the fact that symbols do not necessarily bind a society together, but can also be used to focus a range of different feelings, and consolidate different identities and interests, both of competing groups and of individuals. Durkheimean approaches recognize that collective symbols with long and widely established efficacy are a source of social power in their own right: but this also means that they can be used by individuals and sectional interests to criticize established power; be appropriated by those who stake a new claim to authority; or be desecrated by enemies.

An interesting example of the interplay of personal and collective emotions in relation to a 'collective' symbol is provided by the discussion by Wagner-Pacifici and Schwartz (2002) of the Vietnam Veterans' Memorial in Washington. The erection of a more traditional war memorial depicting male soldiers, symbolizing valour and victory, and inspiring pride and confidence, was rejected as inappropriate for a failed military campaign that had divided the nation. In the end, a small 'traditional' statue was added as a concession. But the main memorial was designed to commemorate not the conflict but those who had died in it. It was not war, but life and death, that were to be the focus of the symbol. It was designed by a woman, and it has no explicit martial reference. The plain black marble bears the names of the dead (originally, it did not even have the name of the war inscribed upon it). The effect was to make this national site a space not so much for the expression of collective emotion but for a wide variety of personal emotions—including anger, grief, celebration, solidarity, and protest.

---

[15] Halbwach's work is further developed in relation to religion by Assmann (2005), who stresses not only the social but also the cultural dimension of collective memory.

The memorial also attracts vast numbers of gifts and objects that individuals deposit there in a sort of symbolic exchange—including flags, flowers, and personal possessions. Here collective and personal emotions and social and symbolic relations twine together in partially scripted and partially unscripted and unpredictable ways, and this polysemic memorial elicits and supports many different, often opposed, feelings and stances towards the war and those who were involved.

Thus symbols do not always compel the whole of a society, nor act in a uniform way to stir a collective mood. They do not merely reproduce and legitimate existing social relations, but help consolidate new solidarities, and they may become a focus of rebellion or be used to express personal and even idiosyncratic feelings. Our understanding of the role of symbols in personal as well as collective sentiment has been enhanced by recent studies in the field of material culture that discuss quotidian symbolic objects such as clothes and ornaments in the context of late-capitalist consumer society (e.g. McCracken 1987; Csikszentmihalyi and Rochberg-Halton 1981; Csikszentmihalyi 1993; Küchler and Miller 2005; Young 2005). The subject matter demands an analysis that takes seriously the ways in which structural, macro-level, factors interplay with the most personal and intimate feelings. We can recognize the sophistication with which design, marketing, and advertising industries seek to elicit emotion, without concluding that personal feeling is simply engineered by these higher powers. On the contrary, a consumer product may also be a symbol for powerful and authentic personal feelings. When a woman tries on a new dress in a shop, for example, what she is weighing up is not just 'me in this dress', but how the dress will affect her relationships. She is making complex calculations about its emotional impact, taking into account the nature of her existing relationships and how the dress with its own particular resonances may affect them. If the purchase is a success, the dress may, over time, become a treasured possession that memorializes and stabilizes the emotions with which it has become associated (for example, a wedding dress as a symbol of a loving, or a failed, relationship). This object, this cultural symbol, is deeply personal, but not merely personal. Not only does it relate to the woman's immediate contexts of relationship (home, work, leisure, and so on), but, in selecting the dress, the 'consumer' invests in an image that has been carefully constructed by designers, marketers, advertisers, and retailers mindful of the signals the dress will give out, of the need to make those appropriate to the target market, and of the imperative to turn the profit on which the capitalist enterprise depends.

Thus symbols mediate, express, and shape social relations, and can take them in new directions. An engagement ring, for example, expresses, establishes, and consolidates feelings between a couple and wider society. It can be used in symbolic gestures that take those emotions in new directions and alter the relations that it cements— for example, if it is flung into the sea, or sold so that something else can be bought. As such, symbols are integral to emotion and social relations, and are not merely a sign or token of them. And their ability to carry intensely personal meanings is not separate from their enmeshment in the structures of late capitalist society, with its symbolic codes, moral values, and emotional expectations.

This whole discussion helps to clarify what we mean by a symbol. Above all, it supports a definition that stresses symbols' *connective* role. Symbols signify beyond their mere appearance or use by establishing relationships between the objects or events they bring together as complexes or concepts (Asad 1993). These connections are not entirely arbitrary, contrary to some forms of post-structuralist semiotics, but are enshrined by established authority, tradition, ritual practice, local convention, and so on. For example, the symbol of God as Father in Christianity makes a connection between a 'source domain' (a human father) and a 'target domain' (God) (Lakoff and Johnson 1993). By bringing them into relation with one another, it 'blends' them in a way that allows our knowledge of the source to structure our understanding of the target, but not in such a way that every aspect of the symbolic source (a human father) is applied to the target (Fauconnier and Turner 2002). Moreover, wider understanding of the target may change the way we think of the source (so our understanding of the heavenly Father may modify our conception of human fatherhood, as pointed out by Soskice 1985). Such a symbol is established and consolidated by repeated convention; its authority is related to that of the religio-political powers that consecrate it; it is tied up with wider patterns of gender relation in family and society; it links to wider liturgical, theological, and historical affirmations. And the connectivity between target and source forges further connections between those who venerate this symbol, between those who depict it and those to whom they communicate and, in the eyes of believers, between heaven and earth.

This is the broadest sense of symbol, but a further distinction can be drawn between 'signs', where one thing stands for another thing in an indexical way (for example, a red light for 'stop') or where one thing is a symptom of something else (for example, a dog bark indicating an approaching visitor), 'symbols', which are more open-ended in reference with a complex range of meanings, uses, and emotional resonances, and 'icons', which have such a close connection with that to which they refer that they bring the referent into being.[16] In religion, the latter sense is often most relevant. Participants normally relate not to a symbol, but to that which it represents: to God, a saint, a spirit, and so on. Here 'symbol' means not a carrier of a fundamental notion, but the 'target' itself. As Birgit Meyer (2006: 9) puts it: 'Sensational forms make the transcendent sense-able... [They] are relatively fixed, authorized modes of invoking, and organizing access to the transcendental, thereby creating and sustaining links between religious practitioners in the context of particular religious organizations.'

Emotions must be integral to this analysis because symbols shape and connect not only objects, images, and concepts, but feelings.[17] The 'source' of a symbol or metaphor is sometimes an early, embodied, repeated, and in that sense 'primary' human experience, like a child's relation to a father. When God is symbolized as a father, some of the emotional complex associated with fathers is transferred to the target concept. This may involve fear, affection, a sense of security, or love, but in a uniquely personal combination. Additional symbols for God and teachings about God within a particular religious tradition will modify those feelings, as the sensibilities of a religious person are 'educated' within a religious system. Thus God the Father becomes

---

[16] This distinction is influenced by Peirce's approach to semiotics (Peirce 1998). A human being uses a symbol in order to indicate something to somebody; symbols are used by human agents in the context of a symbolic community. The symbolic objects as 'representamens' can be regarded mimetically, as an 'icon' involving resemblance to the object, as an 'index', which has an indicative relation to the object, or as a 'symbol', which is a representation referring to an accepted code.

[17] Some treatments of aesthetics and art—literary, visual, and musical—consider the power of artistic objects and performances to express and evoke emotion (e.g., Budd 1985; Johnson 2007; Brown 2008). In an 'arousal' account, such as Matravers's (1998), the work of art serves to arouse emotions by effectively representing situations and relations in which such emotion is appropriate. Such relations may be with the material world as well as with the human: an insight that was foundational within the Romantic tradition; as Gerard Manley Hopkins (1959) expressed it, poetry that expresses the 'inscape' of natural objects and evoke their 'instress'—the unique force and energy that makes the appropriate emotional impression. Such reflections have interesting overlaps with 'rasa theory' in Indian aesthetics (McDaniel 2008).

an important focus of feeling for the believer, somewhat independent of what believers might feel for an actual parent. So important may this relationship be for the believer, that the emotions related to God (for example, trusting confidence) may shape believers' stance in the rest of life, including towards earthly fathers. Thus an emotional complex drawn from one domain of life (here, the religious) impacts back upon sensibilities in other domains (for example, the family), as well as vice versa, with a symbol connecting the two, as well as opening up to wider symbolic links and associations.

Every human experience takes place within a vast background of cultural presuppositions. Cultural assumptions, values, beliefs, and symbols are not a conceptual overlay upon some 'basic' or 'naked' experience. However, even if we grant the culture-laden nature of experience, we can still make distinctions between experiences that are 'more' cultural (like attending a wedding) or 'more' physical (like having sex), and we should not let an interest in symbols blind us to their material dimensions, nor to the impact of material things and places upon emotional life in general.[18] Archaeology is particularly good at stressing the importance of material things qua things: Schiffer (1999: 5), for example, asks why social scientists lavish such attention on sounds and the artefacts that encode them, while ignoring all the other human–artefact interactions? Artefacts, he argues, have irreducibly material as well as symbolic dimensions: a cup is still a certain sort of material thing as well as a symbol with social significance. Roy Rappaport, in his anthropology of ritual, develops this point in relation to emotion. 'It almost goes without saying', he writes, 'that the significata [targets] of ritual representations ... are generally capable of arousing strong emotions.' But 'also obvious, but less frequently remarked upon ... is that the physical nature of some signs themselves, distinct from their significata, carry consciousness away from rational thought toward an awareness characterized more by feeling than by logic' (Rappaport 1999: 259). Rappaport gives the example of the ritual

---

[18] Semiotics, being largely concerned with 'immaterial' language and concepts, has a tendency to neglect this aspect of symbols, and this combines with a tendency in the social sciences more generally to neglect the dimensions of social life. Even in recent studies of material culture the manufacture and use of artefacts are often of interest only for what they tell us about cultural meanings and social relations (e.g. Appadurai 1986; McCracken 1988; Ditmar 1992; Miller 1998). Actor-Network Theory is an interesting departure from this tendency, above all in its insistence on the agency of material, non-human 'actants', and in its interest in the interlinking of 'material' and 'semiotic' relations (e.g. Law and Hassard 1999; Latour 2005). Other disciplines ram home the point.

slaughter and cooking of a pig. The blood, the noise, the food products are, he suggests, inherently 'moving'. He asks: 'whereas wine may be used to represent blood, what can blood itself be representing? Or semen?.... [They] may constitute attempts to push past representation in all its forms to naked, immediate existence' (Rappaport 1999: 261). Recent work on emotion by geographers has also been effective in reminding us of the emotional significance not only of symbolic spaces, but of physical spaces, including natural landscapes, buildings, interiors, and cityscapes (Davidson et al. 2005; Smith et al. 2009). This is not to suggest that there is any completely 'raw' experience of the material world, only to guard against the intellectual's tendency to focus on words, concepts, and culture to the neglect of material–symbolic dimensions of life and their emotional significance.

Emotions, language, and inarticulacy

Just as emotions can be stabilized, objectified, communicated, and shaped by symbolic–material objects, so they can by language. As we have seen, there is no need to draw a sharp distinction between linguistic and non-linguistic forms of communication, since both arise from something more basic, more emotional, and more embodied—namely, those patterns of bodily situational encounter, relation, and discrimination that Johnson (1987) calls 'image schemata'. As Gendlin (1997) argues, the 'continent of feeling' that underlies all meaning, thought, and symbolic expression is not straightforwardly prelinguistic, and the 'felt sense' of a situation is not utterly distinct from words or forms or distinctions. If that were so, we could not have a sense of symbolic expressions as appropriate or inappropriate to the developing meaning of a situation.

This 'felt sense' is full of proto-linguistic possibilities related to patterns of embodied motor activities that give a meaningful structure to physical experience. These possibilities relate to the patterned, recurrent relations between our selves and our social and material settings, which take shape as meaning structures through which our world begins to exhibit a measure of coherence, regularity, and intelligibility. Visual images may be the most basic and compact means by which we bring such patterns to consciousness—and semi-consciousness in dreams—but they can also be articulated by way of words and abstract concepts. As noted above, the two are in fact closely linked, since language works through metaphors—by extending the meaning of a set of more basic, bodily experiences to capture other, related, meanings. Thus image-schema are felt, embodied, understandings of the world that are open to articulation in images and words.

Although the felt sense of life constitutes our most basic form of engagement with the world, it is nevertheless significantly shaped by language, which is not incidental to emotion, but integral to it. This is clear in relation to emotional expression itself. If I express how I feel in words or pictures or bodily enactment, I feel differently, and thereby change my relations with myself and other people and things. If, for example, I respond to another person's rudeness by saying 'that makes me angry', I do not merely issue a report, but position myself in a certain way, attempting to alter the way in which that person behaves towards me. Making this statement rather than expressing my anger physically suggests that I have some awareness and mastery of my emotions, which places pressure on the person who is addressed to make an appropriate response. By expressing personal feelings through a common language, these feelings are interpreted and presented within the shared framework of emotional language. Words have an even closer relation to emotion when used to articulate it directly—as when a person screams 'no!' in response to bad news, swears in frustration, or exclaims 'hallelujah!' in triumph. Such articulations are part of the emotion itself, just as dancing is part of joy and crying is part of sorrow. Similarly, traditional, socially revered linguistic formations can signify emotions independently of the meaning of the words: for example, recitation of the Vedas in Sanskrit for Hindus, or the Mass in Latin for Catholics. Just as meaning can be concentrated material symbolization, so sets of words can become cultural objects with the same power to move and motivate: 'God bless America', 'God save the Queen', 'I have a dream'.

Language can also be used not to express but to conceal feelings and give a false impression of how I stand in relation to others. I can exclaim, 'how lovely to see you!', 'congratulations: I'm so happy for you', or 'I have no interest in material possessions', while having far more complex and contradictory feelings. Politeness and the protocols of good behaviour dictate that people should dissemble in order to avoid hurting others' feelings, while political wisdom ensures that people conceal feelings that might compromise their wider aims. Given human beings' and other animals' expertise in reading emotions from bodily signals, however, it takes the skill of a good actor and manipulator not only to say the right things but to bring body, behaviour, and words into line.

This discussion of emotions, cultural symbols, and language reminds us that human lives are characterized by emotional indeterminacy, which articulation in words and images helps to control. In reality we are often uncertain about how we feel, and need help to work it out. Even when we have some firm grasp on how we feel, we may struggle to clarify our emotions and their consequences. As even William James acknowledges, one reason for such indeterminacy is that physiology alone rarely determines emotion (Carrette 2008). We have no clear touchstones by which to identify our feelings; the causes of those feelings are often mixed or unclear, and our language for expressing them is inadequate. Rosenberg (1990) analyses the various means by which we try to make sense of our emotional experience: by trying to identify the causes of our emotion, searching out social consensus (for example, what others feel about the situation, what similar cultural scenarios tell us), and thinking through the consequences of making one interpretation rather than another. The consequences of emotional determination can be momentous: for example, between interpreting feelings about a marriage as an inconsequential irritation, or a fundamental dissatisfaction.

It is this emotional indeterminacy that explains, in part, why the common tendency to treat emotions 'like stones or ponds or static objects that are given labels' (Denzin 1984: 26) is so misleading. It is equally mistaken to imagine that the general field of emotion can be subdivided into ever more complex general classifications of emotions. Fear, shame, pity, and so on are culturally contingent words with which we try, with varying degrees of inadequacy, to capture aspects of shifting social and material relationships and associated image-schema that always exceed the capacity of our words.[19] Labels such as 'love', 'fear', 'guilt' are never more than loosely fitting umbrella

---

[19] Burkitt (2002) draws a distinction between 'emotions' as the articulated forms of lived emotional experience, and 'feelings' or 'structures of feeling' as the embodied judgements that are expressed as 'emotions'. It is interesting to note that this is the exact opposite of the position advocated by Damasio (2004), who speaks of bodily responses to stimuli mediated through lower brain senses as 'emotions', and higher-level monitoring in the neocortex of such emotions as 'feeling' (the latter being, in his view, the key to consciousness). This linguistic disagreement is symptomatic of a larger disagreement between Damasio's approach to emotions (as discrete inner states of individuals), and our more contextual, cultural, relational account.

terms. It is very rare to have a pure feeling. We are much more likely to feel, say, a mix of grief and relief, or of affection and irritation, or righteous indignation and jealousy. Moreover, even when feelings are less mixed, the use of a single emotion term obscures the differences between feeling, say, love for a dog, for a motorcycle, and for Krishna. This is not to deny that the articulation of emotion is vitally important, but to explain why it remains an art rather than a science.

Emotional regimes

Pulling together the threads so far, we have been developing an account of emotion in dialogue with a wide range of sources (additional sources from the study of religion are discussed in the next chapter). We have argued that 'emotion' is a label for a range of coordinated psychophysical elements, in and through which we relate to other beings and symbols, and in terms of which they relate to us. By virtue of group processes, societal structures, and cultural symbols, emotions also attain intersubjective and supra-individual status, and can be analysed at a range of social scales. Far from being merely inner, private states of the individual, they are generated in interactions between self, society, and objects. There is constant feedback between three elements, resulting in mutual readjustment.

We can consolidate this approach by way of the concept of an emotional regime, as sketched in the Introduction. In acknowledging the coherence, transcendence, and inner logic of emotional structures, this concept has a good deal in common with existing notions of 'emotional culture', 'affective discourses', 'emotional vocabulary', and 'emotionology' (on the latter, see Stearns and Stearns 1985).[20] Unlike these, however, it focuses not only on the cultural sediments of an emotional order, but on the way in which emotional norms are articulated through an entire socio-symbolic structure (such as a business, a family, a religious group).

At the heart of any emotional regime is a unique 'emotional programme'. Using a musical analogy, we can say that such a programme

---

[20] Stearns and Stearns (1985: 813) define emotionology as 'the attitudes or standards that a society, or a definite group within a society, maintains through basic emotions and their appropriate expression; ways that institutions reflect and encourage these attitudes in human conduct'.

is characterized by a distinctive 'scale' of emotional notes. Some have dominant notes of fear, competitiveness, and envy; others of excitement, joy, and fun. Comprehensive programmes—like those of world religions—organize emotional notes into sustainable harmonies. The simplest type of social interplay consists of a monophony, where all participants sound the same notes in the same key. It is more complex to form a harmony with different emotional parts. Since harmonic expressions demand special training and collaboration, participants notice immediately if one emotional performer is out of tune; but successful expressions allow participants to blend feelings in a satisfying unity.

Although every regime has its own emotional programme, not all members of the group are necessarily expected—or allowed—to sound the same emotional notes or play the same emotional roles. The individual is not usually an emotional microcosm for the group, but plays a delimited part in its overall emotional drama. There is room for innovation and variation in playing this role, but not in taking over another person's part, especially not a more powerful part. Jennifer Pierce's research (1995) on emotions in American law firms illustrates this when she finds that the female paralegals must follow quite different emotional rules from the more powerful male lawyers. The former must display care for the lawyers and clients, be constantly patient, cheerful, warm, and nurturing, and avoid displays of anger. By contrast, the male lawyers play the role of the 'Rambo litigator': confident, forceful, competitive, and sometimes angry—some report that they 'psyche themselves up to get mad' prior to a trial (Pierce 1995: 62). But when roles get confused, as when a woman lawyer behaves in a Rambo style, it creates a disharmony in the rehearsed symphony of the law firm, and provokes harsh criticism and sanctions.

As this example shows, emotional 'regimes' go beyond mere programmes by virtue of the fact that their patterns of feeling are enforced by various means. In some regimes emotional standards may be imposed by hierarchical authority, with rulers, teachers, parents, and experts defining standards for an acceptable level of emotions, and punishing disobedience. Emotional conventions can also be set by less formal guidance and more subtle sanctions. Much emotional training occurs through observation and imitation rather than through overt instruction. Those who fail to conform may be sanctioned by no more than a disapproving look or a frosty atmosphere.

Thus Pierce (1995: 99) notes how female paralegals who slip out of emotional role are often greeted with a jokey: 'Why aren't you smiling today?'; 'What's the matter with you, give me a smile!'; 'You look like someone just died.' In individualized modern societies unauthorized emotions are less likely to be blamed on outside agencies (demons, ghosts, ancestors, collective sinfulness) than taken as an indication that an 'individual' is confused, weird, sick, unreliable, crazy, or perverted, and in need of professional, including medical, treatment. As well as sanctioning unauthorized emotions, emotional regimes offer rewards for appropriate emotional display. Those who exhibit the correct emotions in the right settings at the right times and in the right ways receive formal and informal approval. There is extensive informal guidance and help for those who wish to develop these skills in modern societies, including self-help literature and different forms of therapy and techniques of 'self-improvement'. Emotional proficiency need not consist in blind conformity. Emotional creativity and even a degree of subversion of emotional expectations may be acceptable or even highly valued, so long as the underlying rules of the regime are not fundamentally threatened.

It is not only human authorities that set the standards in an emotional regime. Cultural symbols have independent force, and are often hard to countermand. For example, a priest operating in a draughty Victorian church with stiff wooden benches and life-size representations of the crucified Christ cannot easily introduce notes of relaxation, warmth, and fun. Past customs and traditions also help set emotional tone, not only through their continuing material presence, but in the passing-on of established ways of relating and feeling. Standards in surrounding and intersecting emotional regimes also have to be taken into account, in case an unendurable emotional dissonance is created. While it may be possible for individuals to compartmentalize their emotional lives across different regimes—going, say, to a rave on Friday night and a High Mass the following evening—the tension may become so great that one form of participation has to be abandoned.

Emotional regimes exist at all levels of society. Contrary to Reddy (2001), who introduces the term 'emotional regime' in his study of revolutionary France but restricts it to an ordering imposed by a state, we speak of emotional regimes at a range of scales, from that of a family to that of an international organization. A regime is not necessarily singular in a given territory, and there is often a plurality of overlapping and even contradictory emotional regimes in a single time and place. At the macro-level, societies are likely to have extensive, wide-reaching emotional regimes that form a context for a plethora of different regimes at meso- and micro-level. In the case of nation-state societies, such macro-regimes are bound up with socio-material orders constituted by, for example, national political institutions, national symbolic institutions such as monarchy and presidency, national customs and rituals like those memorializing wars and revolutions, and national or transnational cultural norms and symbols, as well as materially supported practices of citizenship such as carrying a passport or ID, or being able to vote. Migrant groups and diasporas transport their own national or transnational emotional regimes, but combine, blend, and rework emotional regimes in their countries of settlement, introducing new forms of emotionality in the process (see, e.g., Warner 2002). Meso-level emotional regimes may nest within the macro-level regime and complement it, may offer emotional alternatives, or may form more complex relations. There is enormous variation in the relations between different meso-level emotional regimes. There can be violent clashes, uncomfortable compartmentalization, or peaceful coexistence and complementarity. At the micro-level, even the most apparently 'private' emotions occur within the framework of wider emotional regimes, whose impress they bear. To take a much-analysed example, the intimate emotional expectations and roles associated with romantic love between a man and a woman are shaped by a wider emotional regime that is carried not only by surrounding social relations, but by a plethora of cultural symbols, material objects, and embodied practices (e.g. Langford 2002; Swidler 2003; Smart 2007). The influence also flows 'upwards' in society—for example, where a differentiation of emotional tasks at the family level makes it harder to bring about change in gendered divisions of labour in the workplace and in political life.

The concept of an emotional regime also opens up to tradition and the past. This is an important corrective to behavioural studies of emotion that think in terms of discrete emotional 'episodes' delimited by a particular situation. In reality, emotions mediate between past, present, and future. Even an experience as apparently discrete as the feeling of fear aroused by seeing a snake is likely to have been shaped by previous encounters with snakes and/or by cultural images and stories about snakes, as well as by wider social and personal emotional tendencies that also have a history. Habituated patterns of emotional engagement help give our lives continuity by linking our past, present, and future. Such tendencies are invoked in talk of 'temperament' and 'disposition', and are a part at least of what is meant by 'character'. Context-specific dispositions are what Hochschild (1998) calls 'emotional habits', which we may distinguish from more general emotional dispositions towards life as a whole, which Mauss (1979) and Bourdieu (1977, 1990) theorize as *habitus*. Obviously the two are closely linked, but there can nevertheless be disjunctions—for example, a normally courageous person may go to pieces when she sees a spider. As psychoanalysis teaches us, emotional habits are laid down in earliest childhood, and are likely to be deep rooted and extremely hard to change. One effect of the stabilization of patterns of emotional relating is to minimize the energy, effort, and emotional upheaval required to negotiate social life; a less desirable one is to lock down patterns of response and action that persist in contexts where they are no longer appropriate.

What the concept of an emotional regime can add is a greater awareness of how habitual personal emotional patterns link to broader social and cultural ones. Karen Horney (1937), the post-Freudian theorist, takes a step in this direction when she argues that it is the competitive-individualist bias of modern societies and cultural symbols, rather than Freud's timeless oedipal conflicts, that engender the characteristic emotional disorders of our times (most notably, narcissism). Implicit in this approach is the awareness that emotional patterns transcend the individual and persist over time and across generations. We would say that they are transmitted by emotional regimes, and communicated by their distinctive cultural symbols, and patterns of relating, over time. Regimes relate back and forward, and carry emotional patterns across history, not in a static way but in a way that develops out of what has been in relation and sometimes reaction to it. It is this that makes it possible for historical studies of emotion to draw on a range of archival and 'archaeological' sources in order to excavate the emotional patterns of a particular time and place, thereby illuminating its characteristic social and material relations (e.g. Stone 1977; Moore 1978; Zeldin 1982; Delumeau 1983, 1989; Stearns and Stearns 1986; Konstan 2005; Rosenwein 2006).

Conclusion

If this chapter had been written for people of another time and place who did not share typically modern preconceptions about emotions, we would have reversed its structure. Instead of starting with emotions in personal, individual experience, we would have started with emotions in social experience and cultural manifestation. For, in reality, individuals are born into pre-existing worlds of feeling that shape their own emotions, supply them with emotional vocabularies, and set the range of their emotional experience. However, such is the power of the individualist mode of thinking, and the prestige of the scientific disciplines that reinforce its framework, that we had to start where we are in order to explain why treating emotions as inner disturbances is not a good place to start—and an even worse place to end.

This chapter tries to cure this typically modern misunderstanding by engaging with some of the most important writers who challenge it and present alternative insights that can be pieced together to form an alternative view of emotion. Several decades ago Gregory Bateson (1973: 113) wrote that:

Anglo-Saxons who are uncomfortable with the idea that feelings and emotions are the outward signs of precise and complex algorithms usually have to be told that these matters, the relationship between self and others, and the relationship between self and environment, are, in fact, the subject matter of what are called 'feelings'—love, hate, fear, confidence, anxiety, etc. It is unfortunate that these abstractions referring to *patterns* of relationship have received names, which are usually handled in ways that assume that the 'feelings' are mainly characterized by quantity rather than precise pattern.

Bateson's observations still hold true: he would be only slightly less dismayed by recent attempts to study 'affect' as a phenomenon reducible to discourse than by attempts to search for the neural-chemical 'causes' of emotion. However, this chapter has also shown how much important work has been undertaken since Bateson wrote these words that corroborates his insights, and gives support to a more relational view of emotion from across a wide range of disciplines. This work complements some of the classical sources we have also drawn upon.

In dialogue with these, we have developed a multidisciplinary and multidimensional understanding of emotion that presents emotion as an active stance towards, and intervention within, a relational context. We are always already located within complex patterns of social and symbolic relationship, and 'emotion' is a name we give to the multidimensional processes by which subjects navigate and negotiate within them. We 'feel' our way through life in an embodied engagement, sometimes dimly and sometimes acutely aware of patterns of relationship and their emotional push and pull on us. As Raymond Williams (1977: 132) puts it: 'We are talking about characteristic elements of impulse, restraint and tone; specifically affective elements of consciousness and relationships: not feeling against thought, but feeling as thought: practical consciousness of a present kind, in a living and interrelating continuity'.

We can engage in reason, thought, and critical reflection retrospectively, once an active process of engagement is past, and we are able to stand back and process what has happened. In the present moment, however, when consciousness is engaged and practical, it is guided by the *feeling* of changing circumstances, and by the sedimented structures of feeling that guide our actions and reactions within them. This is not non-rational, but pre-rational, and prior to articulation and critical investigation.

Our concept of an 'emotional regime' allows us to see how these structures of feeling are not purely personal and idiosyncratic. Rather, we enter into them much as we enter into language: as something intersubjective, supra-personal, and historically pre-existing through which we understand and act. Every society or interactive system, from a family to a nation, has its own emotional programme that, when enforced by formal or informal means, constitutes an emotional regime. These are regimes of practice that may not reflexively propagate their emotional programme, but that normally express, reinforce, and communicate it not only in practice but by means of cultural symbols and material arrangements. This does not mean that individuals are passively disciplined by such regimes, partly because feelings are so hard to constrain and compel, and partly because the variety of different regimes that individuals inhabit allows them to escape the exclusive domination of any one of them.

Thus rather than isolating the self as the privileged site of emotional life, the approach proposed here considers feeling in the context of relations between social agent, structure, and cultural symbols. The next task is to develop this account with reference to religion.

2

Religious Emotion

Having considered the broad question 'what is emotion?' in the previous chapter, we can now turn to the narrower one 'what is religious emotion?' It is helpful to begin by being clear about what religious emotion is *not*. According to the account we develop here, it is not some distinctive experience, sensation, or identifiable set of emotions. When a writer like Rudoph Otto (1924/1931) tries to identify authentic religion with a particular type of feeling (a sense of *mysterium tremedum et fascinans*), or when Karen Armstrong (2007) says that 'all religions are designed to teach us how to live, joyfully, serenely, and kindly, in the midst of suffering', they take a wrong turn. *Any* emotion can be religious: not only awe and serenity, but grief, ecstasy, anxiety, hatred, self-righteousness, and so on. The attempt to isolate essentially religious sentiments is mistaken because, as the previous chapter argued, structures of feeling relate to an endless variety of social and symbolic structures.

What makes an emotion religious is, therefore, the fact that it occurs within a religious context and is integral to its social and symbolic relations.[1] In what follows we argue that religious emotions are, first

---

[1] We do not need to define religion at the outset, since our interpretation will become clear as the chapter develops. We view the term 'religion' as a 'tool' for various purposes, and believe that definitions of religion depend on their purpose and context. That there is no universal, value-free definition has been demonstrated by the expanding literature, which reminds us that many uses of the term 'religion' have associations derived from a Christian–European heritage, and close associations with the Enlightenment and imperial projects (e.g. Luckmann 1967; Smith 1988; Balagangadhara 1994). The meaning of the term has changed again in the latest phase of globalization and with the growth of religious pluralism (Beyer 2006). Although our starting point in this chapter is that a situation or community can be counted as religious (or spiritual) if that is the way in which those involved construct it (a social-constructivist approach to the definition of religion is exemplified and defended by Beckford (1989, 2003)), it will become clear as the chapter

and foremost, those that arise in the context of religious emotional regimes (and we explain why this is more than a tautology). We then go on to address the question whether emotion in such contexts has distinctive characteristics. How, if at all, does religious emotion differ from, say, emotion in the context of families, or politics, or sports, or art? Our starting point in tackling all these questions is a critical engagement with existing literature on religious emotion, in relation to which we develop the concept of a religious emotional regime. By unfolding the wider implications of this concept, we are able to end the chapter by identifying a number of characteristic features of religious emotion, including emotional ordering, emotional transcendence transition, and inspiration orientation.

Religious and theological accounts

Although our approach to this topic is largely informed by empirical studies of religion, it would be blinkered not to begin by acknowledging how much scriptural and theological traditions themselves have to say about religious emotion. For a start, they leave no doubt about the centrality of emotion in religious life. To take just a couple of examples, the Qur'an—which is itself an emotionally self-aware and self-reflective source—repeatedly insists on the importance of feeling, and contains intra-textual prompts on the emotions that it is intended to inspire (Wild 1997). 'Believers', it says, 'are those who, when God is mentioned, feel a tremor in their hearts, and when they hear His signs rehearsed, find their faith strengthened, and put (all) their trust in their Lord' (8: 2) and, 'whereas they who are bent on denying the truth harboured a stubborn disdain in their hearts—the stubborn disdain [born] of ignorance—God bestowed from on high His [gift of] inner peace upon His Apostle and the believers, and bound them to the spirit of God-consciousness' (48: 26). The Bible is also full of reminders of the primacy of emotion and of rhetorical devices to elicit emotion (Olbricht and Sumney 2001). As St Paul's hymn in praise of faith, hope, and love in the New Testament insists: 'If I speak with the tongues of men or angels, but have not love, I am become a sounding

---

progresses how and why we also find it necessary, in the context of this exploration of religious emotion, to challenge thoroughgoing constructivism.

brass, or a clanging symbol' (1 Cor. 13: 1). Neither the Bible nor the Qur'an—nor the Hebrew scriptures—draws the typically modern contrast between reason and emotion, or subordinates the latter to the former. For all of them, 'knowledge' is a matter of 'the heart', within an epistemology that is close to the one proposed here in its refusal to pull apart emotion, bodily sensation, reflection, and motivation.[2]

Many theological writings also reflect on the importance of emotion, despite the fact that such traditions tend by their very nature to prioritize the rational articulation of faith. To confine ourselves to Christian theology, there is a long roll call of theologians who discuss something similar to what we today call 'emotion', both in terms of particular feelings (like love), and by way of general concepts such as 'sentiment', 'passion', and 'affection' (Dixon 2003; Rosenwein 2006). Interest in emotion in a more modern sense, along with an intention to defend it against its rationalist critics, develops from the eighteenth century onwards. One of the most notable examples is the work of Jonathan Edwards (1703–58), written in the context of contemporary evangelical revivals in Massachusetts. Edwards, who had himself experienced a conversion in which 'there came into my soul, and was diffused through it, a sense of the glory of the Divine Being' (Miller 1949/2005), forcefully defended the role of emotion in 'true religion' against its cultured despisers. In his *Treatise Concerning Religious Affections* (1746/1971) Edwards insists that the affections are the 'spring' of all human action, and never more so than in the case of religion: 'True religion is evermore a powerful thing, and the power of it appears, in the first place, in its exercises of the heart, its principle and original seat' (2.1); the person who has 'doctrinal knowledge and speculation only, without affection, never is *engaged* in the business of religion' (2.2; emphasis in original). Edwards considers 'the sense of the heart' (one of his favourite phrases) foundational for thought and action alike. Defending much that he witnessed in the revivals—including his own wife's ecstatic experience of repentance and joy—Edwards nevertheless distinguishes genuine religious emotion from false sentiment. He dismisses mere 'intensity', including above all intensity of expression, and identifies twelve marks of true religious emotion,

---

[2] The 'heart' appears, for example, more than a hundred times in the Qur'an and has a central place in Muslim theology (as, for example, in the work of Imam al-Ghazali (d. 1111), particularly the *Revival of the Religious Sciences*).

which include, above all, attachment to God, and expression in steady moral practice, including charitable action.

In terms of the concepts we use here, Edwards identifies religious emotion by its relation to a religious community and its beliefs, practices, and symbols. His approach differs significantly from that of another major modern theological commentator on religious emotion, Rudoph Otto. In Europe, Friedrich Schleiermacher (1768–1834) had, like Edwards, emphasized the importance of the emotional dimension of religion. He famously identified true religion with *schlechthin abhängig*, 'a feeling of clear and simple dependence', and found in religious emotion a starting point for the new enterprise of religious studies (Capetz 1998). Otto's *Das Heilige* (1917, translated as *The Idea of the Holy* in 1931) builds on Schleiermacher's work, and attempts to specify more precisely the distinctive nature of authentic religious emotion. To a greater extent than Edwards, Otto attempts to identify religious emotion in terms of a distinctive cluster of feelings. He suggests that we can grasp the essence of religion chiefly by sympathy and imaginative intuition. Religion has to do with a unique mental state, which is ineffable and inexpressible, and which he refers to as 'numinous'. It may sweep over the mind 'like a gentle tide', turn into 'a more lasting attitude of the soul', or 'burst in sudden eruption up from the depths of the soul with spasms and eruptions' (Otto 1917/1923: 12–13). Though it cannot be strictly defined, the numinous combines a sense of awe, fascination, wonder, and fear, and arises when the finite individual finds him or herself in the presence of *numen*.

The account of religious emotion we develop here is much closer to Edwards's than to Otto's. Like the former, we argue that religious emotion should be characterized not so much in terms of a particular kind of emotion or set of emotions (that is even more obvious when one looks at other religions besides Christianity), but in relation to the social context in which it arises and which confirms, reinforces, and sanctions it, and in relation to the symbols that inspire it and to which it relates. As Edwards recognizes, community and symbols do not only give rise to personal and collective sentiment; such sentiment binds the believer to them, inspires actions that confirm their importance, and renders them substantial (or, in Edwards's terms, true and Christian). Thus Edwards points us towards the view that religious emotion is not merely a matter of personal, individual affect, but arises in the mutually constitutive relations between an agent, a religious community, and sacred symbols (scriptures, sacraments, and, from the confessional point of view, God).[3]

Psychological 'emotivist' approaches

The tendency to reduce religious emotion to psychological states that is so clear in Otto is also characteristic of some early anthropological accounts of 'primitive' or 'savage' religion. The latter embraced a rationalist agenda that separated emotion from reason and consigned it to the earlier stages of human evolution—and to women and children in general. As E. E. Evans-Pritchard (1965: 5) puts it in his debunking of such work: 'To comprehend what now seem to be obviously faulty interpretations and explanations, we would have to write a treatise on the climate of thought at the time ... a curious mixture of positivism, evolutionism, and the remains of a sentimental religiosity'. But, for all its faults, this approach gave rise to a number of accounts that drew attention to the importance of emotion in religious life, and challenged intellectualist accounts that explained primitive religion as the outcome of faulty reasoning. For example, R. R. Marett, quoted in the Introduction, argued that religion (and magic) had more to do with embodied sensations than rational reflections, had some appreciation of the importance of collective gatherings and the emotions they generated, and emphasized the importance of religion in generating easement, hope, courage, and tenacity. Others emphasized the emotional utility of magic, or religion, or both, and went so far as to identify religion with a specific mode of feeling. For R. H. Lowie, who studied the Crow Indians, for example, religion consists in a sense of awe and amazement, which is often focused upon a person or symbol.[4] And for Paul Radin, who worked among the Winnebago Indians,

---

[3] A similar view is found in the theology of Baron Friedrich von Hügel (1852–1925), who wrote extensively on mysticism, but insisted against thinkers like William James (see below) that religion is not a matter of private sentiment, but arises from the confluence and interplay of feeling and intellect engaged with: 'the clear conceptions, the historic incorporations, the traditional training schools, the visible institutions of the great world-religions' (Hügel 1926: 144).

[4] R. H. Lowie, *Primitive Religion* (1925), discussed by Evans-Pritchard (1965: 38).

religion 'manifests itself in a thrill, a feeling of exhilaration, exaltation and awe and in a complete absorption in internal sensations'.[5]

As Evans-Pritchard (1965) pointed out in his critique of these 'emotivist' accounts, they attempt to identify distinctively religious emotions, such that any person displaying such emotions in any setting would have to be regarded as religious. If religion is a matter of awe, for example, then any activity that generates such a feeling must be counted religious, as must any object or person invested with such an emotion. But on this account not only does the object of emotion cease to count; so do the social and symbolic relations in which it is embedded. Once religion is understood as a matter of emotions of a particular kind experienced by individuals, then religious gatherings and rituals turn into mere epiphenomena of the religious life, and religiously inflected social relations cease to have any significance other than as a convenient but inessential context for personal affective states.

This reductive tendency also afflicts those psychological studies of religious emotion that, though they have much to teach us about the nature and strength of religious emotions in individual experience and biography, neglect the social and symbolic dimensions of experience. This is already evident in William James's early and important *The Varieties of Religious Experience* (1902). Unlike emotivist anthropologists, and unlike Freud, James rejected any attempt to explain—and explain away—religion. He also distanced himself from the enterprise of isolating a distinctive essence of religion, arguing that religion is 'a collective name' that does not stand for any single principle or essence (1902/1981: 46), and that 'the religious sentiment' is a name for 'the many sentiments which religious objects may arouse in alteration', and that 'it probably contains nothing whatever of a psychologically specific nature' (1902/1981: 47). For James there can be religious fear, religious love, religious awe, religious anger, and so on, and there is no ground for assuming a 'religious emotion' to exist as a distinct mental state in itself, present in every religious experience. His rich explorations of autobiographical accounts of religious experience support this argument, and yield many insights, including the famous distinction between the emotional experience of the 'healthy-minded' and of the

---

[5] P. Radin, *Social Anthropology* (1932: 244), quoted by Evans-Pritchard (1965: 39). For a useful introduction to some of the most important early (and later) anthropological approaches to religion, see Bowie (2000).

'twice-born' who move from depressive and pessimistic feelings, through conversion, to a more accepting, serene and hopeful stance. For James there could be no doubt that emotion lay at the heart of religion. Looking back on *The Varieties*, he declared himself 'almost appalled at the amount of emotionality I find in it' (1902/1981: 465), but defended his approach on the grounds that profoundly emotional experiences constituted religion's most profound expression.

Yet James nevertheless insists that it is in private emotional states that we must locate the essence of religion. He chose to focus his exploration of religion upon *'the feelings, acts, and experiences of individual men in their solitude, so far as they apprehend themselves to stand in relation to whatever they may consider divine'* (1902/1981: 50; emphasis in original). He did so not because he considered it helpful to isolate a limited territory for the purpose of analytic exploration, but because he believed that such emotional experience constituted the foundation of all religion. Had the Buddha, Christ, and Muhammad not had such experiences, the religions, institutions, scriptures, and theologies connected with them would not exist. James concluded that 'personal religion should still seem the primordial thing, even to those who esteem it incomplete' (1902/1981: 49), and, despite his insistence that there is no essential religious emotion, he ended up by trying to isolate the distinctively religious emotional state. One of the conclusions of *The Varieties* is that there 'must be something solemn, serious, and tender about any attitude which we denominate religious': 'solemnity and gravity' are defining marks of religious sentiment, and attitudes which imply a 'grin or snicker', 'scream or curse', are profane (1902/1981: 56). The truly religious emotion turns out, for James, to be the opposite of 'morbid-mindedness': it is a 'mystical' state of emotional expansion that embraces reality in a sentiment of loving acceptance and felt significance.

The captivity of these emotivist approaches to the preoccupations of their day seems obvious with the benefit of hindsight. Although he rejected the extreme ethnocentrism of the evolutionary accounts of socio-cultural development, even James seems guilty of confusing the essence of religion with the sensibility of late-nineteenth-century Emersonian mysticism. Ultimately, James's account, like that of the emotivist anthropologists, fails to take seriously the objects of religious emotion and the forms of social relation with which they are intertwined. In this it falls short of most theological accounts, and attracted some interesting criticism from that quarter: for example, the Catholic theologian Friedrich von Hügel wrote to James expressing appreciation for his work but noting his dissatisfaction concerning 'your taking of the religious experience as separable from its institutional-historical occasions and environment'.[6] For James, religious emotion is most likely to occur in the hermit's cave, in the wilderness wanderings of the nature-mystic, or in the solitude of the human heart. It is at best a private relation between man and his God, rather than an integral part of a complex dialogical relation between agent, cultural symbols, and social formations.

Sociological accounts

Although Durkheim was influenced by the emotivist accounts of his day, his approach to religious emotion displays a significant difference. As we saw in the previous chapter, emotion is central to his interpretation of primordial religion, but, rather than viewing it as the product of personal sentiment, Durkheim understands sentiment as the product of religion and society. It is by participating in social rites and beliefs that a person is able to experience intense emotion. Emotions are the product of structured gatherings rather than the experiences of individual men in solitude. And, even though Durkheim identified certain types of emotion as distinctively religious, for him these were distinctively *social* forms of emotion. The most discussed is that which he called 'collective effervescence': an ecstatic sentiment generated by a concentration of members at periodic rituals. In such situations a sort of electricity is formed by the coordinated practices that transport participants into an extraordinary degree of exaltation. Every sentiment expressed finds a place without resistance in other minds, which echo it back; the initial impulse grows as it proceeds, gaining force and momentum like an advancing avalanche; participants feel that they are sharing in unison in sacred power; the experience attaches the individual to the group; emotions are felt to be trustworthy, since all experience them.

Durkheim was also aware of the significance of religious states characterized not by confidence, joy, and enthusiasm, but by fear, grief, and anxiety. For Durkheim these emotions are associated with

---

[6] In Lash (1988: 158 n. 11).

'piacular' rites. Mourning, for example, is first and foremost a duty imposed on individuals by the group. It may have as much to do with respect for custom and fear of social and mythical penalties for non-compliance than with genuine grief, but for Durkheim feelings become real only when collectively confirmed. As he puts it: 'sorrow, like joy, becomes exalted and amplified when leaping from mind to mind, and therefore expresses itself outwardly in the form of exuberant and violent movements' (Durkheim 1912/2001: 400). Thus piacular rites function just like celebratory ones in order to reinforce social solidarity—in this case in the face of an experience like death that threatens to tear a hole in the social fabric. Religious emotions may vary from extreme joy to extreme dejection, but in either case there is a communion of experience, and a comfort resulting from solidarity.

In veering away from psychological reductionism, Durkheim can be accused of falling into the opposite trap of sociological reductionism. It is an exaggeration to say that he presents a theory that reduces religious emotion to social forces without remainder, since he retains some sense of the importance of individual sentiments and appreciates the role of symbolic objects as a focus and stimulant of religious emotion. Nevertheless, both the individual subject and the symbolic-material objects of emotion are significantly subordinated to collective sentiment in Durkheim's scheme. The former is chiefly a channel for social sentiments, and the latter a cipher for them. There is no sense of the power of individual religious sentiment that we find in James, and no appreciation of the independent importance of religious symbols, such as we find in theological accounts. For Durkheim collective sentiment is projected onto arbitrary symbols, and imposed onto empty subjects, and neither has sufficient power to enter into a truly dialectical relationship with society.[7]

A similar criticism can also be made of Karl Marx's treatment of religion, in which religious emotion figures mainly as an epiphenomenon of wider social forces. However, Marx's much briefer and more allusive account contains some additional insights. For Durkheim, religious emotion has the function of social integration. For Marx, it is a symptom of social contradiction. Religious emotion is an expression of real suffering, a protest against it, a distraction from its real

---

[7] This criticism, especially of the neglect of personal religious sentiment, was made by some contemporary critics of *The Elementary Forms*. See the reprinted reviews in Pickering (1994).

causes, and a hindrance to its remedy. All this Marx sums up in his famous statement that 'religion is the sigh of the oppressed creature, the sentiment of a heartless world, and the soul of soulless conditions. It is the opium of the people' (Marx and Engels 1848/1969). This religious false-reflection of this world can only finally vanish when the practical conditions of everyday life offer human beings more satisfactory relations with their fellows and the material world. Thus Marx highlights the emotive aspect of religion, and describes it in terms of both hope and depression. Moreover, he relates religious emotions to the issue of power and relations of social domination: religious distress is a reaction to human powerlessness in oppressive socio-economic relations. Hidden in Marx's critique is an awareness of a repertoire of religious emotions that includes despair, hope, compassion, and love, and an appreciation of the way in which religious emotions relate to wider social structures. Religion may be the only permissible arena in which the oppressed can express their feelings.

Weber understands the connection between religious emotion and social power in a different way. He tends to underplay its importance, since he views it in relation to his central theme of the domination of modern societies by purposive rationality (*Zweckrationalität*) based on a calculation of the most efficient means for a given end. Such calculation is exclusive of historic traditions, and 'irrational' emotions. Weber acknowledged that religion could motivate action, especially 'value-rational' actions that pursue a moral aim in a single-minded and systematic manner, but did not consider the role of emotion here either.[8] Nevertheless, his analysis contains an opening for religious emotion in modern societies, in relation to a third type of authority that he considers capable of breaking up traditional and legal-bureaucratic forms—namely, the charismatic. Such authority can be glimpsed in the extraordinary powers (*ausseralltägliche Kräfte*) of a shaman, a prophet, or a war hero: someone who inspires his followers and confirms his extraordinary power in their eyes. Relations to objects or persons ascribed with charisma are characterized by awe, dread, or enthusiasm, and the bond between a charismatic leader and his followers is primarily emotional. Weber, on the one hand, presents charisma as a special gift of the individual that sets him (or her) apart from the ordinary world, and, on the other, insists on the social dimension

---

[8] See Max Weber, *Die Wirtschaftsethik der Weltreligionen*, S. 1860. Digitale Bibliothek Band 58: Max Weber, S. 7663 (vgl. Weber-RS Bd. 3, S. 303–4).

of charisma. Thus charisma is bestowed on the leader by his (or her) followers, who recognize in him some special powers in which they seek to participate (see Chapter 5).[9]

Cultural and symbolic approaches

Emotivist accounts construe religious emotion primarily in terms of the inner stirrings of the individual, while sociological accounts focus on collective sentiments. A third approach draws attention to the importance of culture and symbols for religious emotion. Here again the most useful work is not that which reduces emotion by looking at only one dimension—in this case, culture and symbols in isolation—but that which relates the cultural dimension to personal experience and social life.

Such an integrative approach recognizes that symbols are not 'natural' carriers of meanings, but that their meanings are shaped by the social relations in which they are embedded, and by their relation with other symbols. As Talal Asad (1993: 28) puts it:

a symbol is not an object or event that serves to carry a meaning but a set of relationships between objects or events uniquely brought together as complexes or as concepts, having at once an intellectual, instrumental, and emotional significance. If we define a symbol along these lines, a number of questions can be raised about the conditions that explain how such complexes and concepts came to be formed, and in particular how their formation is related to varieties of practice.

Although these comments are directed critically at Clifford Geertz's approach to religion as a cultural system, Geertz is not as guilty as many other representatives of the 'cultural turn' of attempting to decode cultural systems without reference to social relations. While the cultural turn in sociology has ignored religion altogether (see Chapter 6), the same is not true of cultural anthropology. The neglect of social relations is clearest in structuralist approaches like that of Lévi-Strauss, where what counts is the ability to decode a symbolic system in terms of its own logic, virtually independent of the social

---

[9] Max Weber, *Wirtschaft und Gesellschaft*, S. 506. Digitale Bibliothek Band 58: Max Weber, S. 1834 (vgl. Weber-WuG, S. 140–1).

system to which it relates (see, e.g., Lévi-Strauss 1963/1974; Henaff 1998). This approach focuses on discursive categories rather than emotion, reducing the latter to a secondary matter. As Lévi-Strauss (2002: 219) puts it, 'emotions... irrupt upon a structure already in place, formed by the architecture of the mind'. For Edmund Leach (1958), collective symbols structure the way a society and its members know the world, but have little emotional significance for individuals. What is significant for individuals are the sort of personal symbols that emerge in dreams and were analysed by Freud: but they are socially insignificant (Leach 1958).

Tellingly, it is when symbols and social relations are held together that emotion is most likely to enter into the analysis of religion. Simmel's reflections on religious emotion and symbolic objects, introduced in the previous chapter, provide a good illustration. For Simmel (1898/1997: 119), the 'power and depth' of religion lie in its 'persistent ability to draw a given item of religious data into the flow of the emotions, whose movements it must renew constantly, like the perpetually changing drops of water that beget the stable image of the rainbow'. Whether emotions relate to scriptures, dogmas, totems, images of God, or sacred buildings, this is a vital part of the process by which they are cultivated, stabilized, communicated, and reinforced or altered. For Simmel, the relations of an individual to others are characterized by certain emotions, and from these there develops a symbolic content: for example, gods who protect these relations. From the subjective faith process there develops an object for that faith, and the object then impacts back upon the faith experience—and, for Simmel, social relations find their substantial and ideal expression in the idea of a deity, which symbolizes the unity of the manifold.

The enterprise of interlinking the dynamic processes that relate religious feeling to symbol and to social relations is further developed in Mary Douglas's later work, where she departs from the more structuralist approach she took in *Purity and Danger* (1966) in order to theorize the relations between natural symbols and social structures. Reproaching Durkheim for failing to follow through his own radical insights about the socially constructed nature of *all* knowledge—including the scientific rationality of the modern academy—she refuses to exempt modern societies from her enterprise (Douglas 1975). In *Natural Symbols* (1970) she offers a comparative analysis that seeks to address the question why some societies—like modern Western ones—give a lesser place to religious ritual and symbol than others. Drawing on Bernstein's theory of social linguistics, and especially his distinction between elaborate and restricted codes, she distinguishes between two dimensions: 'group', or the experience of bounded units, and 'grid', which refers to rules that relate an individual to others. In sociological terms, group corresponds to the dimension of collectivism versus individualism, while grid corresponds to references to normative symbols: '[Grid] is order, classification, the symbolic system. [Group] is pressure, the experience of having no option but to consent to the overwhelming demands of other people' (Douglas 1970: 81). Group and grid are proposed as alternative modes of integration, with different symbolic implications. This gives two axes along which different types of social and symbolic formation can be plotted. Using this approach, Douglas points out provocative parallels between, for example, modern society and communities like those of the Pygmies, both of which integrate autonomous individuals through loose formal rules rather than by group cohesion, and both of which rotate around 'Big Men' who establish their authority through success in competitive struggles.

Religion and emotions are recurrent minor themes in Douglas's presentation. She notices how religious symbols (particularly images of deities) and religious rituals correspond with social structure (1970: 35). Her model identifies the social conditions for ritualism and effervescence (the focus of Durkheim's interest) as well as for religious and symbolic informality (1970: 71), and thereby contrasts formal, ritualistic religions and informal, mystical ones. For example, emphasis on internal emotional states is to be expected in societies where group and grid are weak, and emphasis on external symbols, signs, and rituals and dogmatic formalism where grid and group are strong.

Although Douglas's account does not wholly escape the tendency to subordinate symbols to social structure and to deny the latter independent power, Douglas nevertheless goes further than Durkheim in appreciating the socially and culturally inflected diversity of religious emotion. She raises the possibility that Durkheim's account of religious emotion as essentially a matter of socially integrative collective effervescence and solidarity was true only in the context of the sort of small-scale, bounded, totemic culture in which he was interested (Douglas 1975). Douglas argues that, far from being typical of all 'primitive' societies, let alone all societies, Durkheim's account is characteristic of a particular societal form. If he had considered the shamanic societies investigated by Lowie and Radin, or modern Western societies, he might have drawn a rather different portrait of religious emotion, in which collective feeling was not so totally overwhelming of personal emotion.

Finally, in the discussion of cultural approaches to religious emotion, we must return to Geertz, since Geertz not only puts emotion at the very heart of his general account of religion, but succeeds in highlighting some of the most important and distinctive features of religious emotion. As he puts it in his justly famous definition of 'religion as a cultural system', religion is

(1) a system of symbols (2) which acts to establish powerful, pervasive and long-lasting moods and motivations in men (3) by formulating conceptions of a general order of existence and (4) clothing these conceptions with such an aura of factuality that (5) the moods and motivations seem uniquely realistic. (Geertz 1971: 4)

We take up a number of features of this account in our delineation of religious emotion below, including Geertz's recognition that religious emotions are characteristically encompassing in their scope and enduring in their influence, and that they have a special role in providing value direction and motivation. What this definition also highlights is the way in which religio-symbolic orders provoke emotions, while the emotions produce the religio-symbolic orders. Thus the conviction and power of a symbolic system are tied up with the emotions it inspires, while the emotions it inspires give it power and conviction. The process is dialectical: our feelings shape our reality, and what we take to be real shapes our feelings.

All the cultural approaches to emotion considered so far share a preoccupation with *collective* symbols—as does Durkheim. It is less common for theorists to consider the significance of *personal* symbols in religion. The assumption seems to be that the really important emotional interactions are those between groups and their symbols, and that individuals' emotional relations with religious symbols are merely derivative from these. But collective gatherings are not the focal point in the same way for all types of religion, and, even when they are, subgroups that are at a distance from the agenda of the religious elite may have alternative practices of their own that are of equal or greater significance, and that often centre around personal forms of devotion focused on domestic, local, or dispersed sites and symbols. Too great a focus on the collective ignores the way in which individuals can manipulate symbols for their own ends and in order to resist, change, or stake a new claim within, an emotional regime. It neglects the fact that collective symbols often develop out of individual visions and symbolic creations. And it forgets that the power of collective symbols is not unrelated to their ability to provoke profound personal reactions and devotions.

A psychological approach lends itself to study of this subject, and the contribution that has most influenced our approach is that of the psychologically informed anthropologist Gananath Obeyesekere (1978, 1981, 1990).[10] Obeyesekere dwells with equal seriousness on the deeply felt and highly personal religious emotions bound up with unique autobiographies (which he interprets with the help of tools from psychoanalysis), and the wider social and symbolic contexts to which they relate. While not ignoring the importance of these contexts, he balances this with attention to the ways in which cultural symbols are articulated with individual experience. He is interested in 'personal symbols', which is his term for 'cultural symbols operating on the level of personality and of culture at the same time' (Obeyesekere 1981: 2). Obeyesekere's studies reveal how such symbols are appropriated and creatively reinterpreted by individuals, who use them not only to make sense of their own situations, but to negotiate complex social relations and, very often, to attain some leverage within them, thereby effecting changes in personal standing and circumstance that would otherwise be impossible. In *Medusa's Hair* (1981), for example, he considers the meanings of a single symbol—matted hair—and the relation of that symbol to personal life crises and their resolution. He shows how the difficult and complex life experiences of his informants—three female Hindu ascetics in the pilgrimage centre of Kataragama in Sri Lanka—are crystallized in this personal–public symbol, which is personally appropriated and drawn into the autobiographical process. He suggests that matted locks of hair, which may originally emerge as a psychological symptom, are transformed into symbols through the cultural patterning of consciousness, which in turn helps the individuals concerned to integrate and resolve painful emotional experiences: unhappy experiences of *eros* are transformed into *agape*, and the status of victim or patient is transformed into that of a religious virtuoso—signalled by the locks of matted hair.

---

[10] Some recent ethnographic accounts add to our understanding of relations between material symbols and emotions in practice, including those by Humphrey (2002), Küchler (2002), and Kwon (2007).

Citing G. H. Mead's work (1934) on symbolic communication with the self, Obeyesekere (1981: 46) points out the deep motivational and intra-communicative significance that personal symbols can have for individuals. Religious idioms are used to objectify personal emotions. Individuals can objectify emotions in new ways, or can appropriate collective symbols and run away with their meaning, turning it in new directions, and to new ends. In the process they can change that meaning, adding new layers of emotional significance in the process. Sometimes personal symbols are 'returned' to the community, and may lead to a reconfiguration of symbolic meaning and emotional significance. Since they are embedded in social relations, this return may lead to adjustments that help raise the status of certain individuals, or negotiate some new advantage for a certain class of persons. As Obeyesekere (1981: 99) sums up his study of matted hair: 'we are once again confronted with the capacity of the symbolic idiom to operate simultaneously at different levels—intrapsychic, interpersonal or sociological, and cultural'.

Religious emotional regimes

Pulling together the threads from these very different perspectives on emotion—from the theological to the cultural—and relating them to the discussion of emotion in the previous chapter, we can now answer the question 'what is religious emotion?' in terms that revolve around the concept of a religious emotional regime.

The previous chapter introduced the general concept of an emotional regime, which serves to bring together the personal, symbolic, and social aspects of emotion, and captures the way in which emotions relate embodied agents to their wider social and material-symbolic interactions. anchor and communicate the emotional agenda, and serve as normative points of reference. This concept of an emotional regime has direct applicability in the field of religion. Part of what distinguishes religious emotional regimes from non-religious ones, particularly in functionally differentiated modern societies, is simply the fact that they are socially constructed as religious—whether by insiders, or outsiders, or both. Such construction involves political claim-making, and is always historically and culturally contingent (what counts as religious in one society may not count in another, and the reasons for wanting to be identified as religious—or not—are related to the advantages and disadvantages that accrue in a particular time and place). Where we go beyond the constructivist approach, however, is by claiming that an additional part of what makes an emotional regime religious is the way in which it represents its emotional programme as relating to an 'alternate ordering' that goes beyond the orderings of everyday life.[11] In this sense, religion has to do with transcendence, though such transcendence does not necessarily imply other-worldliness: alternate orderings may be this-worldly in focus, and may claim to disclose the true contours of this life rather than pointing to an existence beyond this one (as, for example, in many versions of Zen Buddhism).

By offering to order emotional lives not just differently, but in accordance with a truer, more foundational, more satisfying pattern, religion proposes a new structuring of relationships, and with it an emotional restructuring. Religions reconfigure emotions by reconfiguring earthly and heavenly relationships, as well as vice versa. To become a devout Roman Catholic, for example, is to enter into a new set of relations not only with other human beings, especially fellow Catholics and 'non-Catholics', but with a pantheon of beings who are symbolically represented within the religious regime, and whose presence is felt. It is, for example, to fall in love with Jesus, to seek comfort and inspiration from Mary, to vent frustrations on St Anthony, and to bolster one's courage by invoking St Christopher. Philosophical debate about the existence of such beings does not by itself establish or undermine their emotional reality. As Robert Orsi says of his dying Italian-American Catholic mother clasping a tiny blue statue of Our Lady of Fatima, the latter's power to evoke love, trust, and calm was 'real enough' (Orsi 2005: 18). And, for the working-class Anglican women in Newcastle-upon-Tyne interviewed by Clark-King (2004), the romantic, tender, and faithful figure of Jesus Christ was as real and emotionally significant as their often absent, sometimes violent, and generally disappointing real-life lovers and husbands. Equally real for many people are the evil spirits, vengeful powers and fates who

[11] The term 'alternate ordering' comes from Quaker theology (see Dandelion 2004). It has interesting overlaps with the concept of heterotopia in postmodern thought. We prefer it to 'higher' order, because it may be this-worldly as well as other-worldly in focus. The point is that it offers some significant difference from, and leverage against, the current emotional and relational order-of-things, as that is perceived by the social group in question.

must be appeased and placated, and whose destructive potential must be averted by active measures, both moral and magical. Such beings crowd together in the religious imagination and provide additional and alternate relations to those of everyday life. They serve to temper, manage, adjust, and transfigure feelings, and so impact back upon life and society.

Such 'symbolic relations' are closely connected to the patternings of human relations within a religious regime. Gods, good and evil spirits, and other beings are evoked and felt to be present in ritual gatherings and scripted enactments, as well as in domestic symbols and rituals. Authorized emotions are expressed, imitated, enforced, and internalized in formal and informal social gatherings and interactions. Personal feelings towards such beings are learnt, stabilized, reinforced, or undermined by observing the emotional actions and reactions of other participants, and by practising and performing prescribed kinds of bodily action (for example, kneeling in prayer, receiving communion, wearing special dress). Religious elites and authorities prescribe and proscribe what can and cannot be felt, expressed, and enacted according to the agenda they uphold. Punishments and reinforcements may be used to maintain appropriate standards, but more importantly social acceptance or disapproval, plus the threat of rejection or exclusion, serve to maintain the sanctioned order.

The harmonized interconnection of symbolic, material, and social elements in a religious emotional regime can have powerful effects on feeling and sensibility. The combination of a beautiful and richly furnished religious building (or a dedicated religious site in a natural landscape); music, drumming, and other sounds; use of natural and artificial light; fragrances and scents; coordinated bodily actions; scripted performances; symbolic foci of attention; the recitation of traditional words and texts—all can 'move' participants into a different realm of feeling and relating. This may be experienced as taking them out of their everyday emotional lives, or rooting them more securely within what is important in those lives, or both. The emotional impact can be one-off—as, for example, in an initiation rite or other rite of passage—or related to regular repetition and a consequent accrual of significance (Whitehouse and Laidlaw 2004). In any case, the overall effect is to bring an alternate ordering to life, making its reality so deeply felt that, in Geertz's words, that 'order of existence' and the 'moods and motivations' associated with it become 'uniquely realistic'.

This emphasis on the emotional power that can be generated by the coordination of symbolic and social means should not, however, lead to a neglect of the importance of individual emotional agency, or give the impression that personal feelings are swept away on waves of collective emotion. In the wider context of religious emotional regimes, individuals forge their own emotional relations with particular symbols, and have a certain freedom of emotional expression in the collective context. Even in regimes where emotional protocols are tight, individual emotions can never be completely controlled, and even in the most coordinated ritual gatherings, individuals can always fail to be moved appropriately, or simply feel bored. They may fail to internalize all the correct emotions, even when they appear to follow emotional scripts to the letter. Or, by adding a new tone or variation to an emotional performance, they may be able to effect change in the programme, especially if they are able to influence others to feel similarly. Individual virtuosi may demonstrate such a level of emotional skill (for example, in interpreting and improving the emotions of others) that they are given a dispensation for special emotional performances. Moreover, the symbolic repertoire of most religions is sufficiently varied and open to allow individuals to relate in their own ways to the favoured deities, thereby creating orderings within orderings. Appeal to collective symbols can also be made as a way of challenging religious elites or drawing them back to an emotional standard from which they are thought to have departed.

Like any emotional regime, a religious one helps structure a system of power relations. Emotional authorities take many forms, some interlocking and mutually reinforcing, and some conflictual and mutually checking. The charismatic leader can set emotional standards by word, deed, and example. Traditional forms of authority are more common, and range from groups of elders in small-scale societies, to religious professionals and scholarly elites in larger religious communities who can afford to finance a religious elite. Such human authority rarely operates independently of symbolic authority. Islamic authority, for example, reaches back to the prophet Muhammad, 'the beautiful model', whose life and teaching set the model and standard for all human perfection, and provide the basis of subsequent legal and ethical reflection. Thus heavenly and human, past and present, orderings interpret and reinforce one another, and mediate a structure of feeling. Moreover, as we have repeatedly emphasized, emotions are not just inner states but relational stances. To say, for example, that

I am angry about how I was treated in my last job is less likely to be a report on how I am currently feeling (I may feel nothing) than an account of a relational situation.

Variations

Different religious emotional regimes can be distinguished by their varied emotional scales, harmonies, and discords. At the most general and 'ideal-typical' level the emotional regime of, say, Christianity is different from that of Hinduism. At a lower but still highly abstract level, that of Roman Catholicism is different from that of Calvinism, or that of Vaishnavism different from that of Shaivism. Emotions gain their meaning and particular tone from their place within the broad, symbolically- and textually-inscribed, programme. This helps to explain why religious emotions vary so widely between religious traditions, even with regard to what appears in translation as the same. Take 'love', for example. Just a few quotations from the sacred texts of different religions can illustrate its breadth of meaning and significance. For Paul in the New Testament, 'love is patient, love is kind. It does not envy, it does not boast, it is not proud. It is not rude, it is not self-seeking, it is not easily angered, it keeps no record of wrongs' (1 Cor. 13). The *Gita Govinda*, which celebrates Rādhā's union with Krishna, tells us that 'arrows of Love went through his eyes, arrows which were her nail-scratched bosom, her reddened sleep-denied eyes, her crimson lips from a bath of kisses, her hair disarranged with the flowers awry, and her girdle all loose and slipping' (Sura XII). And the *Dhammapada* warns: 'Let no man love anything; loss of the beloved is evil. Those who love nothing, and hate nothing, have no fetters...He who in his mind is satisfied, and whose thoughts are not bewildered by love, is called *ūrdhvaṃsrotas* (carried upwards by the stream)' (XVI).

Variations in the emotional scales and characteristic notes of religious emotional regimes multiply as tradition-inscribed repertoires are translated into actual social forms. Although they may all belong to a much broader emotional 'type', religious communities on the ground embody this in interestingly different ways. For example, in research in the small town of Kendal, Cumbria, we found congregations with the same churchmanship and theological position that differed significantly in terms of their emotional regimes. One evangelical congregation had an emotional scale that made sorrow the dominant note and relief and gratitude at sins forgiven its counterpoint, while another, which in terms of its teachings was virtually identical, had a scale in which joy was the dominant note and repentance its counterpoint. These differences were reflected and reinforced by different church furnishings, styles of dress, music, and comportment. (Not surprisingly, the two congregations had a very uneasy relationship with one another.) The salience of emotional diversity within a single religious tradition is high, and many internal divisions, schisms, and bitter rivalries centre, in part, around emotional differences within a single tradition.

There is also variation in the extent to which religious emotional regimes cover social and cultural life. They do not necessarily dominate the whole of life—even in the case of very devout individuals—or saturate a whole society—even in the case of a theocracy. Anthropological studies, including Durkheim's, typically deal with societies that do not have differentiated social spheres with their own distinctive emotional standards. In such cases it makes little sense to speak of a 'religious' emotional regime as something different from the regime of society *per se*. The situation in modern societies, discussed in detail in Chapter 6, is strikingly different. Here an advanced degree of differentiation, combined with cultural and religious pluralism, means that individuals and groups find themselves shaped and confronted by a range of different, sometimes contradictory, emotional regimes. Religious emotional regimes must take their place alongside many different, and often competing, emotional regimes, including those of the workplace, the law court, the hospital, and so on. As we will see, they face a range of options, including social encapsulation, transformation in ways that diminish the dissonance with other emotional regimes, and acceptance of diminished influence over only certain aspects of their adherent's emotional life.[12]

Religious emotional regimes also differ in terms of their 'coverage' of individual life. We can draw a distinction between 'comprehensive regimes' and 'fragmentary regimes'. The former offer a complete emo-

---

[12] It is wrong to assume that there is a neat contrast between 'simple' and 'plural' societies that overlaps neatly with that between pre-modern and modern societies. For millennia it has been the normal condition of many religious regimes, including those of all the so-called world religions to compete with alternative regimes, often within the same territory. The degree of religio-cultural pluralism was often at least as high as that of contemporary Western societies.

tional ordering that serves to shape and direct emotional life from cradle to grave for all types and conditions of person, and for the whole of life. Comprehensive regimes are typically bound to universalizing religions with extensive influence and power. Thus Western Christendom, for example, provided an emotional regime that not only provided a framework for the whole life course, but also gave emotional patterning to time by shaping the week and the year according to a rhythm of feasts (joys, loves, and convivialities), fasts (sorrows and repentance), and rests (peace, calm, devotion). By contrast, emotional life may be scripted by a range of different diverse regimes, or fragments of regimes, that apply to only limited aspects of life. When assembled together, however, they may constitute a broad programme. In Japan, for example, births are often conducted according to Shinto rites, weddings with Christian rites, and funerals following Buddhist traditions. The rest of life is shaped by a range of regimes, both religious and secular (Reader and Tanabe 1998). Obeyesekere (1981) gives a more local example from his study in Kataragama, explaining how pilgrims to the site first cross a river to visit the main (Hindu) shrine to Katgaragama, before walking down a long street crammed with the lame and sick in order to visit the nearby Kiri Vehara (Buddhist stupa). At the former the mood is one of joyous celebration, at the latter one of serenity, calm, and stillness:

If the predominant colour of Kataragama is red, the colour of the Kiri Vehara is white; if one place represents the celebration of the senses, the other celebrates their transcendence . . . The pilgrim has made his full progress: he crosses the river and leaves the everyday realty of mundane existence; from there he goes on to the passion and sensuality of Kataragama; then to the shock of life's suffering and misery; and finally to a realization of release from both passion and misery—all aspects of impermanence—into the serenity and calm of the Kiri Vehara. (Obeyesekere 1981: 4–5)

Finally, we can also draw a distinction—at different ends of a spectrum—between emotionally explicit regimes, which deal directly with emotions, and emotionally implicit regimes, which evoke feeling in more indirect ways. The former make promises to effect emotional change and improvement, pay a great deal of attention to the articulation and transformation of emotional states, and have instrumental techniques for effecting such change. For example, the current Dalai Lama presents Tibetan Buddhism as a religion that offers 'a systematic way to reduce the negative emotions' aimed at 'the complete elimination of negative emotions', by way of techniques like guided meditation.[13] By contrast, emotionally implicit forms may be no less emotionally transformative or effective, but affect feeling by way of symbols and practices (like those at Kataragama, or in a Catholic High Mass), rather than by making direct appeal to the emotions. Here the focus falls less on the self and its subjective states than on the gods, spirits, and community in relation to which a person and community is moved. This distinction leads onto another one. All religions offer some sort of emotional programme, and all aim to shape sensibilities to some degree. But the shaping of emotional patterns and dispositions may not itself generate emotion. For example, McGuire (2008) rightly points out that participation in rituals is often a matter of practice, of going through the emotions, rather than of feeling—and this is often all that is expected. For example, a monk saying the offices every day is unlikely to be overcome with emotion each time. But such regular practice may nevertheless have a significant effect in shaping a structure of feeling, and laying down affective dispositions.

Key characteristics of religious emotion

From this discussion of religious emotional regimes, we can pull out a number of features that seem to be particularly characteristic of religious emotion: emotional ordering, emotional transcendence-transition, and inspiration-orientation.

Emotional ordering

Religious emotional regimes help to order and pattern emotional life. The same can, of course, be said of emotional regimes in other spheres of life, including the family and politics. But religious regimes invoke an 'alternate ordering' that provides the reference point for orienting moods and motivations. Just as everyday emotions are configured in relation to situations composed of symbolic, material, and social elements, so religious emotions are structured by relation to a symboli-

---

[13] 'H. H. the Dalai Lama Answers Questions at Life as a Western Buddhist Nun', www2.hawaii.edu/~tsomo/ordination/hh_q_a.html (accessed Jan. 2008).

cally mediated ideal ordering—a paradise of harmonious human and material relations. This shapes an emotional template that may extend over the whole of life, and override other emotional programmes. For example, if self-sacrificial love is the dominant emotional note in a religious regime, it should infuse all relations, and overrule incompatible emotional demands. When a believer feels aggrieved, proud, or angry, such emotions have to be suppressed. Over time and with the appropriate religious disciplines, it may be possible to banish them completely; in the meantime they may be categorized as sins or temptations, personified as demons, or lures of an evil power. Because religion has a reference point beyond the mundane, religious emotional orders also integrate feelings related to death, loss, and bereavement, and maintain emotional bonds with the dead as well as the living.

Emotional ordering occurs at the individual level, the group level, the societal level, or all three. For the individual, religion can foster a general sense of hope and trust that orients human life despite experiences that threaten to engender fear and anguish. Trust in a merciful God may inspire a sense of assurance in the face of worldly disruption; alternatively, belief in a vengeful God, malevolent spirits, or witchcraft may engender a pervading sense of guilt or mistrustful anxiety. At the group level, symbolic relations with the alternate ordering serve to orient and stabilize collective emotion. As we have noted, sophisticated symbolic systems are able to inspire complex polyphonic emotional expressions within a religious community. Religious groups can control and eliminate discordant emotions, and bring members into line emotionally. Positive and negative emotional feedbacks sustain an emotional harmony that can nevertheless change and adapt over time (see Chapters 3 and 4). When a religious emotional ordering is embodied at societal as well as group level, its notes and rhythms structure life in a more comprehensive fashion. In medieval Western Christendom, for example, the life of Christ and the saints became the template by which time, space, and social hierarchy were ordered, thus providing an encompassing template for collective and personal emotion (Woodhead 2004).

Ordering implies offering a coherent programme for emotional life that clarifies which emotional notes must be sounded and which must not, which emotions should be foregrounded, and which should appear only on the 'back stage' or not at all. It includes providing guidance, inspiration, and support. This is inseparable from particular patterns of social and symbolic relations. To love, for example, is not merely to feel something but to relate to others and oneself in new ways. A religion that exhorts love and defines what is meant by love and also guides love towards its proper objects, regulates its expressions, rules out inappropriate loves, and sanctions incompatible emotions. Thus emotional ordering involves emotional clarification and emotional focusing. By means of ritual, symbolism, and living examples, religious emotional regimes embody normative patterns of feeling and relating that shape both personal and collective life.

Such emotional ordering is not static. It is constantly produced, disrupted, and reproduced in the lives of religious communities and their members, often through innovation and adjustment below a fully conscious level. People 'feel their way' along emotional paths and patternings, and in doing so consolidate patterns of action and reaction. A memorable example drawn from our own participant observation in an evangelical-charismatic Sunday service in Kendal illustrates the process. In the service the previous week a vase had broken, and the elder in charge on the day we attended had taken as his theme: 'being ready to be broken'. The first part of the ritual was scripted accordingly, with songs and prayers chosen to sound notes of sorrow, melancholy, and abnegation. After about half an hour of this, with an intense emotional tone, we noticed the senior church pastor crouching down behind the lectern whispering to the elder who was leading the service. The leader then got up and said: 'I don't know if anyone else is feeling this too, but I'm sensing a conflict here.' He asked us to imagine Jesus walking up the main street of Kendal that very morning surrounded by disciples celebrating that the King of Love had come. What should we do? Should we be out there praising him? Or would there be a group of people stuck in this church saying, 'Lord, am I ready enough to be broken?' Everyone laughed and there was an almost palpable release of tension. The leader called for 'King of Love' to be played again, but this time people sang loudly and joyfully, with smiles on their faces.[14] This intervention was spontaneous, but unusual. In a congregation that prided itself on lay leadership, it was an uncharacteristically authoritarian gesture, reflecting how serious the situation was felt to be. The effect was to reassert the dominant emotional order and relieve the tension generated by the introduction of discordant emotional notes. Thus the borders as well as the inner contours of a

---

[14] From field notes recorded at the time by Karin Tusting.

religion are often marked out by feeling to such an extent that adherents will know 'intuitively' (emotionally) if something is 'out of place', if another group's worship is authentically religious, whether their neighbour counts as a godly person or not, what counts as sacrilegious and blasphemous. Emotional orderings serve to identify not only who genuinely belongs to a group (and is not just pretending, feigning, or going through the motions), and who is an outsider. Thus the boundaries between sacred and profane and religious and secular are emotional as well as cognitive and symbolic.

The nature and strength of religious emotional orderings are illuminated by many anthropological studies of small-scale, bounded communities. Ruth Benedict's *Patterns of Culture* (1935) is an early and influential example. A major part of her purpose was to show that, however bizarre different cultural orderings may seem from the standpoint of a different order (particularly Western individualism), they have a logic that makes perfect sense on its own terms. Benedict contrasts different cases selected to demonstrate how diverse human cultures can be, and how they can integrate traits that are regarded as deviant and even repugnant in ours. Emotions figure quite largely in her analysis—for example, in the contrasts she draws between emotionally expressive 'Dionysian' cultures and emotionally self-controlled 'Apollonian' ones. With this and other examples, she draws attention to 'fundamental and distinctive cultural configurations that pattern existence and condition the thoughts and emotions of the individuals who participate in those cultures' (Benedict 1935: 55).[15] Gregory Bateson's *Naven* (1936/1958) is even more explicit in its reflections on emotional ordering. In this study of the Iatmul in what

---

[15] The Zuñi in the South-West desert of the USA, represent an Apollonian case. Even family members prefer not to display deep feeling. Whether it is anger or love or jealousy or grief, moderation is the first virtue. Death is a discomfort which must be put out of the way as quick and discreetly as possible. Their relation with the supernatural power is also characterized by formality and sobriety. The spirits have no animus against man, and there is no placation of evil forces. 'Abnormal' individuals who trespass the norms of moderation are branded as witches and excluded from social life. The Dobu who live on an island close to New Guinea represent another case discussed by Benedict. They are sorcerers who use magical formulae to attract yams from their neighbours or harm others. There is no propitiation of supernatural beings, which are only associated with a few secret names, and not referred to as a common source of meaning. Any magically obtained benefit for one person involves a loss for another. Jealousy, suspicion and fierce exclusiveness of ownership are characteristic emotions. The prevailing mood is described by Benedict as dour, prudish, and passionate, consumed with jealousy and suspicion and resentment. The emotional regime of the Dobu exalts animosity and malignancy as life virtues in their cut-throat struggle for existence in a malign world.

is now Papua New Guinea, Bateson introduced the concepts of *ethos* and *eidos*. Whereas the latter has to do with cognitive patterning, the former refers to 'the characteristic spirit, prevalent tone of sentiment of a people or a community' (1936/1958: 2). 'Ethological relationships' may be observed to exist between the emotional aspects of the culture as a whole, and details of individual emotional life. They constitute 'affective relationships, between details of cultural behaviour and the basic or derived emotional needs and desires of individuals: the affective motivation of details of behaviour' (1936/1958: 29–30). Bateson operationalizes these ideas in his analysis of the Iatmul male ethos, whose dominant notes are pride, fearlessness, display, and confidence marked by spectacular achievement and appropriate symbolic reinforcements. He contrasts this with the modest ethos of Iatmul women, whose shy emotionality is more often expressed in private and without the same symbolic reinforcement.[16]

There is a danger in approaches that are calibrated to perceive social order and cohesion that they overlook emotional tensions, imbalances, and disorders and the social change that they may entail. Emotional disorder makes most sense in relation to an emotional ordering. Some religious emotional regimes allow for a significant degree of disorder. Carnivals and saturnalia, for example, deliberately turn the social order of things 'upside down' for a brief period of time, and allow the expression of emotions that are not normally sanctioned (Bakhtin 1993). Spirit possession allows certain categories of person to express emotions they would not normally feel, and that run contrary to what an emotional regime dictates for them, and thereby serves not only as a release valve, but as a way of reinforcing the dominant order that is restored when the spirit departs (Lambek 1981). Witchcraft may be a less controlled and controllable—and hence more dangerous and frightening—imaginative inversion of dominant norms and values, especially those associated with nurture, kindness, and reciprocity. The witch personifies emotions that are proscribed for a certain category of person. He or she is often accused of feeling the exact opposite of what is sanctioned in relation to a particular object—for example, sexual violence towards children, envy towards property, mockery of sacred rites and symbols (Roper 1994).

---

[16] See the illuminating discussion of these positions by Klass (1995: 41–8).

A few 'emotions out of place' do not represent a serious challenge to an emotional regime. For example, tears at church weddings are a little discordant with the mood of joy and celebration, but are considered harmless if shed quietly by women, especially by the mother of the bride (in some wedding rituals—for example, many Hindu ones—there may even be a ritual time for women to cry). But other disorderly emotions can be much more problematic. For example, the expression of sadness and grief is problematic in many regimes of contemporary Western societies, where such a high premium is placed on happiness (Chapter 6). This contrasts with older European cultures in which there was much more room for the expression of grief, and in which 'ritual weeping' was considered a mark of sanctity (Christian 2004; Ebersole 2004).

In the following chapters we propose a framework for analysing not only ordered emotional regimes, but regimes in which there is disorder and disconnection. Such imbalance does not merely consist in individual expressions of unauthorized emotion, but involves symbols that clash by failing to communicate appropriate emotions, and emotional programmes proposed by religious elites that are resisted by participants. Such resistance may be reinforced by the introduction of symbols that contradict with the dominant agenda. As we will see, emotional disorder may be actively pursued with the purpose of instigating disruption or bringing about change, or may result from wider circumstance, including the presence of competing emotional regimes.

Emotional transcendence-transition

Religious emotional regimes enable transcendence over everyday emotional states, both collective and personal. It is worth emphasizing again that such transcendence need not imply other-worldiness (though it sometimes does), since it is also focused upon alteration of relations with and within this world. To embark on a course of meditation practice, to gather together a community to celebrate a harvest, to participate in a funeral service, or to seek advice from a shaman, is likely to result in some emotional change—even if this is not its primary purpose, and even if it is not explicitly acknowledged. By multifarious means, religions offer some distance from everyday emotions, some critical purchase over them, some ability to review, alter, or selectively confirm them. Generally, religions promise emotional ease-ment and amelioration. This does not necessarily mean that they offer to make people feel better. On the contrary, they may make them feel worse—for example, by highlighting the evil, transitory, and painful nature of existence, by calling for self-examination and confession of sin and failure, or by provoking grief. Emotional transcendence does not mean leaving behind what modern psychologists categorize as 'negative emotions', but bringing emotions into relation with alter-nate orderings in a way that enhances order, control, and change. It has less to do with 'feeling better' in the narrow, modern sense of feeling happier, and more to do with being able to symbolize, order, and hence gain some control over emotions.

This also means that religion often facilitates emotional transition. This is a dramatic form of emotional transcendence, partly because it usually takes place over a much shorter time, and often involves more intense emotions. An emotional transition is a significant shift in the structure of personal sensibility that involves a dis-ordering and re-ordering of emotion, a de-patterning and re-patterning. William James's distinction between the 'healthy-minded', whose religious lives follow a smooth line of commitment, and the 'twice-born', who adopt a new religious disposition in a dramatic change of life, captures something of this, but he draws the line too sharply. In practice most religions combine routine, ritualized means of patterning religious sensibility with more dramatic rites and techniques to make and mark more dramatic shifts. Often the two are entirely complementary, with a dramatic transition (like baptism) being reinforced and recapi-tulated over a lifetime in a repeated ritual (participation in the Eucha-rist). We speak of emotional 'transcendence-transition' in order to hold these aspects together, but we can nevertheless distinguish between dramatic emotional transitions, and emotional transcendence effected through regular means operating over a longer time span.

To begin with the latter, we can consider the example of liturgical church worship. Sunday services in many historic Christian denomi-nations can give visitors the impression that no feeling, let alone transformation of feeling, is involved at all. It is true, of course, that forms of religion can lose their emotional appeal and simply be expe-rienced as boring and 'meaningless'. But our research in the churches in Kendal led us to think that there was more to be said. We noticed not only their power to order emotion, but the subtle forms of emotion-al transcendence they engendered. The ancient architecture, beautiful furnishings, choral music, and scripted words evoked no obvious displays of emotion. In interviews members of the churches did not refer to their feelings in great detail, but many (women in particular) spoke of love as being at the heart of their faith, and others (both men and women) spoke of the sense of calm and peace that they experienced in church. We also noticed that small incidents, including changes within the community and its worship, could evoke tremendous passion, suggesting that it is sometimes in the disruption of ritual, rather than in its routine performance, that its emotional significance can be most clearly glimpsed. The overall impression was that this form of religion served to ground and stabilize a particular structure of feeling that was felt to be under threat from the emotional regimes of wider society. Such religion provided emotional transcendence by allowing people to escape everyday emotional pressures and enter a familiar space in which few explicit emotional demands were made, yet which nevertheless served to reinforce and anchor a distinctive sensibility.

In other kinds of church, emotional transcendence is much easier to observe. In the course of research in Asheville, for example, Woodhead observed a largely Hispanic Pentecostal church in a poor suburb. Preparations for the Sunday morning service began an hour before it started. They involved the choir and the leaders of the service not only rehearsing their lines and their music, but working themselves into an appropriate mood—here, one of upbeat, energetic, infectious, excitable joy and celebration. The chief pastor literally paced up and down the stage by himself, praying and invoking God. At the same time, the choir leader rehearsed young men and women to praise the Lord and to 'SMILE!' as they sang. Once the congregation started to flow in, they were greeted with a compelling emotional atmosphere that seemed instantly to transport participants into a mood of joy. They joined in a swelling chorus of extempore prayer and praise, swaying, clapping, and smiling. But there was more to this ritual than celebration. Participants whose lives were marked by considerable hardship were not simply being offered an 'opiate', because the hardship was being acknowledged and honoured in various ways. The preacher, for example, spoke from the heart of recent events that had 'blindsided' him, leading him to feel frustration, anger, and a desire for revenge. The congregation joined in the sermon by shouting out in sympathy and appreciation of what had been said, adding 'amens' and 'yes brothers'. The crescendo came with the preacher's affirmation that he had overcome the temptation to seek revenge, under the conviction that he had a powerful Father God who was trustworthy, loving, and 'slow to anger'. Frustration, pain, and anger must therefore be transformed into love and the courage to continue. The service ended with songs reaffirming trust, joy, hope, confidence, and pride.

Although emotional transcendence—and transition—is very evident in this example, it is implicit in the sense that the church does not foreground explicit promises to transform feeling. In other cases the offer of emotional transformation is openly advertised. For example, many forms of contemporary spirituality promise emotional 'well-being'. They assist individuals with understanding and expressing how they feel, and help them to monitor and 'manage' emotions more effectively (Sointu and Woodhead 2008). An explicit focus on emotional transformation is also found in some Christian communities. For example, in the course of the same research in Asheville, we observed an independent Christian congregation influenced by alternative spirituality that advertised its Sunday services with the following themes:

> From Sorrow to Joy
> From Broken to Whole
> From Fear to Faith
> From Distraction to Connection
> From Anxiety to Assurance
> From Ebb to Flow
> From Apathy to Awe.[17]

In Sunday worship the theme was announced at the start and skilfully woven through the event in a range of ways: in symbols, readings, songs, and hymns, in the sermon, and through ritualized enactment. By creating powerful collective sentiments of whichever emotion was on the menu that week, the ritual helped participants experience that mood. As the service titles indicate, the process was dynamic, moving from invocation of an unwanted emotion to its banishment by a valued one. In keeping with an individualist ethos, space was also provided for individuals to express their own, perhaps discordant, feelings in a 'healing' section of the service, as well as in counselling services offered outside it.

---

[17] Brochure, 'Seeds for Celebration', Spring 2006. Woodhead and Berger carried out this research.

In analysing forms of emotional transcendence in which the element of transition is prominent, Victor Turner's scheme for interpreting rites of passage is helpful. Drawing on van Gennep's work (1908/1960), Turner (1967) characterizes them as drawing participants from an existing emotional state, through a liminal stage, into a new life. Turner focuses particularly on the liminal phase in which participants are betwixt and between their former and later identities, assigned with an ambivalent status, and subject to degradation that will be reversed when they are aggregated back into society and a new role. In many cultures rites of passage that lead from childhood to adulthood involve elements of fear and pain. Initiates are taught first to abstain from the emotional regime of their former status—childish emotions—and then to conform with the new roles ascribed to them fitting their new status. Such transformation is intended to be permanent; the new emotional disposition and patterning will shape life into the unknown future.

Adapting Turner, we propose a simpler scheme with just two stages: emotional de-patterning and re-patterning, or what Mol (1976) calls emotional 'stripping' and 'welding'. This corresponds with a transition from one emotional programme to another, the latter being that of the religious regime whose ordering is being internalized. Such emotional restructuring takes place in so many ways, for so many different reasons, and under such different conditions that it is hard to generalize about it (Turner's account of liminality and *communitas* is only one example). Instead, we can illustrate with a few examples, moving from the macro to the micro level.

It is widely recognized that historical periods of social upheaval often involve a loosening of mores, leading to social change and altered behaviour. Periods of disruption are also associated with religious change—as, for example, during the period of Civil War in England, which led to an outburst of new forms of individual and group prophecy and piety (see Chapter 4). Something similar can be observed when change is imposed from the outside, as, for example, when colonization and/or capitalism disrupt existing social order. Millenarian movements are common in both situations. They centre around a revelation (*apocalypsis*) of an alternate ordering that is to be imminently realized in a form that will supplant the existing order of things. Such movements actively embrace the destruction of existing social relations and cultural symbols (or some portion of them) in anticipation of what is to come. For example, the Melanesian cargo cults as analysed by Worsley (1957) are precipitated by the arrival of a form of colonial capitalism that involves indigenous people in new modes of production without allowing them full access to the rewards of consumption. The cults look forward to the imminent destruction of the existing order and the arrival of ancestors and gods with goods hijacked by the white man. Selective destruction was sometimes carried out by cult followers in order to make the wheel of history turn more quickly. Worsley views such religion as a reasonable proto-political response to a situation that offers little or no other option for marginalized people trying to gain some control over an intolerable situation. Emotionally, such millenarianism involves a stripping of existing loyalties, hopes, and commitments in order to engage with a new structure of feeling that involves joyous expectation of a state in which humiliation and injustice will end, and spiritual and material needs will be satisfied.[18] From this perspective, the claim that millenarianism is not futile despite its failed predictions makes sense: the de-patterning and re-patterning of emotion effects emotional amelioration, gives a sense of control, and shifts sensibility in ways that may lead to lasting personal and political change (see Chapter 5 on 'The Power of Religious Emotion').

The phenomenon of religious conversion can also be illuminated by taking the emotional element seriously (e.g. Barker 1984; Rambo 1993). Conversion normally depends upon there being existing emotional regimes to convert to and from, and is particularly relevant for entry into religious regimes with tight boundaries. The latter usually have existing narratives, rituals, symbols, and practices of conversion, which embody the process of emotional stripping as well as welding. In evangelical Christian conversion narratives, for example, converts typically recall their experience of how a life of emotional chaos, dissolution, despair, and depression gave way in conversion to one of hope, trust, faith, and overwhelming gratitude and love (Csordas 1997). As well as such conversion *into* a new regime, there can be conversion *within* an existing religious regime, as emotional patterning is more closely conformed to an emotional programme over time. Here, too, destruction of bad habits of feeling is prominent, whether in the destruction of negative emotions in Buddhist meditation practices,

---

[18] For an overview and analysis of the anthropological literature on cargo cults, see Morris (2006: 257–70).

or in the process of confession, penance, repentance, and absolution in Catholic Christianity.

Finally, we must mention those forms of emotional transcendence-transition that involve the suspension of everyday feeling as individuals enter into states of 'altered consciousness'. In the proposed scheme, these can be classified as religious if they are part of a religious emotional regime. They include trances, spirit journeys, drug-induced states, ecstasies, possessions, and channelling. There is considerable and continuing debate about how to define and draw the line between such states.[19] Without entering into this, it is enough to point out that all seem to involve some form of emotional dissociation and de-patterning prior to a re-patterning (which may simply involve return to normal). Lambek's study of trance (1981) in Mayotte provides a vivid example that shows how the common experience of spirit possession allows individuals, especially women, not just to feel and act out very different emotional repertoires from those the emotional regime would normally allow, but actually to be possessed by a new 'spirit'—a complete de-patterning and re-patterning within socially accepted boundaries, and on a temporary basis. Convention has it that during trance the host herself is absent from her own body.[20] An enormous range of means are used in different religious contexts to loosen existing emotional patterns, including bodily modifications (for example, postures, fasting, dancing, experiencing extremes of temperature) and sensory stimulation (for example, rhythmic drumming, strong smells, and foods), plus the use of symbols and objects (for example, symbols of the gods), together with wider social reinforcements.

It is the exception rather than the rule that such experiences, though intensely 'individual', take place in solitude or without reference to cultural symbols. In the case of shamanism, for example, initiation is often preceded by long and arduous apprenticeships, which may involve dramatic dissociative experiences. The role of the shaman is to help members of their community deal with a range of problems, including cases of emotional and bodily disturbance and illness (the two being treated as inseparable). In treating such disturbance, shamans employ various means to disassociate from their existing

---

[19] For useful discussions, see Lambek (1981), Winkelman (1997), and Morris (2006).

[20] As Lambek (1981: 41) puts it, 'the opposition between two discrete entities, host and spirit, is the single most crucial element, the axiom, upon which the entire system of possession rests. If it is not maintained, the case is simply not possession.'

state of consciousness and enter a new one. This may involve trance states, negotiation with good and evil spirits, or possession, usually in the presence of the afflicted and other family and community members. The culmination is the diagnosis and attempted cure. To effect this, shamans creatively deploy their own emotional insight, the repertoire of signs and symbols common to the culture, traditional rituals, and the collective spirit of those who are gathered (Desjarlais 1992). Thus personal emotional troubles are transfigured in relation to accepted social roles and commitments, and deviant feelings are 'healed' by being interpreted and reintegrated into an existing emotional regime (Vitebsky 1993).

When revived in the context of contemporary societies, shamanism takes a more individualistic form, with trances and spirit journeys (rarely possession) being undertaken by individuals using packaged techniques, sometimes in the privacy of their own homes, and with the purpose of effecting personal change (Jakobsen 1999; Wallis 2003). There is an explicit attempt to dissociate from routine patterns of thinking and feeling, to enter deeper into the 'psyche' to glimpse new patterns and possibilities, and to return emotionally renewed, refreshed, and freed from limiting patterns. Modern appropriations of magical practices, such as Wicca, share some of the same characteristics, with many practitioners happily embracing the idea that they are casting spells or brewing potions or undertaking rituals for the primary purpose of transforming consciousness. Many who carry out, say, a ritual for banishing an unwanted person from their territory has no expectation that it will ensure they never return, but they know it helps banish him or her from the mind and dispel feelings of anger, resentment, and anxiety (Berger 2005; Berger and Ezzy 2007). Still, the contrast between modern and 'traditional' forms should not be overdrawn. As Godfrey Lienhardt (1961) argued in his study of the Dinka, a hunter who is late for his dinner and knots a piece of grass (symbolizing a constriction) as he hurries home does not really believe it will delay the culinary preparations. Rather, when he makes an external, physical representation of a well-formed mental intention, 'he has produced a model of his desires and hopes, upon which to base renewed practical endeavour' (Lienhardt 1961: 283). In terms of the account of emotions we developed in the previous chapter, we can add that a change of feeling involves a change of relational stance that, in an important sense, changes one's world.

Inspiration-orientation

Geertz points to another characteristic feature of religious emotion when he speaks of 'powerful, pervasive and long-lasting moods and motivations'. Although religions can produce short-lived moments of emotional intensity, their ability to shape emotional dispositions, and hence permanent relational stances, is more notable. As such, religious emotional regimes affect human character rather than offering only passing sensation. This is part of the reason why religion differs from, say, a movie or some other art or entertainment, despite the latter's capacity to move people profoundly. 'Long-lasting' captures much of this, but 'pervasive' adds another element, pointing to the universal or cosmic reference of religious emotion. Emotions like hope, compassion, and submission are cosmic emotions in the sense that they are universally applicable. It is tempting to argue that any emotion that 'goes cosmic' can count as a religious emotion, though we would argue that this applies fully only to those that are integrated into a religious programme (and there are many religious emotions that are not as pervasive). Nevertheless, the reference of religious emotion to a higher, alternate, ordering of things, often lends it characteristic 'pervasiveness'.

With its mention of 'motivation', Geertz's compact definition also covers the active and inspiring quality of religious emotion: the way in which it readies for action, guides that action, and fires or inhibits particular courses of action. Again, he points out that this motivation has wide scope and reference, and is also 'powerful'. This captures the way in which it may transcend and override other motivations. This is bound up with the way in which it relates agents to a standpoint from which everyday order is interpreted, judged, and revitalized. From this perspective, it may even make sense to sacrifice one's life, which is no longer considered of ultimate value. This is not so much a matter of rational judgement, as of being impelled by feelings like love, devotion, hope, and trust. Since emotions are what orient us within our life worlds, and since religions claim to reveal what is truly sacred, valuable, and meaningful, the emotional orientation they provide often has a particularly strong bearing on how adherents live out their lives, and what inspires their ultimate loyalty.

In other words, religion provides fundamental inspiration *and* orientation—both an engine and a direction of travel. Religious emotions have an important part to play in setting value direction, not least by training emotions of love and devotion to become attached to their 'proper' objects and detached from 'improper' ones. In this they have a great deal in common with the emotions of family life, which also bind to love objects, and also provide powerful motivation and orientation (Bowlby 1982; Klein 1997). They also have things in common with political emotions, in so far as these provide a symbolic focus of attachment and striving. Here, too, adherents may become convinced they are subject to a higher power that demands their allegiance, commitment, and submission—though disillusionment is more likely with human than heavenly gods (Smith 2003). Many religions recognize the threat of competing familial and political objects of devotion, and have various means for putting them in their place, and for reorienting emotions after a lapse has taken place—of which apostasy is the most serious. Religions inspire and orient by providing a focus not only of devotion, but of fear, anxiety, repulsion, disgust, and aversion. That which threatens the objects of emotional trust and devotion is likely to be feared and condemned. Regimes that are experienced as incompatible, yet threatening, may be hated and aggressively attacked. Rogue emotions within a regime may be equally abjured. Internal deviants may be stigmatized, banished, accused of sin or witchcraft, or subjected to practices designed to change their feelings and motivations, perhaps by driving out a disordered or evil 'spirit'. From the point of view of those outside a religious order, or outside religion altogether, the power of the passions it can inspire may seem fantastic, fanatical, dangerous, and irrational. Religious passion can inspire people to kill and to sacrifice their own lives.

Emotional cultivation

The 'power' and 'pervasiveness' of religious emotion are bound up with its characteristic means of cultivation. The aim is nothing less than a change of heart—a metaphor that nicely sums up its deep embodiment. The means are holistic, drawing in not just thought, but habit, bodily posture, and 'standing' (Mellor and Shilling 1997). Cultivation often begins in earliest childhood and extends across a lifetime. The multidimensional account of emotion proposed in the previous chapter explains how and why emotions are shaped by such various means. It also explains why emotional patterning is so far-reaching in its effects, which shape how individuals and groups relate to the worlds they encounter. Indeed, such patterning may be so integral to identity that even individuals who have drifted away from religious commitment find it hard to cast off the emotional habits that unconsciously influence them to observe religious standards, or that condemn them in their own hearts when they fall short—even though they have intellectually abandoned them.

Material and symbolic objects and spatial organization play an important role in religious emotional cultivation. Even before a child can read, and even at the periphery of rational awareness, religious images convey powerful emotive messages and shape sensibilities. They serve as overdetermined compact symbols (Ortner 2002) that not only communicate emotional dispositions approved by a religious regime, but become entwined in autobiographies and anchor personal emotional moods and memories (Hoskins 1998; Carsten 2007). Sometimes symbols are embedded within stories, narratives, or myths, which serve to anchor, interpret, and shape emotions, dramatically enact and reconcile a basic cultural conflict, memorably represent aspects of alternate orderings, and so on. Myths also serve to relate individual feelings and memories to collective sentiments and memories, and to connect individuals to a living tradition that forms a bridge to sacred time. Internal pictures are sequences connected to external ones by repeated encounter with images, and a number of spiritual disciplines have to do with building up a mental repertoire of salient images and 'visions' that shape understanding and engagement with the world (Carruthers 1998).

Religious images and narratives rarely exist in isolation, but rather in relation to sacred texts and spaces, including buildings and landscapes (Recht 2008). Sacred images are often located within controlled zones, accessible only to certain persons or at certain times. Such spaces are themselves emotionally impactful and sacred (Knott 2005). Constructed spaces are deliberately planned to evoke certain feelings, such as a sense of security and communion in an enclosed, circular space, or a sense of awe in a soaring vertical space. Natural landscapes can also become dense with emotional significance, a significance related not only to their unique natural form, but to human constructions upon them, including the myths, symbols, and other cultural products associated with them that mediate their significance (Ivakhiv 2001).

The power and significance of these various means of emotional cultivation may be enhanced and clarified in collective settings, and their coordination is often characteristic of the diverse practices that some scholars attempt to gather together under the heading of 'ritual' (Bowie 2000: 151–89; Lambek 2002: 327–446). Ritual engages individuals in orchestrated and formalized social performances, and serves to coordinate bodily movements in synchronized and harmonious ways that can often reinforce and intensify certain feelings, and banish others. Emotion may, thereby, be focused more effectively by and upon certain symbols and myths. As Jonathan Z. Smith (1988) puts it, ritual serves as a 'focusing lens' creating what is in effect a 'controlled environment' that can simplify and concentrate the confusions of everyday experience by focusing attention on what really matters and how one should feel about it. In other words, ritual brings an alternate ordering to life. Although performative (as well as cognitive) interpretations of ritual often downplay the emotional aspects of ritual, it is hard to explain how ritual can have lasting effects without paying some attention to its emotional aspects, and difficult to explain how it conjures the sacred without noticing how it generates certain feelings. Even Rappaport's performative analysis of ritual (1999) acknowledges ritual's ability to 'intensify emotion' and, by way of the 'significata of ritual representations', to alter consciousness (1999: 258–9).[21]

But although it may be true that many powerful states of altered consciousness occur in collective, ritualized settings, not all collective rituals generate powerful emotions or, indeed, much emotion at all. The effectiveness of ritual is not as assured as some theorists assume. Nor is the category as clear-cut. As Bell (1997) suggests, it is more helpful to think in terms of 'ritualization' than to view ritual as a fixed category assigned to a special place in social life. This also helps to avoid isolating ritual from the other elements of religious and emotional life in relation to which it makes sense. Rather than concentrate too exclusively on the emotional power of orchestrated, usually male-led, ritual practices, it is important, for example, to take account of domestic and intimate practices that are often not recognized as ritual at all, but that may have profound emotional signifi-

---

[21] Although Smith's approach is intellectualist and emphasizes thinking, reflecting, and recollecting, its cognitive perspective can be enlarged to take account of emotion. See Klassen (2008: 145–6).

cance for participants (McGuire 2008). Public rituals that find no reinforcement in other spheres of society may provide nostalgia or entertainment or fleeting intense emotion, but are unlikely to be able to feed 'powerful and long-lasting' moods and motivations. Practices that are regularly carried out in the home and a domestic setting may have equal or greater emotional impact, as will those that find reinforcement in other spheres of public life, such as the educational and political. Thus emotional cultivation has to do not only with crowds and intensity and authorized orchestration, but with duration, repetition, and reinforcement. Practices that are 'bred in the bone' from a very early age are likely to retain great emotional power, not only when re-enacted, but even when merely recalled. Moreover, those religious practices that harness feelings generated in other spheres of life (the love of a parent for a child, the grief of a bereaved person at their loss, and so on), bring them to a ritual and symbolic focus, and relate them to an alternate ordering of significance may be most moving and motivating.

Conclusion

This chapter addresses the question 'what is religious emotion?' It does not answer by trying to isolate a uniquely religious experience, or by overstressing the distinctiveness of religious emotion. Religious emotions may have similarities to emotions in other spheres. Similar feelings may, for example, arise when viewing a favourite movie, listening to a piece of music, or joining in a political rally or a festival. There is also a close similarity with emotions in family and personal life, which also have to do with the intense attachment to 'objects' of devotion and, sometimes, feelings associated with the loss of the beloved or once-beloved.

However, a religious emotion—which can be any emotion—can be distinguished by its place within a religion's emotional programme, and hence by its relation to the symbols, persons, and practices that constitute such a programme. Religious emotion in general is simply emotion in the context of a religious regime. The latter makes reference to an alternate ordering that is experienced as foundational, a frame of reference by which to interpret and live in the everyday world. Such an ordering engenders special bonds, obligations, and exclusions. Demands for submission, sacrifice, and commitment to the cause of the nation, the corporation, or a political party may have close parallels, but the transcendent reference of religious emotion gives it a scope that goes beyond the limitations of worldliness.

This has some special consequences, not only for some self-contained set of 'religious emotions', but for emotional life in general. By relating individuals and groups to an alternate ordering that supplements and complements everyday life, emotions are configured in a wider perspective. Family emotions are connected not just to kin but to ancestral families, lineages of holy men and women, and a heavenly family. Political emotions are connected not just to a given people, territory, and set of customs, but to a sacred geography (for example, one centred on Rome, Mecca, Benares, Jerusalem), and a more perfect sacred community in an eternal setting. Religious emotions relate not just to an 'as-if' world of artistic imagination, but to a reality that shapes and interprets what we usually take to be real. The emotional focus may become the eye of God or the perspective of the religious community, time may be eternalized and spatial limitations suspended, and personal memories and their emotional weight may be subsumed into collective ones. Thus religious emotion characteristically serves to order emotional experience, offer emotional transcendence, and provide powerful inspiration and orientation. It may offer an emotional gyroscope to stabilize the buffeting of everyday emotions, an emotional compass to provide a sense of purpose and direction, and the emotional energy and coordination to pursue that vision collectively.

3

Dynamics of Religious Emotion I: Connections of Self, Society, and Symbols

Having established in the preceding chapters what we mean by emotion, and indicated some of the characteristic features of religious emotion, we can now develop our scheme for analysing religious emotional regimes. We begin by looking at regimes in which there are balanced and reinforcing interactions between constituent parts: individual agents, a social group, and symbols. In the next chapter we consider what happens when disruptions and disconnections occur, and balance is lost. To avoid misunderstanding it is important to emphasize at the outset that the term 'balance' does not imply any sort of normative judgement: a 'balanced' emotional regime is not inherently better or worse than a 'one-sided' one, simply different in structure.

Because the constituent elements of an emotional regime are not merely interactive but mutually constituting, we speak of them as 'dialectically' related. Dialectics refer to formative two-way processes, in which the *relata* are affected and shaped by the relation. An implication here is that novel processes emerge from the interaction of the parts that are irreducible to those parts. This is more than mere 'interaction' and covers more than mutual actions between agents: it also embraces relations between agents, community, and symbols. Dialectical relations form an entity, which is something more than the sum of its parts.

Within the framework we propose, religious emotions arise when individuals relate emotionally to religious symbols within the context of a religious community. This involves three sets of relations, which this chapter sets out to clarify and illustrate with concrete examples from a range of different religious settings and traditions.

Objectification and subjectification

We begin, not with sociology's preferred dialectic between individual and society, but with that between persons and symbols, because for religious emotion this is as important but more neglected. Religion involves a multitude of sacred objects imbued with emotional significance. Such symbolic expressions take a range of forms including architecture, painting, sculpture, and music. All are products of human agency, yet they are ascribed supra-human qualities. As Morgan (1998: 9), in his study of the role of mass-produced images in Protestantism, puts it, the gap between signifier and signified is at least partially closed for the believer, so that the image 'possesses its referent within itself' (see also Neville 1996; Morgan 2005). An icon may seem to perform miracles by itself, entirely independent of its human producer. When a devout woman visits an Orthodox church and kisses an icon, it seems to provoke tears by its own power rather than her volition. The power of such objects is enhanced by personal and collective associations, and they often become the basis for a chain of memories. They may obtain a history and existence and 'biography' of their own, beyond that of their producers.

In this example, 'objectification' refers to the act of production which is aimed at expressing and evoking certain emotions through the icon. More broadly, objectification in our use refers to the expression of personal emotions in a symbolic object, and to that extent, in a public idiom.[1] This does not imply that an individual is in some constant state of personal emotional arousal in relation to the object. The painter of an icon, for example, may not personally feel the

---

[1] The term 'objectification' is used by Berger and Luckmann (1966), where it refers to the project where society emerges as an objective reality, with a history that seems independent of its human producers. This is dialectically related to processes of 'internalization' and 'externalization'. Our usage of 'objectification' differs, since it here relates to the human production of symbols, rather than to the human construction of a world view. It seemed logical to counterpoint the term objectification with the term 'subjectification'. Our concepts should be read as a dialectical pairs, and do not therefore refer to an object/subject duality.

emotions expressed by the icon (at least not all the time), but will have some awareness of the emotional effect he or she wishes to achieve, and the work will usually be inspired and directed by existing icons, which have proven themselves in this regard. As Baggley (1995: 55) puts it: 'the true iconographer is engaged in a work of spiritual expression; he is not merely repeating a form, but externalizing a spiritual reality that is part of the Orthodox tradition, and should have become a part of himself.' Although some of the most powerful religious objects are likely to be those that express their creators' deep emotions, their power also resides in their ability to evoke feeling in others.[2] Religious objectification refers to the creation of an object that aims to capture and provoke emotions that are classified as religious. This classification normally involves relating the emotions to the emotional regime of a religious order, which deems it sacred. At this point there is, therefore, a social aspect to the process, which is discussed in the next section.

A piece of sacred art such as a painting, a composition, a sculpture, or a building represents a tangible and permanent example of objectification expressing certain emotions. Rituals, drama, and music are also objectified expressions of religious emotions that have a relatively manifest and permanent form. Objectifications additionally include less tangible or permanent forms, such as telling a myth, singing a song, writing a book, or preparing a meal. Through acts of objectification, emotional expressions become fixed and communicable. Outsiders and new generations can be affected by the objects, and gain a sense of the wider regime to which they belong. The objects may also serve as emotional mediators between people, expressing feelings that would not otherwise be communicated. Many religious symbols are relatively fixed—like the authorized image of a deity. They have a permanent place in the pantheon. But each symbol may be experienced afresh by individuals in their own emotional

---

[2] In the orthodox tradition, an icon was painted by a monk in a monastery. The creative process took place in a group under the guidance of an experienced artist, while a monk read passages from the Bible or a saint's biography. Painting was a contemplative or meditative act, not just a technical one. The guidance of the master could ensure a necessary technical standard and that the style followed tradition. However, icons were not just esteemed by their craftsmanship or veneration for tradition. A true icon is supposed to be a manifestation of divine energies, and thus create a meeting point where a human can enter into the unseen world of the Spirit.

experience, as subjective experiences are canalized in terms of objective culture.

The range of emotions that may be conveyed by objectifications is unlimited. Moreover, the emotions provoked by sacred objects are underdetermined. The same sacred building, for example, can humble some of those who enter it and fill others with awe. As Stringer (1999) finds, part of the power of a ritual lies in its ability to provoke very different feelings—or none at all—in different participants. Nevertheless, the form of an object often has some relation to the range of emotions it evokes. Depictions of the Buddha, for example, may instil something of the serenity or joy that the image expresses. Other depictions of sacred beings have their effects by provoking, not imitation, but relationship—such as maternal tenderness for the infant Krishna, gratitude and sorrow for the crucified Christ, or fear of a heavenly Judge. An image may provoke a flash memory that helps one to cope with difficult life situations and reorient emotions—as when a taxi-driver glimpses the image of a special deity hanging from the mirror of the car. An opus of music may provoke different emotions by its harmonies, tempo, and rhythmic force. Consider Hildegard von Bingen's contemplative harmonies, Johann Sebastian Bach's strictly organized Masses, Ludwig van Beethoven's romantic Ninth Symphony, or Camille Saint-Saëns's overwhelming Third Symphony. Each is related to a different religious order and corresponds with a certain emotional scale.

Objectification does not only refer to virtuosi who create religious art for elites. It includes everyday acts such as lighting a candle, thumbing rosary beads, placing a veil over one's hair, reciting scripture, burning incense, tracing an image in the mud—or writing out a Bible by hand. The latter example comes from Park's study (2009) of Bible-copying in Korea, a recent practice that has become increasingly popular. Ninety-year-old Mrs Choi, whom Park interviews, has completed twelve handwritten copies of the whole Bible. Park explains the appeal of Bible-copying as a form of prayer and spiritual concern for the family, especially children who will inherit a Bible. When Mrs Choi copies the Bible, she has two objects in front of her besides her manuscript: a printed 'master' copy of the Bible, and photos of her children (Park 2009: 214). Objectification may also include acts of creative destruction, such as the removal or obstructions to religious practice, and acts of cleansing that remove matter from a sacred context in which it is 'out of place' (Mary Douglas's concept (1966) of dirt).

Thus, voluntary work decorating or cleaning a church, synagogue, temple, or mosque may be interpreted as objectification when it expresses religious sentiment. Even where religious objects are common and mass produced, the emotions they provoke can be deeply meaningful to those who feel them. They crystallize and elevate, not some generic experience, but an experience that is also unique to the person who has it. An icon carried in the pocket, a set of prayer beads fingered repeatedly, a prayer mat used five times a day, a tattered image of Ganesha on the wall—these objects, which may appear like rubbish to others, can have an irreplaceable emotional power for those to whom they belong. Their power accrues over time, and with repeated association. As Pratt (1920: 602) comments, 'nearly all religious symbolism that ever becomes really potent in an individual's experience comes into his life in childhood': songs sung in infancy, pictures gazed on at school, words repeated at every mealtime, smells encountered when worshipping—these may be powerful enough to provoke tidal waves of emotion in later life. Likewise, religious objects handed down over generations, ancestors worshipped at a household shrine, words repeated at the funeral of father, grandfather, and great grandfather, may have an emotional force so strong that it is either cherished—or rejected in an act of life-changing rebellion (Hervieu-Léger 2000).

This brings us to the subjective aspect of the dialectical relation. 'Subjectification' involves more than perceiving the object through the senses and understanding its emotional message intellectually, and more even than altering bodily practice in response to a material setting.[3] In religious subjectification, an object provokes an emotional reaction that is considered religious. In many religious contexts, the

---

[3] Obeyesekere (1981: 123) also writes that 'subjectification is the opposite of objectification: cultural ideas are used to justify the introduction of innovative acts and meanings. Subjective imagery is to subjectification what personal symbols are to objectification. The former help externalized (but do not objectify) internal psychic states; yet such subjective externalizations do not, and cannot, constitute a part of the publicly accepted culture.' The theme of subjectification has been discussed in literature on 'religious experience' by psychologists of religion, such as Allport's well-known contrast (1950) between an 'extrinsic', institution-oriented, and an 'intrinsic', interior-oriented religiosity. An 'intrinsic' interior-oriented religious person lives her (or his) religion. Instead of focusing on the very dramatic instances of a religious emotional subjectification, as described by the great mystics or extreme psychological cases, we consider its more routine occurrences, and we resist a dualism between intrinsic and extrinsic religion, seeing them rather as dialectically linked.

ability to feel emotions sanctioned by the wider regime when in the presence of its sacred objects is taken to be a proof of piety (see, e.g., Csordas 1997; Meyer 2006 on the process of incorporation into Charismatic Christianity). One may not understand the sacred narrative to which an object belongs, one may doubt the truth of the dogma surrounding it, but, if it provokes appropriate emotions, its sanctity is confirmed by the reaction. The tears shed before the icon confirm that one is a true believer, and confirm that the icon, and the saint it represents, is holy.

To see what is at stake, we can note the difference between people looking at a religious painting in an art gallery, and others venerating it in the context of a church service; or between an audience watching an actor playing a vicar and a congregation being led by a vicar in worship; or between a group of students in a lecture on Kierkegaard and a congregation listening to a preacher make reference to the same philosopher. The objects are the same: the difference lies in the emotional subjectifications. In the process of subjectification cultural objects may be used to produce, and thereafter justify, innovative acts, meanings, or images that help express the emotions of individuals.

Some forms of religion place more stress on the subjective side of the dialectic than others. In most forms of Evangelical Christianity, for example, it is vital to witness to one's conversion and personal devotion with some show of emotion. Many forms of holistic 'mind, body, spirit' spirituality also place a high premium on personal, inward experience, and rather less on outward, external forms (Heelas and Woodhead 2005). As in charismatic religion, the most personal and deeply felt emotions can be stimulated by the most external and objective array of material and symbolic configurations. People entering such a context for the first time may be overwhelmed and terrified by what they feel to be the emotional coercion of such a setting. Nevertheless, even powerful objectifications cannot force a corresponding subjectivization. A novice who enters a convent in medieval Italy may find that the silence, the cold, stark buildings, and images of the crucified Christ fill her with dread or numbness— or with the expected religious emotions. Some who desperately want to feel the approved emotions of a religious regime, and who contemplate the objects that inspire such feelings in others, may fail. Or entirely inappropriate objects may stimulate profoundly pious emotion: like the parrot Loulou who is experienced as the Holy Ghost by the maid Félicité in Flaubert's *A Simple Heart*.

When successful for the regime, the process of objectivization–subjectivization involves a focusing of emotional life, in which approved emotions are brought to the fore; a clarifying in which extraneous emotions are suppressed; and an emotional transcendence that opens a new emotional perspective. In the process the individual may feel him or herself redefined through divine encounter. Religious objects become levers of emotional life. They serve to bring forward certain emotions, and to push others into the background. By contemplating the crucifix, for example, one may cultivate compassion for others, and by contemplating Mary and the Christ child, a mother may refresh unconditional love for a child. Intellectual discourses on dogma may provoke nothing but doubt and confusion; contemplation of a holy object may force a solution. Nouwen (2000: 21) provides an example in recollecting his contemplation of an icon that represents the holy trinity as three angel-like figures sitting at a table:

During a hard period of my life in which verbal prayer has become nearly impossible and during which mental and emotional fatigue had made me the victim of feelings of despair and fear, a long and quiet presence to this icon became the beginning of my healing. As I sat for long hours in front of Rublev's Trinity, I noticed how gradually my gaze became a prayer. This silent prayer slowly made my inner restlessness melt away and lifted me into the circle of love, a circle that could not be broken by the powers of the world . . . Through the contemplation of this icon we come to see with our inner eyes that all engagements in this world can bear fruit only when they take place within this divine circle.

Emotional life flows in real time as a continuous stream. It is only occasionally that individuals stand outside the stream to confront their emotions—an occurrence that is often provoked by some emotional dissonance. Religion also allows individuals to confront their emotions, whether through techniques honed for the purpose—such as shamanic rituals like those recorded in Nepal by Desjarlais (1992), or confessional practices like those developed in Catholicism (Mahoney 1989). The core issue of confession relates to inner emotions rather than outward trespasses, and forgiveness depends on an emotional recognition of having trespassed. As Goffman (1971) and Hochschild (1983) remind us, modern secular regimes provoke individuals to ask whether their emotional behaviour corresponds with their feelings 'backstage'. In such contexts sacred space may also serve as a back stage where people can withdraw from the role plays of the public front stage, and enter an alternate ordering. Many religions offer practical approaches to emotional work. It may be performed in solitary meditation or prayer; in dialogue with an elder or confessor; in a group in collective ritual; in rituals of exorcism and healing; in relation to objects of devotion.

A person's relation to a religious object intensifies as its dialectical character unfolds. This means that it no longer becomes a formal encounter between a person and an external, religious object. The person merges with the symbol through the dialectical bond between objectification and subjectification. The person relates to the symbol in a way that manifestly ascribes it with religious associations. These are evoked as the person observes the object. This relation may hold only for a specific person. However, such relations are transferable in a community with a shared emotional programme. Other members of the community are able to recognize symbolic objects and they react in a similar manner when they observe the object. An emotional bond also grows between an individual and a community of persons—past and present—who share the same emotional reactions to the same object, and solidarity is enhanced. As John Wesley put it: if your heart is as my heart, give me your hand.[4]

Consecration and insignation

Although we have tried to focus the discussion of subjectification and objectification exclusively on emotional relations between individual and symbol, the social aspects of the process have kept creeping in. We have seen that the objects that are the subject of religious feeling are often collective symbols, that the intensity of subjectification is increased when others feel deeply about the same symbols, and that symbols created to express religious emotions may be adopted by a community and used to focus its identity and clarify its boundaries. In order to analyse more precisely the emotional significance of relations between the symbols and social groups in our conceptual scheme, we use the terms 'consecration' and 'insignation'. By consecration we mean the process by which a religious community, and/or its elite, legitimates an object as a religious sign that binds the community and

---

[4] Sermon 34: 'Catholic Spirit'; 2 Kgs 10: 15.

helps to define its identity. Although formal or informal religious leaders may play an important role in consecration, symbols once consecrated accrue their own power, which may eventually balance or outweigh that of the leaders—whose authority is then legitimated by reference to such symbols. Consecrated symbols help define the emotional regime of a religious group, act as points of emotional focus, communicate the emotional norms of the community, and define the identity of the group.

There are parallels between consecration and objectification, though objectification refers to a process that occurs at an individual level, and consecration refers to a collective process. Just as the dialectical counter-process of objectification is subjectification, so that of consecration is insignation. 'Insignation' refers to the process whereby a community is moved and inspired by a religious symbol. Insignation is the process whereby symbols are refashioned and proposed, a sort of wellspring of cultural creation. If a consecrated object fails to evoke appropriate emotional reactions in a religious group, the dialectic is disrupted (see Chapter 4). Contrariwise, if an object inspires powerful collective emotions in a group, but is not taken up and officially legitimized, the dialectical process is interrupted. Where the dialectical process is in balance, there is a positive feedback between consecrated symbols and collective emotions, each reinforcing the power of the other.

A strong form of consecration occurs when a state establishes standards for religious symbols. A law against blasphemy, for example, invokes legal power to ensure that religious objects should not provoke inappropriate emotions. The leaders of a religious group can also set and enforce standards for emotional expression 'from above' through their consecration of symbols—as Pope Pius IX did in establishing the piety of 'Fortress Catholicism' (Woodhead 2004: 312–14). There is always the possibility, however, that such consecration will not attract an appropriate emotional response from the community, and that insignation will fail. A softer kind of consecration can be traced in a group that evolves its own tales, symbols, and rituals as focal points in its emotional regime. Consecrated symbols may eventually come to be regarded as natural symbols that do not demand further legitimation. By means of the consecrated symbols it is possible to evaluate which emotions are sacred and appropriate and which are unholy, blasphemous, or even demonic. Thus the symbols form a shared language by which the community can communicate shared experiences. This language contains a vocabulary of symbolic references and a grammar for ordering complex, confusing, and contradictory emotional experiences. Its symbols are referents that can maintain emotional associations and memories beyond the actual experiences. They are also media for transferring emotional experiences and interpretations to new members of the community.

Consecrated symbols not only enable the community to have shared emotional experiences; they also restrict the range of emotions that are accepted as religious by the community. They serve as a resource for emotional appeals by the leadership, but they also bind the leaders to the agenda that led to their consecration. The consecrated symbols determine the agenda for the emotional regime. Even if the leadership tries to change the programme of the community, this calls for reference to the consecrated symbols. As we will see in Chapter 5, this means that collective symbols have their own power. Even if the elite dismiss the symbols as outdated and primitive, they linger as memories that evoke good or bad emotions among members. Symbols that have established their ability to provoke religious sentiment—which are firmly insignated—can be reinterpreted or 'desecrated' by elites, but cannot be ignored or easily suppressed.

The process of insignation may be based on individual subjectification but proposes a collective symbol. As Durkheim (1912/2001) recognizes, emotional experiences are amplified and justified by being shared, and emotional encounters with a religious symbol are heightened: 'within a crowd moved by a common passion, we become susceptible to feelings and actions of which we are incapable on our own' (1912/2001: 157). We can often observe that emotions relating to a symbol form a chain reaction. At first, individuals may hesitate to show their feelings. However, after the first participant has shown an emotional reaction, others allow themselves to follow. Individual emotions grow by following a collective trend, and emotional expressions are amplified by being shared. Durkheim sees how symbols can focus, crystallize and communicate such emotion and sustain it over time: 'Religious force', he comments, 'is the feeling the collectivity inspires in its members, but projected and objectified by the minds which feel it. It becomes objectified by being anchored in an object which then becomes sacred, but any object can play this role' (1912/2001: 174).

Though close to ours, Durkheim's approach does not identify situations in which the dialectic between consecration and insignation is disrupted or ceases to work (see next chapter), nor pay sufficient attention to the 'content' of symbols and their 'fittingness' to carry the emotions characteristic of a particular emotional regime. There is often more of a fit between object and emotional inspiration than he acknowledges. A religious community may have a sacred text that explicitly points to a sacred symbol—such as the rainbow in Genesis for the Jewish people—without utilizing that symbol. Even though it is not self-evident which symbols will be accepted by a religious community for communal veneration, in retrospect the logic can often be discerned. The logic of choosing symbolic objects depends on many factors, crucially upon whether members of the group are able to insignify it—to relate to it with appropriate feeling. Religious communities establish internal standards for accepted forms of symbol. Some themes and forms are taboo. For instance, Jewish religion, Islam, and Calvinism prohibit the representation of God by painting or sculpture, but not by poetry or music. Sometimes a community engages in heated battles about whether an object is an appropriate symbol for it or not. Emotional issues are often hidden in the heated debates about which symbolic forms are right or wrong. Reactions are especially strong if a work of art or a piece of music provokes emotions that some find discordant with the wider emotional regime. Rational protestations do not suffice when the core issue is emotional and the other party seems to be deaf to clashing emotional notes.

An object is also more likely to be ascribed with emotional significance when it is significant in other social domains. For instance, objects that are associated with a socio-cultural elite are likely to be consecrated and accepted by religious communities that seek legitimacy. Obversely, some religious communities may consecrate objects that are rejected by the socio-cultural elite in order to demonstrate their distance from it. Many Christian cathedrals and 'high' churches have impressive and ancient architecture, sophisticated choral music, and priceless art. The panoply is impressive and expensive, signifying tradition and accepted style. The setting calls for a sense of awe, solemnity, deference, and respect. This can be contrasted with the setting of a low-church meeting in a modified workshop with few symbols. Here it is the preaching, music, and the dramaturgical choreography that form the objectified framework for evoking religious emotions. The setting lends itself to feeling by participating by song, testimony, speaking in tongues, and falling into trance.

Symbols can also become sacred by their placement as well as their content and wider associations. A painting, for example, may become sacred when placed in a church, where its symbolism is associated with other religious symbols and it is received accordingly. When a popular song is used in a church, it becomes ascribed with a new, religious meaning by its affiliation to the ritual: for instance, Mendelssohn's incidental music for *A Midsummer Night's Dream* and Wagner's march from *Lohengrin* became standard music for weddings. An interesting example of the process is offered by the introduction of new murals in the ancient Cathedral of Ribe (948). Its apse now presents abstract fresco murals and painted windows by Carl-Henning Petersen (1913–2007), a well-respected painter who belonged to the Cobra group. However, the artist was not a member of the state church and did not consider himself a Christian. At the viewing, he explained his work as a celebration of life, not of God: the pastor retorted that his views were pantheistic and pagan. After long debate, the congregation accepted the murals, and they achieved an insignation corresponding to their placement. Worshippers began to ascribe the abstract forms with new meanings. Memories from services, baptisms, marriages, or burials became associated with the abstract forms, and they began to elicit emotions appropriate to the regime in which they were set.

Emotional reactions to religious symbols also depend on social factors, such as the size of the community, its relation with majority society, and its cultural heterogeneity. A closed circle of connoisseurs or afficionados, or a group of specially selected persons, can establish more intense and intimate relations than a wide network of people. The use of esoteric symbols and 'shibboleths' indicates membership of a tight circle, and may evoke the whole heritage of the group. One example is provided by sectarian groups that seek to maintain a distance from wider society, and who employ complex and demanding rituals and symbols. Another is provided by diasporic communities whose members experience collective emotion provoked by shared symbols brought from the homeland (though the symbols and their meanings may change significantly in the new setting). Members of a minority can feel that they belong together because their emotional reactions to certain symbols are similar—and serve to separate them from the majority. Thus Danish expatriates in Australia gather for 'a real Christmas' and commemorate rituals associated with the darkest and coldest period of the year at beach parties, and Vietnamese immigrants gather in the Roman Catholic church in Kristiansand or in the Buddhist temple at Aarhus to affirm that they are not alone in a sea of strangers but belong to a community of shared sensibility. The exhibition of shared religious symbols can be an effective means by which marginal and minority groups redefine identities ascribed them by a majority, and assert their identity in their own terms. A group may even accept a symbol that was ascribed for it by its oppressors as a symbol of exclusion—such as the six-pointed star for Judaism. Rountree (2004) gives a rich account of how goddess worshippers and 'witches' manipulate symbols in order to redefine the status of women. A similar analysis can be given of the way in which religious dress has been deployed by minority religions in Europe. Controversies surrounding Sikh turbans and Muslim headscarves are 'passionate' because the symbols carry a set of values and associated emotions into the heart of regimes where many secular or Christian Europeans feel they do not belong. One reaction is to ban such symbols, another is to ridicule them. The Danish cartoonists took the latter route, and the anger that this provoked among many Muslims related not only to their being subject to ridicule, but to the emotional dissonance that the cartoons provoke. Although the ban on pictorial images of Muhammad is not absolute, his depiction in cartoons—let alone as a terrorist—can affect believers' ability to retain personal and largely unobjectified images and feelings about him as the perfect human being.

Very often people are alienated by symbols that do not fit with the emotional regime they consider religious. However, the strangeness of an emotional symbolism can also offer an exotic appeal, and a means for social change. It came as a surprise to many of the older generation in Western societies when varieties of Eastern religion became popular among young people in the 1960s. Many of the so-called new religions were deliberately challenging to existing emotional regimes—including Christian ones that stressed deference, solemnity, and emotional self-control. Eastern religions offered a storehouse of clashing symbols and alternative emotional possibilities, including sensual and ecstatic ones. The movement founded by Bhagwan Shree Rajneesh, for example, exalted sexual love and valued cathartic emotional expressions. Bhagwan stated that: 'Sitting in a group, in an encounter group, or in a group touching each other's bodies, you become part of the community. Touching each other's hand, holding each other's hand, or lying on top of each other in a pile, you feel oneness—a religious elation happens' (Mullan 1983: 111). The emotional tone of the blessing darshans at Poona was described by a participant in these words: 'the atmosphere was filled with joy and festivity... other sannyasins danced ecstatically around him [Baghwan] in a semicircle and the group swayed to the music. The whole experience was like opening out or being totally receptive to the flow of energy' (Mullan 1983: 26). Although many new religious movements seemed at first to expand the emotional repertoire, over time they might appear to restrict it. We can see a historical example in the development of Shaker worship. At first, services were emotional and spontaneous: 'When they meet for their worship, they fall on groaning and trembling, and every one acts alone for himself' (Roberts 1990: 177). Later, the services became ritualized and the symbols fixed, and tightly controlled group dances evolved with men dancing as one group and women as a separate unit.

Since a community and its cultural context change over time, the symbolic references change as well. Symbols may lose their inspirational capacity when they become distant from or discordant with emotional regimes in other social domains. We explore this process in relation to late modern, highly differentiated societies in Chapter 6. For those who share their emotional experiences with others in their encounter with a religious symbol, that symbol may cease to be merely a symbol and becomes a direct manifestation of the divine. For outsiders, however, the same symbol may be meaningless, banal, or kitsch. There is a difference between relating to sacred objects as symbols and regarding them as possessing divine power. While intellectuals tend to take the former position, devotees take the latter. There is, however, internal religious scepticism towards objectifications in religion, as we have noted in relation to Judaism, early Christianity, Islam, and iconoclastic Protestantism. Religious reforms often attempt to purify religious symbolism and excise 'idolatry'. Clear theological distinctions may be drawn between 'veneration' of an icon (approved) and 'worship' (disapproved), and missionary encounters with non-Christian religions prompted lengthy treatises by Hindu and Buddhist reformers on the non-idolatrous nature of their religions. What we see here, in effect, are attempts by religious elites to impose order on popular emotions, and to purify religious emotional regimes. In some cases new consecrations, re-consecrations, or de-consecrations are attempted. Generally speaking, a perfect harmony between consecration and insignation is probably the exception rather than the norm: the most perfectly orchestrated rituals can fail to evoke the expected emotions, and those emotions may instead attach themselves to symbols that no elite had authorized.

Externalization and internalization

Berger and Luckmann's cognitive theory (1966) explores the dialectic between 'externalization' and 'internalization', showing how society makes an impression on the minds of individuals (internalization), and individuals give their ideas social expression (externalization). This analysis can be broadened and extended to apply not only to cognition narrowly defined, but to emotions as well. Individual emotional experiences and social sentiments are closely related.

Internalization refers to the ways in which a community influences individuals' emotional lives. It is directly related to externalization. The emotional programme set by the religious regime becomes effective only as it is internalized in the lives, actions, bodies, and feelings of those whom it binds together. The community acts, and individuals respond; individuals respond, and the community acts. Emotional externalizations affect the wider group, and can amplify, confirm, or confront, other people's feelings. By externalizing emotions in a harmonious and coordinated way, emotional standards are established that confirm personal sentiments, and help create an emotional regime that transcends them. Externalization refers to the process by which an individual feels something for him or herself and is moved by it. It is deeply personal, but is not normally private. People's feelings are noticed by others, and have an effect on them. People express their feelings through acts, and actions consolidate emotions. Actions seem more sincere and intense when they are carried by a clear personal feeling. Moreover, by performing an emotional act, the feeling is clarified and intensified. To externalize emotion by creating a communal sentiment involves encouraging and supporting appropriate individual emotions, and curtailing and sanctioning deviant ones.

A useful example for illuminating the process is provided by Benjamin Zablocki's study (1971) of the Pietistic community of Bruderhof, which points to a number of different mechanisms by which a community may shape collective sentiment: it may provide a trigger mechanism for personal emotional experiences (for example, when its elders model and express a mood), it may intensify selected emotions among its members (for example, by setting an experience within a positive framework of interpretation), it may stabilize certain emotions and moods (for example, by dampening their sporadic nature and controlling their intensity), and it may sanction emotions that deviate from the regime. Through processes of socialization, members of the community are predisposed to have certain emotional experiences and not others, to identify appropriate emotions, and to internalize norms for emotional expression in certain situations. The community prepares its members for certain experiences by forming social contexts that inspire these emotions, and orchestrating the participants' acts. It organizes events that stimulate emotions in correspondence with its regime. It may define the situation in a way that highlights certain emotions. It may refer to symbols that are ascribed with an emotional content. It may filter a spectrum of emotions by stimulating those that fit into its programme and subduing others.

There is a difference between an emotional programme (which refers to the emotions a community aims to establish) and emotional norms (which refer to how emotional acts are evaluated by a community).[5] Some emotional expressions are obligatory in a certain situation, some are accepted, some are frowned upon, and some are forbidden or unthinkable. The norms depend on the definition of the situation. A specific situation may call for sorrow, joy, happiness, gratitude, solemnity, or disgust. The definition of the appropriate emotions for the situation depends on the group, and the emotional standard of each participant is influenced by the norms of the group. In a closely integrated community with a clear structure of authority, such as Bruderhof, the norms are especially strong.

In a loosely connected religious community with a weak authority structure, such as a Danish Lutheran congregation, the emotional norms are less well defined. However, it is still possible to track emotional norms by how other people react. Internalization implies that a person recognizes the collective emotional programme and accepts its norms for emotional behaviour in relevant situations. Spontaneous, ambiguous, and overwhelming personal feelings can be interpreted, controlled, and directed by referring to the wider regime. A religious event may be disrupted if it is subject to too many spontaneous emotional outbursts. Shared emotional norms help to integrate a community, as emotional energies are channelled into a common stream. The members accept a common frame of reference for their emotions, and they have common standards for what they ought to feel and how

---

[5] This corresponds to the distinction made by Hochschild (1998).

to express these emotions in a relevant situation. Thereby emotional ambiguities, uncertainties, and dissonances are diminished, and conflicts are controlled.

Deviant emotional expressions can spoil the communal sentiment for other participants and undermine its leadership. In an authoritarian community, people who deviate from the collective emotional norms can be subject to harsh sanctions. An omission of emotional expressions in a situation where they are required may be interpreted as a provocation. Some acts aim directly at transgressing the norms. At a Lutheran confirmation in Denmark, a boy took the chalice of wine and said 'cheers'. The expected laughter did not arise. Ice-cold stares from adult participants told the boy that a serious norm had been transgressed. Even if it is well known that few of the confirmed recognize the religious meaning of the event, they are still supposed to perform their roles in accordance with the programme. The act of spontaneous provocation disrupted the collective sentiment.

Emotional norms can often be decoded by observing what constitutes a transgression. In Richard Curtis's 1994 film *Four Weddings and a Funeral*, the solemn emotional programme is disturbed by the vicar's mispronouncing of the 'holy ghost' as 'the holy goat'. In a similar manner, Rowan Atkinson's 'Mr Bean' acts in an awkward manner that reveals the norms by his transgressions. When he attends a church service, he disturbs others and falls asleep on the floor during the sermon. We can identify with such failed internalizations and laugh at them in the cinema, but they are more likely to be experienced as embarrassing or annoying in real life. Emotionally misaligned acts provoke emotional tensions among other participants that often result in anger. In many cases, however, emotional deviations are not a conscious provocation. For instance, children may play in a graveyard because they see it as just a park without recognizing a demand for solemnity. When children transgress norms for religious emotions, adults are expected to educate them. By indicating that the park is not for amusement, children can be taught to obey the appropriate emotional norms. An emotional act is not acceptable just because of its personal sincerity.

Religious emotions may demarcate the borderline that separates insiders from outsiders. A religious community may draw a line of distinction between the flock of true believers who are encompassed by bonds of love, and outsiders who are regarded as unworthy of affection, or as dangerous and deviant. Such a boundary is especially sharp in 'religions of difference' (Heelas and Woodhead 2001). Someone who breaks the norms of an Amish community, for example, may be shunned and treated as an outsider. Some sectarian groups are bound by norms of hospitality to the stranger, but for others openness to outsiders poses a risk of spiritual contamination. As Douglas (1966) shows, purity laws are effective ways of demarcating and defending social and personal boundaries: emotions of horror and disgust and bodily contamination can encompass not only intimate bodily practices such as eating and sexual intercourse, but attitudes towards outsiders who threaten the integrity of the community. In some historical instances, a specific religious institution can dominate society and define its emotive norms in an authoritative manner. In such instances, transgressions of the emotional norms are regarded as both a sacrilege and an anti-social provocation. Acts that transgress the emotional norms can be explained in religious terms as an effect of demon possession or witchcraft. Witches display and inspire the wrong emotions within a community, personifying feelings like envy, enmity, and vindictiveness.

Puritanism is characterized by strongly internalized emotions, with a regime that calls for personal submission. The emotional scale is narrowed down to love of God and one's neighbour and fear for one's salvation. According to Puritan preachers, men are 'guilty before God, of all the sins that swarm and roar in the whole world at this day, for God looks to the heart' (Morgan 1966: 2). Salvation does not depend on good deeds, but on receiving God's grace by faith. Spontaneous emotions are dangerous: 'if you live at random at your heart's desire you may be sure you are no believer' (Morgan 1966: 5). Good Christians are bound by a covenant with God, and must relinquish their own feelings and desires to his demands: 'a Christian may and ought to desire many things as meanes, but God alone, as his End, as his last end . . . no Creature that is finite can be the end of the Soul, nor give satisfaction to it' (Morgan 1966: 15–16). Puritan asceticism did not, however, mean a celibate life or abstention from good food and drink. Good and natural gifts from God should not be refused, but Christians must be thankful to the giver of these gifts, and not indulge in them, because they are a foretaste of the greater and eternal gifts that believers receive in heaven. The only important aim is salvation, and indulgence in the illusory, short-term benefits of this life can hinder people from a spiritual life in search for eternal bliss. Any act that could lead to frivolous emotional expression—especially erotic emotions involved in dancing and boisterous feasts—was forbidden. Puritans were seen by outsiders as killjoys: they saw themselves as carrying a permanent and true religious joy in contrast to the short-term satisfactions of sinners that ended first with a hangover and eventually with damnation.

For Puritan theology, the Fall has deprived human beings of control over their passions and affections. The consequence is not that affections should be banished, but that they should be educated, controlled, disciplined, and purified. Puritan love letters demonstrate controlled affections: 'lest we should forget our selves and love this world too much, and not set our affections on heaven wheare all true happiness is for ever' (Morgan 1966: 51). Even sexual desire and satisfaction are acceptable within the context of marriage. Love, including sexual love, is a mutual duty between the couple, a solemn obligation imposed by God. The husband stands before the wife in the place of God, and is obliged to protect her and furnish her with the fruits of the earth. A wife must submit joyfully to her husband's instructions and commands: true conjugal affection demands that wives look at their husbands not for their own ends but to be better fitted for God's service. If husband and wife fail to love each other appropriately, they disobey God. But the highest love must be reserved for God himself. To prize human relations too highly is to upset the proper order of love. Man and wife should not, therefore, be so 'transported with affection' that they forget their maker. Romantic love that transgresses these limits is regarded as a demonic temptation. A widow or widower should not demonstrate immoderate grief, but keep sentiment within bounds, and hope to meet the beloved again in the afterlife. Human affections must maintain proper moderation. A dying pastor sends his wife away from his deathbed and instructs her to go and pray alone with the words: 'I fear lest thou look too much upon this affliction.' True believers in God's providence must exercise patience and meekness in all losses and crosses in this life. They are required to restrain their spontaneous emotions and internalize the emotional regime of Puritanism.

The Puritan regime also illustrates how certain emotional norms may refer only to a segment of the community or to special roles within it. For instance, many regimes allow women to cry publicly at a funeral, while men are supposed to control their feelings. In order to be in tune with the emotions of a community, a person has to sense its emotional programme and have a notion of its potential harmony.

To tune into an emotional programme involves an acute awareness of emotional signals from other participants: it represents a social art that is acquired through experience. Certain roles call for extensive training in order to join in the performance. People practise from childhood to demonstrate emotions in a manner that others can interpret, and teenagers especially like to experiment with emotional expressions. A religious community designates religious roles that include specific emotional norms. A shaman, prophet, sibyl, witch, or rabbi is expected to demonstrate certain emotions and abstain from others. The norms also cover everyday life, where a holder of a religious role is expected to demonstrate a special emotional stance towards others. Again, the norms can be decoded by looking at transgressions, such as a Danish female pastor who drove her motorbike down to the harbour in order to drink and gossip with the sailors; or the stereotypical Anglican vicar in whose presence people monitor their language, curtail their swearing, and try to express only 'polite' sentiment.

Internalization is constantly balanced—or challenged—by externalization. Contrary to the impression that Durkheim gives of collective emotions being irresistibly imposed upon individuals in a religious setting, each individual is likely to have personal standards for what they ought to feel in a situation and how their feelings may be expressed. In order to form a correspondence between the communal programme and the individual standards, a link must be formed between the community and its members. For the latter simply to 'go through the motions' and feign feelings is not sufficient to sustain the regime. Feelings are social acts as well as personal ones. They are performed in a direct or indirect interaction with other people, and they lead to immediate or delayed emotional reactions. Both the actor and the audience can read expressions of sorrow, joy, tension, awe, disgust, hatred, and anxiety. Such emotions form a basic element in social interaction: the small and great dramas of social life revolve around them. A person's emotional expressions have a social reference: they can express a stance to oneself, to specific persons, to a community, or to society at large. Even to escape and seek solitude forms part of a social pattern and makes a social statement.

Rosabeth Kanter's study (1972) of utopian communities shows that those that survived over a generation depended not so much on ideological coercion by elites, nor self-interested calculation by members, but on establishing affective moral commitments. The former involved a dual process of 'renunciation' of former ties and 'communion' with the new group, and the latter a 'mortification' of egotism and existing commitments and a 'transcendence' whereby the cause of the group seems compellingly true, eternal, and just. Mortification involves feelings of humility and worthlessness, while transcendence involves the exhilaration and joy experienced by individuals who merge with the group. Kanter (1972: 105) writes: 'the use of mortification is a sign that the group cares about the individual, about his thoughts and feelings, about the content in this world. The group cares enough to pay great attention to the person's behaviour, and to promise him warmth, intimacy, and love . . . if he indicates he can accept these gifts without abuse.' Membership generates a sense of mystery and a feeling of awe for the leaders. In our terms, a closed community like Oneida succeeded in balancing internalization with externalization in such a way that members experienced the costs of sacrificing material interests, external bonds, and individual self-interest as outweighed by the emotional gain of merging with the group.

Demonstrations of religious emotion have wider social consequences beyond the religious community. By externalizing religious emotions, individuals adopt a social stance that may lead to active engagement in wider society, a universalist love for humanity that provokes humanitarian concern for the distant others, loyalty to one's cultural, ethnic, or familial kin and suspicion of others, retreat from an evil and corrupt society, or violence and hostility towards that society. A religious setting may allow people to feel and express emotions that are suppressed in everyday life, may help people redefine or redirect their social emotions, or may support and sustain the acceptable emotional norms of the wider community.

Although religious norms may be presented as timeless and indisputable, they are constantly subject to challenge and redefinition. If the members fail to internalize them, leaders have to make the norms more explicit and appeal to them, or redefine and revise them. If the processes of externalization are inoperative, internalizations become dampened and dissonant. The community will eventually find such a state unsatisfactory. Some members may drift away; others may try to voice a critique. However, it is extremely difficult to change the emotional programme of a religious community, and where change does take place it may have to be masked (Halbwachs 1992; Repstad 2008). Nevertheless, a dysfunctional programme will eventually lead to a passive and uncommitted membership or to a major re-formation or split. This theme will be followed up in the next chapter.

Dialectical feedback

The proposed approach recognizes that many social processes are characterized by mutually interacting factors, rather than being the effect of a series of isolated causes. The emotional processes operative in religious regimes have a two-way character. They can stabilize, amplify, modify, or extinguish each other through feedbacks and adjustments.[6] What this means is that an outcome is not merely the static and self-contained effect of a cause, but that it has a positive or negative impact on its preconditions. Thus emotions may increase social solidarity, bring about personal change, lead to adjustments of power, and reinforce the power of a collective symbol. Similarly, if a religious service fails to elicit appropriate emotions on the part of some participants, that may lead to an adjustment of the ritual and symbols, a challenge to leadership, the use of guidance or sanctions to enforce conformity, and so on.

In relation to human emotions in general, and religious emotions in particular, simple, mechanical processes—like the individualist–behaviourist ideal-typical model of an emotional stimulus causing an emotional response—are the exception rather than the norm. With dramatic exceptions—like a man who kills another because he feels insulted—emotional relations are more often two way than one way. Dialectics may certainly involve juxtapositions and contradictions, as Hegelian and Marxist traditions emphasize.[7] However, as Georges Gurwitch (1962) points out, a dialectical process need not imply polarization.[8] Among other possible outcomes are complementarity, mutual involvement, ambivalence, or mutual immanence. In this

---

[6] The notions of positive and negative feedback, derived from cybernetics, are inadequate to capture the range of processes involved, which include approval, reinforcement, sanctioning, amplification, mirroring, disapproval, refinement, punishment and so on.

[7] Karl Marx's work is one of the major sources for social dialectics. He said: 'As society itself produces man as a man, so is society produced by him' (Marx 1964: 137). His approach has inspired both the Frankfurt School and French post-war sociology, including Jean-Paul Sartre (1960) and Merleau-Ponty (1964). Horkheimer and Adorno discussed the dialectic of the enlightenment project, which aimed at human control over nature by way of demystified science and technology, but ended with a reified world that controls human life. Merleau-Ponty (1964: 20) argued that man appears as a product-producer, the locus where necessity can turn into concrete liberty.

[8] Gurwitch (1962) pointed in his micro-sociology to the reciprocity of perspectives between the I, the Other, and the We, and in his macro-sociology to the forces of structuration, destructuration, and restructuration. His analysis included symbols as mediators between the contents and the collective and individual agents, and thereby resembles our approach.

chapter we focus on relations of complementarity and mutual involvement; in the next on ambivalence and polarity. The normal focus of sociological interest is on the dialectics between social agent and structure. We have drawn on a number of different traditions in developing this element of our scheme, including Simmel,[9] Berger and Luckman,[10] Giddens,[11] Archer and Bhaskar.[12] But we have extended the reference of 'dialectics' by applying it to relations between individual agents and symbols, as well as to relations between society and symbols. There are precedents for this, not least in the work of Marx for whom dialectics includes not only relations between agents and social structure, but those between material conditions of production and social relations of production, and between production and reproduction. For Durkheim, as we have seen, the dialectic between society and collective symbol was of prime importance; for Simmel, that between individual agent and symbol was also significant. Clearly the nature of the dialectics between agent and symbol is not identical with those between social agents, and processes of

---

[9] Simmel's dialectics are influenced by the Neo-Kantian distinction between form and content. He speaks of 'a dialectic without reconciliation' between human life and social forms: 'The individual is contained in sociation and, at the same time, finds himself confronted by it. He is both a link in the organism of sociation and an autonomous organic whole; he exists both for society and for himself' (Simmel 1908/1971b: 17). Simmel discusses dialectical relations between strife and sociation, imitation and distinction, distance and closeness.

[10] Peter Berger and Thomas Luckmann developed a dialectical constellation of theses derived from Weber, Durkheim, and the young Marx: 'Society is a human product. Society is an objective reality. Man is a social product' (Berger and Luckmann 1966: 61). Their approach ties the subject and the social world together by dialectical processes of cognitive internalization, objectification, and externalization.

[11] Anthony Giddens's structuration theory (1979) can be read as a dialectical attempt to combine philosophy of action with theories of social structure. Giddens sees the production and reproduction of society as a skilled performance on the part of its members, but human agency is bounded. Human beings produce society as historically located actors. Structure is constituted through action and it both enables and constrains agents (Giddens 1976/1993). Giddens (1979: 6) especially refers to the 'dialectic of control' as the central problem of social theory, which points to an intrinsic relation between agency and power.

[12] Critical-realist theory based on Roy Bhaskar (in Archer 1998) distinguishes between the genesis of human action and the structures governing social activities. These form distinct strata of social reality. Critical-realist research analyses the processes by which structure and agency shape and reshape one another. The linkage between structure and agency depends on a 'mediating system' consisting of the positions occupied and the practices that the occupants engage in. By distinguishing between structure and agency, critical realism is able to identify contextual restraints on our freedoms and to specify strategic uses of our freedoms for social transformation (Archer 1998). Our approach follows this distinction. However, we have not been able to follow Bhaskar's dialectical theory (1993) completely.

feedback are not necessarily communicative in the same ways. Yet we follow Durkheim and Simmel in maintaining that there can nevertheless be reciprocity and mutual constitution, and we have shown in the examples above that these processes can be every bit as significant for emotional life as those between persons.

The processes that constitute a balanced religious emotional regime can be represented diagrammatically, as in Fig. 1. In such a regime an agent's emotions are shaped by internalizing norms enacted by a community, and by subjectifying emotions related to sacred symbols. The agent may objectify religious emotion by creating or appropriating symbols that are emotionally meaningful to him or her. Feelings relating to such symbols are shared with others in the process of insignation, and insignation is disciplined by consecration. The collective expression of emotions reinforces the emotional standards of the religious community, which agents internalize.

The feedback between these different processes may lead to reinforcement or adjustment. If, for example, consecrated symbols do not elicit appropriate feeling, the community may solve the discrepancy by altering the symbols or guiding its members. Symbols that seem hollow because people are not able to summon the expected feelings towards them may be dismissed or recreated. Alternatively, a religious elite may feel so bound by the symbols that they are forced to admonish, punish, or even expel those who do not express appropriate sentiments and actions.

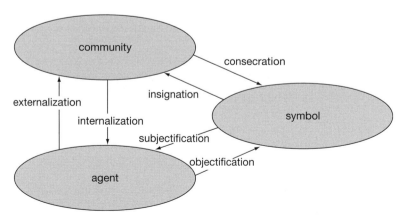

Figure 1 Dialectical relations

The emotional power of religious symbols is dependent on processes of insignation and subjectification. It is necessary that members can relate personally to the symbols, and that they also provoke appropriate collective sentiment. A religious symbol may have an appeal to a single person, perhaps as an expression of a personal memory, but it has a stronger and more stable emotional appeal if others feel similarly. Then feelings are confirmed and enhanced by the dialectical interactions.

Thus the different dialectical processes are linked together by feedback mechanisms, which can serve to reinforce an emotional regime or lead to change. By picturing the processes as operating in a circle, we can point out a clockwise and anti-clockwise spiral of feedback (Figs. 2 and 3). Although it is only possible to represent a circular process here, a spiral is perhaps a more appropriate image, since reinforcing processes do not necessarily lead to a regime that 'goes round in circles' without alteration, but to regimes that 'take another turn' through adjustments that maintain their balance. The clockwise spiral illustrated in Fig. 2 involves processes of consecration–subjectification–externalization. It may start—to give one example—with a community's consecration of a religious symbol as an exemplary expression of religious emotions. Inspired by the consecration, individual agents may subjectivize the emotions associated with it. They may also externalize their emotions in the context of the religious community.

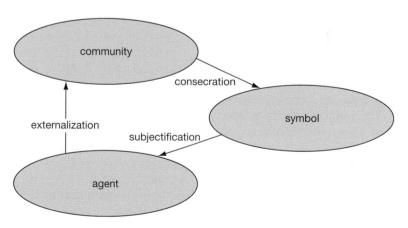

Figure 2 Relational feedback, example 1

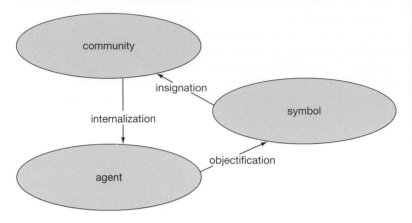

Figure 3 Relational feedback, example 2

This entire process may confirm consecrated symbols, or lead to new subjectifications among individual members.

An anti-clockwise spiral can also be pictured (Fig. 3) that involves processes of objectification–insignation–internalization. For example, an agent who experiences religious feelings may express them by creating or appropriating a religious symbol (objectification). That symbol is then felt to be meaningful by others in the community in a collective context (insignation). The emotions relating to the symbol may then be internalized by members of the community. This may in turn lead other individuals to objectify their religious emotion by relating to the symbol, whether by recreating, altering, or rejecting it. Thereby the symbol is affected, which leads to further processes of insignation by the community.

Although for the sake of visual clarity we have represented each of these feedback processes separately in Figs. 2 and 3, in balanced emotional regimes they operate simultaneously. If only one is operative, there is an unbalanced dialectic, as discussed in the next chapter. Our conceptual scheme is merely an analytical tool that works by dissecting the holistic flow of religious emotions within a regime. The dialectics separates out interrelated aspects of a unity, and needs to be put together again to make sense of real emotional regimes.

In reality, balanced regimes are likely to be the exception rather than the rule. But, by beginning with this case, we can go on to analyse instances when the processes are one-sided and become 'un-dialectic'.

This may occur, for example, when a regime's emotional standards are influenced by symbolic insignations that are not consecrated, or when objectifications do not correspond with the regime's emotional standards, or when externalizations are not balanced by internalization. Thus the conceptual scheme can also help pinpoint where relations become strained and positive feedback mechanisms do not operate. These themes are taken up in the next chapter.

Conclusion

This chapter proposes a framework for analysing religious emotional regimes characterized by balanced dialectical connections between self, society, and symbols. In such a regime the relations between agents, the community, and the symbols are mutually constitutive, and there is a correspondence between the emotional symbols, the community's emotional programme, and the individual emotions of the participants. Of course, it is artificial to split up the regime between these parts, because the symbols in such a situation express what the community feels collectively and the members experience individually. Each one confirms, amplifies, and empowers the others: the power of the symbols is strenghtened as they are venerated by the community and subjectified by individuals, the power of the community to move its members is enhanced as it refers to accepted symbols and as members participate in it, and religious emotions among participants are intensified as they participate in collective rituals or relate to established symbols.

A balanced regime has several mechanisms of adjustment and feedback for addressing situations where emotional dissonances or discrepancies arise. If members do not internalize and express the emotions authorized by the regime, they are guided and corrected. Protests may be talked down or suggestions and critique from members may be accepted, rules may be adjusted, symbols rejuvenated or changed, deviations controlled, and constant nuisances condemned, made to repent, or expelled. This does not guarantee success or longevity. Balanced regimes can lack structural pressures towards innovation, reform, and adaptation to new emotional challenges, and focus more on conformity, consensus, and continuity. They may refer to the intense feelings of the founders and point to inherited symbols that originally evoked passionate emotions; but such emotions need to be renewed and revitalized in the ritual practices and symbols of the community and the spiritual lives of the members. Moreover, as we will see in later chapters, religious emotional regimes are rarely closed systems. The ways in which they and their participants relate to other emotional regimes in society also impact upon their internal dynamics.

1. Private prayer in a church in Rome. Sacred spaces influence the cultivation and expression of emotion, and help to set a particular emotional tone.

2. Charismatic prayer and praise in a megachurch in Singapore. Notes of joy, hope, repentance and commitment are prominent.

3. A healer at a spiritual festival in Kristiansand, Norway channels the power of the Holy Spirit.

4. Burning incense outside a Chinese temple in Singapore. The incense carries hopes, fears, intentions and pleas to the gods.

5. Afternoon prayer in a mosque in Bangkok, Thailand (The Islamic Center of Thailand): 'Glory be to my Lord Almighty'. Bodily posture, and the co-ordination of bodily movement, serves to shape as well as to express emotion.

6. Bernini's statue of Saint Teresa of Ávila, Santa Maria della Vittoria, Rome. A depiction of religious ecstasy which aroused the displeasure of some church leaders. It refers to a passage in Teresa's autobiography where an angel stabs her in the heart, indicating God's love, and provoking feeling beyond mundane joy.

7. From the Thaipusam celebration in Penang, Malaysia: 'To Murugan with Love'. The ritual involves participants threading weighted needles through their flesh without showing pain. This collective practice is in praise of Lord Murugan and in fulfillment of vows.

8. Hindu and Catholic statues mingle on a market stall in Singapore. Pluralistic religious cultures may mix emotional elements from several religions, often in relation to different aspects of social and personal life.

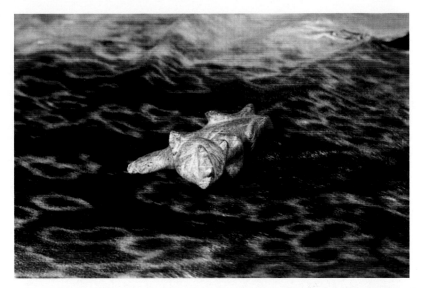

9. A carved stone from the collection of Moesgaard Museum, Denmark, possibly a *tupilaq*. Among the Greenland Inuit such objects might be employed for malevolent purposes. Depicting a mix of life and death, human and animal, they focus hatred, jealousy, and fear.

10. A personal shrine on an office windowsill in Norway. It mixes traditional religious symbols with icons of celebrity culture, and brings together objects of emotional significance to an individual.

11. The holy well in the Chalice Well Gardens, Glastonbury, England, is in the foreground of this picture, and statues of goddesses are in the niches in the wall. This ancient Christian site is now a centre of feminised alternative spirituality. The setting, symbols and uses of the garden support a mood of meditative calm and nurture.

12. 'Viking Card Reading' (using symbols from norse mythology) at a spiritual festival in Kristiansand, Norway. The seriousness with which this engagement with personal hopes and fears is undertaken is indicated by the picture.

4

Dynamics of Religious Emotion II: Disconnections of Self, Society, and Symbols

This chapter offers a framework for analysing imbalances in emotional regimes, where mutually constitutive interactive processes are blocked, weakened, or inhibited. As we have seen, a balanced regime involves ongoing adjustments between its constituent parts, which serve to regulate and control an emotional flow. In an unbalanced regime these feedbacks cease to operate as effectively and may lead to a 'tilt' towards agent, community, or symbol, and a fracturing of the relations between them. Emotions may become highly individualized (for example, in spontaneous, uncontrolled expressions), intensely concentrated on a particular symbol, or imposed by the community despite a clash with individual sensibilities. Such regimes are less well able to integrate the emotions of individual members and the group as a whole within the symbolic framework of the regime. This does not necessarily mean that emotions are dampened or extinguished. Unbalanced regimes cover an emotional range from ecstasy and intensity to emotional tedium and hypocrisy, and from suppression and tension to emotional eruptions that call for change.

Many religious communities and theologies consider balanced regimes to be ideal. From a sociological perspective, however, there is nothing normative about the idea of a balanced or an unbalanced regime. The fact that dialectics are in balance implies nothing about how sound, beneficial, or moral a regime might be. Some people would consider the moral and political programme of, say, the New England Puritans offensive and dehumanizing. Yet such regimes are dialectically balanced in so far as their programmes express emotions that are deeply felt by their members without obvious coercion, which relate to symbols that are experienced by them as sacred, and that sustain great communal solidarity. From a moral point of view, the 'unbalancing' of a regime with an offensive moral and emotional programme may sometimes be a desirable outcome.

Relations between a community, human agents, and symbols are not inherently balanced, and do not 'naturally' tend towards a state of equilibrium. For analytic purposes, balanced emotional regimes form a standard by contrast with which cases of imbalance may be identified. A dialectical approach allows us to identify emotional relations as more or less reciprocal. For each of the three dialectical relations we have identified in the previous chapter, there are two ways in which the balance can tilt. It is these imbalances and 'extremes' in religious emotions and regimes that we examine here.

Ultra-externalization versus ultra-internalization

We begin with imbalance in the relationship between a community and its members. At one extreme, an unbalanced emotional regime can maintain tight standards defined and controlled by the community; at the other its members are free to express their feelings without hindrance. Ruth Benedict's distinction (1935) between 'Dionysian' and 'Apollonian' cultures captures these ideal-typical extremes. While Dionysian culture is characterized by extreme individual expressions lacking collective convergence and control, Apollonian culture is characterized by a stern collective demand for emotional self-control that does not permit any spontaneity. In our terms, an Appollonian culture illustrates one-sided internalization, while a Dionysian culture illustrates one-sided externalization.

Ultra-internalization occurs in a regime that considers the 'true' religious emotions to be only those that conform with the authorized framework and guidance of the community. Individual, incongruent feelings are regarded as dangerous or evil. In order to function, this type of regime generally calls for external control by the community and self-control among the members (or for an astonishing degree of collective cohesion, such as may occur in a period of religious enthusiasm). Such a regime is likely to emphasize submission to religious authority and distrust of human nature. True religious emotions are considered to be those that guide humans towards the purposes of God, the gods, the community and its leaders. Genuine religious emotion depends upon agents suppressing their personal feelings in order to join in collective emotion that unites them in a preordained harmony. Members must be guided, trained, and controlled and they must learn to feel appropriately. Spontaneous emotional outbursts will upset the harmony of the group, and challenge the proper order. Such expressions may be taken as an indication that someone does not really belong, is a sinner, a witch, or possessed by an evil spirit. A range of remedies are used by different regimes to eliminate the disturbing emotions and restore emotional harmony to the group, including various forms of exorcism and ritual reintegration.

Regimes that control emotions and suppress individual expressions display strong structural power combined with a low degree of individual empowerment. In order to formulate a strong emotional regime and to impose its norms, the structure of domination must be regarded as legitimate, and the members have to be convinced about their own need for control and self-discipline. This may be legitimized by presenting individuals as animals who need to be tamed, as savages who need to be civilized, as naive persons who need to be instructed, as sinners who need to be disciplined and purified, or as spirit-possessed who need to be exorcized.

Some of the examples we have discussed illustrate such imbalance. We have referred many times to Durkheim's example of collective effervescence. This can tilt from a balanced to a one-sided regime in situations where personal feelings are suppressed and the collective mood overwhelms. Such a shift may be a reaction to outside influences. For instance, in order to re-establish a religion threatened by dissolution under the influence of another culture, a strong socialization is called for. The Puritan case was presented in the previous chapter as a balanced regime. However, this is only the case as long as the agents identify with it and support it as an institutionalization of their own emotions. Although this was often the case among the first generations of Puritan settlers, who struggled to establish their own communities under external opposition, as Puritan regimes became established and obtained an institutional power, the children of founding members were automatically socialized into its emotional regime. Some came to harbour doubts about the regime—both spiritual doubt and self-criticism, but also a potential critique of the communal authorities who prescribed and controlled the regime. Thereby, the precarious balance of the regime was upset. While the community's leaders tried to enforce the regime more sternly, lingering individual doubt and outward rebellion grew.

There are many other examples that can be given. Classical Chinese philosophy is an interesting one, since it was well aware of the tensions inherent in emotional regimes (Nielsen 2003). In the work of Zisi, emotional dispositions (*qing*) are thought of as flowing appropriately from human nature (*xing*), but some later Confucian philosophy, especially that of Xunsi, became more critical of *xing*. To give way to natural desires and emotions was interpreted as a danger to society, unless *xing* is cultivated by *li*—a concept that includes not only rituals but the right path indicated by the wise ancestral kings. *Li* demarcates limits of actions, and cultivates the heart. Humans do not spontaneously wish to follow *li*, but must learn to do so. Rituals are carriers of proper emotions. By following *li*, the natural affects are joined with the rational mind and thereby the right emotions are cultivated for becoming a noble person (*junzi*). Thus heaven and earth are joined through *li*. Xunsi's emotional programme was congruent with his political ideology in its demand for social control based on a suspicion of human nature. Xunsi was relatively extreme, but several other varieties of Confucianism shared the aim of regulating, controlling, and cultivating human emotions. Late Confucianism stressed propriety, emotional cultivation, ritual participation, and respectful manners. In order to ensure that public officials had the qualities of a *junzi*, Confucian rulers established a system that gave candidates for public service a rigorous schooling.

The classical Chinese stress on *li* corresponds with a general pattern of religious ritualism that demands meticulous conformity with little consideration for its correspondence with the inner feelings of the actors (McGuire 2008). We noted in Chapter 1 that Norbert Elias's interpretation of the European process of civilization stresses the internalization of emotional norms. This corresponds with a religious conventionalism, which considers outward manners more important than their emotional resonance.[1]

---

[1] This aspect has been stressed by the psychologist of religion, Gordon Allport (1950). He described an 'extrinsic' type of religion that conforms with demands for outward deference as less sincere and mature than 'intrinsic' religiosity. Further psychological research followed this up, and affiliated extrinsic religiosity with narcissism, guilt, fear of death, and prejudice. Whereas this psychological pattern is debatable, Allport's extrinsic religiosity corresponds with our notion of unbalanced emotional regimes, and it may help

An interesting example occurs when a population is forcibly converted to a new religion. During such a process religious and/or political leaders strive to secure conformity with new standards and suppress externalizations that are considered deviant. In the Christianization of Europe, for example, many tribes were converted by force and mass baptism. The Nordic tribes were converted through their kings or chiefs. According to the *Saga of Hakon the Good* by Snorre Sturlason, the King demanded the commoners of Trondelag to be baptized, believe in one God, Christ, son of Mary, refrain from pagan rites (*bloting*), refrain from work and fast on Sundays (Sturlason 1899/2009: 85). This was refused by the commoners, who pressed the King to honour the pagan rites for Midwinter. Christianity was eventually established by King Olav, often by pressure and force. Some of the pagan rituals were reinterpreted and merged into the new Christian regime, including Yule as Christmas and Midsummer as St John's Day. The written—Christian—sources indicate that Christianity represented an alien emotional regime to the Nordic warrior lords, who considered feelings such as compassion and humility signs of weakness. Their gradual conversion was achieved by persuasive means, such as presenting St George as the ideal warrior: defender of the weak and martyr for the faith. The gradual establishment of monastic orders, of lay brethren, and eventually of Protestantism can be interpreted as moves in a historical process whereby the emotional regime of Christianity was gradually internalized to such a degree that the Nordic people eventually identified with it as divinely ordained and genuinely human.

As these examples show, a strong internalization may involve the suppression of agents or voluntary submission by agents, and implies accepting and even welcoming the submission of personal feelings to collective standards—a 'mortification of the self'. As we saw in the previous chapter, this process is discussed by Rosabeth Kanter (1972) in her study of utopian communes, most of which were religious. In order to become a member of such a commune, a new identity was provided that reduced the member's sense of a separate, private,

us to understand why some people accept to be subject to a strongly societalized emotional control. To some people, religious conventionalism provides an emotional stability. Such people accept the authorities behind the regime because it provides them with that stability.

unconnected ego, while the power and meaningfulness of group membership was stressed (1972: 103). The theme of mortification was directly expressed in a Shaker hymn: 'That big I, I'll mortify' (1972: 106). Suppression and submission can occur within the same community at different historical stages, or among different segments of the membership at the same time.

Where there is an ultra-internalized emotional regime, and that regime is bound up with social power, it can lead to a demonstration of emotions that do not correspond with peoples' innermost feelings. People's bodies may go through the motions of religious observance automatically, while they experience what Whitehouse (2000) calls a 'tedium effect'. Hypocrisy refers to emotional acts that do not correspond with subjective feelings, but that confer some advantage—usually social respectability. It is often tolerated, because it does not challenge a regime openly. An extreme form of hypocrisy involves the presentation of actions that are seriously dissonant with a person's feelings. Such dissonance is most likely to occur under a regime that is able to impose an emotional programme on its members, sanction them for not acting in correspondence with it, and offer significant rewards for conformity. The theme of hypocrisy is well known among the monotheistic religions. Jesus condemned the Pharisees for their outward holiness (Matt. 27–8). Islam condemns hypocrisy as *munafiq* (Quran 63: 1; 4: 145) and demands a sincere belief (Al Baqarah 8–12). Pretended belief is considered worse than deviant belief or open disbelief.

Though the term hypocrisy implies morally reprehensible and self-interested acts, emotional expressions that conform to the accepted standards of a regime but rebel in personal feeling can also represent a form of moral protest. The Catholic Inquisition, for example, included inquisitions that assessed conformity not only of belief, but of dreams and feelings (Ginzburg 1991). *Conversos*, people converted from Judaism or Islam, or people in contact with Cathars or Protestants, were especially suspected of hiding their true religious commitment. Even people who demonstrated a strong religious commitment to the Church were suspected of being overtly conforming while hiding a private form of mysticism. Both Theresa of Avila and Juan de la Cruz were accused of heresy despite their expressed Catholic allegiance.

As in these examples, a sincere person may feel obliged to demonstrate emotions that do not entirely correspond with innermost feelings. This may simply be a matter of politeness. But emotional change often takes place by expressing emotions that are not truly felt in the hope that the 'heart' will follow. This is a common form of religious training and disciplining, which may be willingly embraced. Any religious person is sometimes confronted with the challenge of performing rituals despite an inner state of doubt, emptiness, or protest. Very often, people participate in religious acts without much emotional identification. For instance, a person may participate in a service in order to please a relative. By participating, emotions are evoked. Despite being doubtful in private, people can develop a commitment when they participate in a collective context. Acts that may at first be stamped as hypocritical can thereby lead from belonging to believing.[2]

The contrasting emotional imbalance to ultra-internalization is ultra-externalization, which is most obvious when personal emotions are given powerful expression by an individual, an expression that is only loosely connected to or controlled by the community. Some religious emotional regimes are tilted in this direction, with genuinely religious emotions presented as those based on personal experiences and spontaneous expressions. The personal authenticity of the emotions confirms their divine origin. The regime invites members to loosen their inhibitions and freely express their emotions. It provides a framework for expressing, affirming, and giving meaning to spontaneous personal feelings. Members may be invited to take an emotional journey, through which they experience a sacred cosmos emotionally—for example, in neo-shamanism (Wallis 2003). In order to succeed, they must abandon cultivated restrictions and cast off their normal roles and masks. They must open themselves to the guidance of supernatural powers or even allow their bodies to become vessels taken over by such powers. In such a setting, extraordinary and extreme emotions are allowed and even welcomed. Even 'inhuman'

---

[2] In some cases, hypocrisy can be a recognized and accepted state. Spectators at a drama know that the performance is an illusion. The dramatist and the director may even stress the illusory character of the play, as Brecht did. Nevertheless, a dramatic performance appeals to an emotional identification among the spectators. One obvious case of illusory act is the imitator, who solicits an emotional reaction in the observer of the presented schema. This example is discussed in Jean-Paul Sartre's sketch of a theory of emotions. According to Sartre, an impersonation works because the spectators recognize the model and hold an intentional affective reaction it. The spectator has seen Chevalier on the stage or screen, accompanied by an affective reaction, and a well-performed impersonation of him reawakens and incorporates this affective reaction in 'the intentional synthesis' (Sartre in Cumming 1992: 62).

emotional expressions, such as animal imitations and transgression of sexual taboos, may be accepted. However, unrestrained emotions are usually allowed only under special conditions and for selected persons.

Emotional regimes characterized by ultra-externalization are common in many contemporary societies. From their perspective, true emotions are located within an individual; they are deep, internal, and intimate, they are private and secret, and they are spontaneous and natural. People can hide their feelings from others but not from themselves. Such a dialectical imbalance implies a tilt away from internalization and attachment to prescribed collective symbols. True religious emotions are those that an individual feels so deeply they are experienced as an explosion from inside, unbound by the emotional regime, or those that a person objectifies without regard to the established agenda. Even in the case of an extreme tilt towards externalization in a regime, however, there is rarely a complete break in dialectics. Some human or symbolic authorities remain to give guidance about which emotions are deeper, higher, truer, or more natural than others—otherwise a regime might dissolve in an emotional anarchy.

However, despite the fact that externalization occurs in a context of social and symbolic reinforcement, its emotional stance involves a general distrust of authoritative emotive norms, orchestrated emotional events, and prescribed symbols and dogmas. Emotional programmes are seen as stiff and inhibiting, and emotional norms as encouraging hypocrisy. Such an attitude rests upon a basic distrust of structural formations that interfere with a person's subjective life (Heelas and Woodhead 2005). It is often based on a general distrust towards the dominant cultural forms, and a search for 'naturalness'—as exemplified by Alan Watts's autobiography *In My Own Way* (1973). Such critique of internalization emerges in certain periods and in certain segments of society. As we will see in the following chapter, it is often associated with social segments characterized by status discrepancy and lack of power relative to other groups or 'mainstream' society. Such a critical stance may inspire spiritual seekers to merge as a group. However, a strongly expressive religiosity lacks coordination and continuation and is therefore unpredictable. A group of seekers may take a step towards organizing a programme and common standards. This may lead to establishing a religious cult with a distinct emotional regime. However, it is also possible that such a group dissolves after a while as different emotional programmes prove incompatible.

Ultra-externalization is sometimes permitted under controlled conditions *within* strongly internalized regimes. Sometimes such expressions are threatening to the regime, and have to occur in another space, but in some circumstances certain individuals may be authorized to have 'extraordinary' emotional experiences within prescribed everyday settings, as in the case of much shamanism. A good example is documented by the Arctic ethnographer Knud Rasmussen. One of his accounts tells of a man who felt a mystical vocation to become an *angakkoq* or shaman. He sought instruction from established shamans in vain. He then wandered off to the wilderness. Although it was part of the normal training to learn to withstand loneliness, this would normally take place under the supervision of a trained shaman. In Greenland it is dangerous to leave the group and walk alone into the land of ice; you not only risk your life; you also risk becoming a *qivitoq*, a wandering mountain spirit. The informant told Rasmussen:

I soon became melancholy. I would sometimes fall to weeping and feel unhappy without knowing why. Then for no reason, all would suddenly be changed, and I felt a great, inexplicable joy, a joy so powerful that I could not restrain it, but had to break into song, a mighty song, with room for only one word: joy, joy! And I had to use the full strength of my voice. And then in the midst of such a fit of mysterious and overwhelming delight, I became a shaman, not knowing myself how it came about. But I was a shaman. I could see and hear in a totally different way. I had gained my enlightenment, the shaman's light of brain and body. (Quoted by Lewis 1989: 32)

Like Rasmussen's informant, those who are called to become shamans are often persons who have experienced grief or illness, who are able to stand up against such afflictions, and who can help others through similar afflictions (Desjarlais 1992). They are part of a regime, but their unique formation and experiences fit them for their social role. In our perspective, shamans may be seen as people who are special vessels for suppressed emotions in a strongly regulated regime. They are allowed to express emotions that are otherwise withheld, and to help others to do so in a controlled situation. They are allowed to castigate wrongdoers and they are allowed to express anger, hatred, envy, disappointment, and jealousy—and allow others to do so—in specific ritualized situations. A shaman has access to several spirits who aid and serve him (or in some cases, her). When a possession comes to a shaman in Greenland, he moans and shudders, then jumps up and begins to intone a monotonous tune, louder and louder, with ever wilder gesticulations. The spirits warn him of diseases or their cure, help him find 'lost souls', or aid him in his journey to Nerrivik, the mistress of the sea animals, when the catch is missing. Those who attend the ceremony do not feel the spirit, but they cry to the shaman to pursue the task and render his message. The advice is normally a declaration of taboos and rules that may re-establish order.

A somewhat different example of contained ultra-externalization emerges in I. M. Lewis's famous study of ecstatic religion, based on fieldwork among Somali pastoralists in a strong patrilineal society where male domination is supported by Islam, and all the positions of religious authority and prestige are dominated by men. Lewis describes the male culture as puritanical and stiff-lipped. We may characterize it as a one-sided regime, where emotional expression is strictly controlled. The open display of love between men and women is unmanly and sentimental and must be suppressed. The love of God, in contrast, is highly approved and rapturously praised in poetry. Similar feelings between men and women are totally out of place, and if they occur it must be due to a sprit, *jinn*, or *sar*, which has 'entered' the victim. *Jinns* lurk in dark corners and strike bypassers capriciously. They are consumed by envy and greed, and hunger after luxuries. The victim is typically a girl, because women are notoriously weak, submissive creatures. When possessed, she withdraws, shows extreme lassitude and even signs of physical illness. Lewis observes that the victim is often a hard-pressed wife, struggling to survive and feed her children, and liable to neglect or suppression by her husband. Maybe he is absent and following his manly pastoral pursuits, and maybe she suspects that he is looking for another spouse. A possessed woman begins to speak in a strange language, that of the spirit, and she has to call female shamans in order to interpret it. They interpret the message as demanding gifts from the menfolk, and organize a cathartic dance, called 'mounting the *sar*', attended by other women. Only after this can the patient be expected to recover. However, the relief may be only temporary. If the spirits reappear, the woman may eventually move into a circle of *sar* devotees. The Somali men believe in *jinns*, but are somewhat sceptical about whether this possession is genuine or blackmail. They normally accept a few bouts, if they are not too costly, but, if the affliction becomes chronic, the man may beat the wife or threaten with divorce. Lewis (1989: 68) interprets such spirit possession as the means by which women 'both air their grievances obliquely, and gain some satisfaction'.[3] He depicts a state of mutual suspicion between men and women in the Somali culture, which erupts in ecstatic possession. In our terms, the cult of *sar* forms a mechanism for individual emotional expression—and protest—in a tightly controlled emotional regime where the control weighs particularly heavily on women.

As the next chapter shows, hierarchical and unequal societies are often bound up with emotional regimes that establish a programme of emotions congruent with the rulers' interests and experiences. For instance, rulers and powerful groups—including in terms of gender, class, and ethnicity—may present obedience, subservience, respect, humility, and endurance as ideal emotions for ordinary people. This may succeed to some degree. However, it may eventually accumulate a series of emotional tensions as people find they cannot internalize the emotions decreed by the regime. If they cannot confront the ideology of the power structure, their emotional tensions may lead to physical and psychic illness, and their confused and ambivalent anger may be voiced involuntarily through spirits. Such an expression is interpreted not as a voice of rebellion but as an involuntary act sanctioned by the same religious symbols that legitimate the emotional regime.

Ultra-objectification versus ultra-subjectification

It will be recalled that the relation between what we refer to as objectification and subjectification has to do with that between an individual and religious symbols. This relation can tilt in two directions. On the one hand, a human agent may stand in relation to symbols that have a religious reference, but may fail to be emotionally affected to a significant degree. Here the object is just an object, with no emotional significance, and the dialectical relation weakens: a case of 'ultra-objectification'. On the other hand, the emotions that arise in relation to a religious symbol may be so overwhelming that the individual is overcome with emotion to such a degree that the symbol seems to be

---

[3] Lewis's analysis has been subject to critique for its functionalist approach. However, this point is not central in our discussion. We focus on the emotional dialectic. Ecstatic rituals may in some situations contribute to releasing social pressure, and in others they manage risk in everyday life by negotiating with supernatural beings.

a powerful agent in its own right: this represents a case of 'ultra-subjectification'.

In ultra-subjectification a symbol seems to possess an inner force that compels its subject to react emotionally. It is experienced not as created or chosen by humans, embedded in a cultural pattern, internalized through socialization, and legitimated by a community or society—but as an emotional agent in its own right. In his study of conversion in adolescence, Stanley Hall (1904) paralleled religion with sexual passion. In certain situations, people become fanatically dedicated to the object of devotion, hallow the sites with which it is associated, and attribute vitality to the object (Hall 1904: 2). Such a stance can be labelled 'fetishism', a term now rendered suspect because of its association with ethnocentric studies of 'primitive religion'. If we draw on Marx (1887/1974: 76), however, the term can be used to signal a misrepresentation which leads to the estrangement of human products from human beings' control.

In a religious context this may mean an object that is venerated as if it were alive, powerful, and potentially dangerous to humans. It is beyond human control, or at least beyond the control of all but an elite that is ascribed with the ability to approach, handle, and interpret the symbol. On Bellona Island, for example, the sacred pole, ritual mats, spears, and other objects were considered *tapu*. If a person touched them, he or she would become afflicted. Only the religious officials who were themselves *tapu* could touch them (Monberg 1966: 125). The elite may coincide with the political rulers, such as Pharaohs or divine Emperors, or it may consist of specially qualified persons, such as shamans, or specially trained people, such as priests. In other situations, powerful sacred objects may come into the possession of individuals or institutions that can accrue power by means of the association—as happened with relics in medieval Europe. In such a case ultra-subjectification may represent a potential challenge towards established power in society. By evoking strong passions with a supra-human source of reference, emotions may move beyond social control.

Practices labelled 'magical' may involve ultra-subjectification if the manipulation of objects *per se* is held to effect certain ends irrespective of human intention and agency. In fact, as Mauss (1902/2006) argued, most magic involves dialectics between object, practitioner, and client or audience; but the regime may be strongly balanced towards subjectification. An example is provided by the role of the *tupilaq* among the Greenland inuit. A *tupilaq* is normally a figure, often carved in bone, with animal and human features that indicate life and death. It represents a constellation of categories that are normally held apart, and thus symbolizes disruption and chaos (Bringsværd 2006). A *tupilaq* is an objectification of jealousy or hatred. For instance, when an old and weak hunter harpoons a walrus while a younger hunter is out of luck for days, the humiliated youth may produce a *tupilaq* in secret, bring it to life, and direct it against his rival. A *tupilaq* is more than a symbol of enmity: it is an object that is brought to life by magical acts, potent to spread dread, danger, and illness. It makes people behave in strange ways that jeopardize life itself. When a carved *tupilaq* is found in a camp, people know that they have become the target of a strong hatred. An equally strong magic is needed to avert the danger or divert it back to its origin.

For those who do not feel the same emotions towards a religious object, ultra-subjectification appears as a form of primitive superstition. It is interpreted as irrational and often immoral—whether it is focused on religious symbols, money, or status symbols. Many religions contain an internal critique of 'idolatry'. However, 'fetishism' remains widespread in modern societies, and applies even to cherished symbols of modernity, such as national flags and memorabilia of celebrities like Elvis. One man's idol may be another man's God or 'self-evident truth'. Nordic tourists in Southern Europe may wonder why natives are enthralled by the gilded statue of a saint. The faithful can see the aesthetic quality of the statue, but they can also see something more. For them, it contains an emotive message. Back home, the same Nordic tourists may have something like an altar with framed portraits and other small artefacts, and may spend a good deal of time communicating with these things. Ultra-subjectification can even be seen where people ascribe forms of art with a power that transcends the craftsmanship of its human creator.

Religious and theological critiques of ultra-subjectification often insist that true religious emotions are those that focus on common, consecrated symbols, and relate to the common good. From this perspective, individuals who are wrapped up in feelings related to personally meaningful objects may be castigated as deluded, self-centred, and dangerous. The opposition between 'religion' and 'magic' often relates to this critique. However, ultra-subjectification may provide an emotional support and inspiration that serves to counterbalance marginality in relation to wider social or religious power. By venerating sacred objects at home—on a personal shrine, for example—an individual claims direct access to a power that might otherwise be mediated and controlled by religious authorities. This may be viewed by those authorities as legitimate and pious, or as subversive of their own authority, depending on the circumstances and wider symbolic and emotional regime of the religion.

The dialectical relation of subjectification and objectification may also tilt towards a one-sided 'ultra-objectification', where symbolic forms lack appropriate emotional resonance. This can be based on a religious scepticism towards all attempts at representing the divine by material means. For such iconoclasm, objects get in the way of a true 'spiritual' relation to the divine. Religious texts form an intermediate category. They may be venerated as objects, or revered solely for the spiritual message they convey. Some forms of mysticism seek an inner, spiritual enlightenment that rejects the material world as a hindrance. A moderate variety of religious ultra-objectification considers sacred objects to be socially produced, but appreciates their worth and their ability to stimulate genuine religious emotion. More utilitarian forms of ultra-objectification appreciate a symbol for its emotional effect, but discard it and move to another when the emotional effect wears down.

An example of emotional distancing from religious symbols occurs in the case of artefacts considered 'kitsch' by cognoscenti. These symbols may be taken seriously by superstitious and ignorant people, but sophisticates recognize them as commodities, which may evoke memories of a visit to an exotic culture, but with little regard for any deeper significance. By mocking their original significance, it is possible to demonstrate greater sophistication and a more refined sense of irony. A related but somewhat different example of ultra-objectification is provided by religious art that is appreciated purely for its aesthetic or economic value. Museums and galleries generally offer a framework for presenting religious symbols that creates a distance from the emotional regimes in which they were originally embedded. A religious masterpiece may still be venerated in a museum context, but as much for its aesthetic as its religious qualities. Some may observe it with awe or deep feeling, but, unless they are members of the regime in which it originated, they are unlikely to grasp its original emotive force.

The aesthetic quality of cheap, simplified religious art does not hinder it from evoking powerful religious emotions. Some of the simplest and brashest symbols are the most effective in conveying emotional messages that can be deciphered by people, including those whose status does not depend on a display of 'taste'. Abstract dogmatic or philosophical texts have more appeal to educated, 'sophisticated' people who need to cultivate cultural capital (Bourdieu 1984). The symbols that gain greatest popularity have simpler, more focused emotional appeals. To the cultivated elite, this thematic purity may seem emotionally manipulative—a reaction that indicates a struggle for emotional autonomy. For people with little cultural capital, the abstracted symbolism favoured by the elite is unengaging. Most societies are characterized by a split of religious symbolism between popular and sophisticated symbols, high and low culture (Singer 1960), but it is the objects of popular culture that most explicitly express basic motifs of an emotional regime. Religious elites may be suspicious of popular religious symbolism, because it seems to over-accentuate peripheral themes. For instance, at Christmas, Santa Claus, angels, and the baby Jesus are very popular, while the doctrine of incarnation is absent. So the clergy welcomes the event and its moods, but deplores the way in which what should be central according to their interpretation gets lost in popular enthusiasm.

Ultra-consecration versus ultra-insignation

Relations between a religious community and its collective symbols need not be dialectically balanced. Where collective symbols have a power that overwhelms individuals, but may bear no relation to authorized consecrations, there is a dialectic tipped strongly towards insignation—a case of 'ultra-insignation'. And where religious elites treat religious symbols as purely instrumental objects that can be changed or discarded to suit the needs of the regime with little reference to collective emotions, we have a dialectic tipped towards consecration—a case of 'ultra-consecration'.

It is more common for religious communities to ascribe their symbols with an inherent emotional power that pervades the whole community than for the community to take an instrumentalist approach, and assess its symbols in terms of their usefulness. Nevertheless, a more instrumentalist approach may occur when a leadership seeks to re-establish or redefine an emotional regime. This leads to a consideration of which symbols may best communicate and inspire a fresh, or adjusted, scale of emotions.

Dramatic symbolic revisions are rare and are often met with protest. The reforms of the Second Vatican Council (1962–5) aimed at an *aggiornamento* (a bringing up to date) of the Church, and led to a significant adjustment of liturgy and symbols. The local implementation often involved ritual experimentation and a 'cleansing' of symbols. For Catholics inspired by the Council and its aims, there was a readiness to respond to new symbolic formations as more appropriate to the new siprit of the regime. But many felt alienated by the changes, and raised objections to the innovations. The reforms of Vatican II may be interpreted, in part, as an attempt to reformulate the emotional regime of the Church, and the strength of the counter-reaction may be explained in terms of dissonance with the new emotional notes being introduced (for example, joy and light-heartedness in place of respect and awe).[4]

Religious regimes' symbolic systems are continually subject to smaller-scale, more incremental revision. For instance, fir trees and cute angels have sneaked into the Christmas symbolism in many Protestant churches, despite theological protests when the practice was introduced from Germany in the nineteenth century. This change goes hand in hand with a corresponding emotional shift— perhaps towards more 'cosy' sentiments of family and fellow feeling. While Calvinist and Pietist churches were once purified of all visual symbols, human or divine, today they have paintings and even carved images. For example, the Herrnhut church at Christiansfeld, Denmark, exhibits a copy of Thorvaldsen's statue of the resurrected Christ. Again, such changes may be interpreted as a demonstration of a changed emotional regime, which accommodates a new emotional tone. It is common for leaders of religious communities to consider whether religious symbols correspond well with its emotional regime, and to try to consecrate more appropriate symbols. It is when the leadership takes a purely instrumentalist attitude to the symbols that the relationship tilts into ultra-consecration.[5]

---

[4] Works of art that are objectified as religious are not automatically consecrated as such. The German-Danish painter Emil Nolde made several paintings for churches. His most important set of religious paintings was rejected by the congregation that originally ordered it, because Jesus was depicted in vivid colours as a charismatic—maybe crazed—person with Jewish features. Eventually, these religious paintings ended up in his art museum at Seebül and became aesthetic objects rather than a source for spiritual meditation.

[5] Sociological analyses of symbols often follow a similar functionalist approach, where the symbols are seen as arbitrary signs. This may be the case, if the dialectic is tilted. However, the symbols may also be media for emotionally charged memories that refer to community's regime.

When a symbol that has intense emotional power for religious people is treated as 'merely an object', or is ridiculed or attacked, a 'desecration' occurs. For those for whom the symbol has no emotional resonance, the emotional reaction seems extreme and 'irrational'. For those who understand its emotional resonance, but wish to counter the symbol with some alternative, the reaction is intended. Desecration or 'iconoclasm' in a narrow sense refers to the destruction and banning of visual symbols. Iconoclasm may serve to purify emotional life by excluding emotionally evocative symbols, and is typically a consequence of enhancing the status of texts, doctrines, and their interpreters (Whitehouse 2000). A stronger form of iconoclasm occurs when one religious emotional regime is directly challenged and confronted by another. This may be an intra- or an inter-religious process. Both can be glimpsed in the iconoclasm based on the passage in Exodus 20: 4: 'Thou shalt not make unto thee any graven image, or any likeness of any thing that is in heaven above, or that is in the earth beneath, or that is in the water under the earth.' The Jewish people had left Egypt, where statues were venerated as living expressions of the gods, and the Mosaic ban helped demarcate a distance from Egypt. By rejecting all known images of divinity, it also allowed a new beginning, based on the more abstract idea of a God who could not be expressed adequately by material objects created by human beings.

When a religious symbol has been consecrated by a community and thereby associated with a particular set of emotions, its veneration may eventually become habitual. Later members of the community may feel less attached to the original emotional programme and its symbols, and the dialectic may tip towards ultra-consecration. Some sense that the emotions appealed to by their leaders are hollow. If a leadership crisis occurs, critical members may refer to symbols that expressed the original emotional programme in order to raise a critique of its discrepancy with the actual regime. Symbols associated with humility, asceticism, and equality may be used to confront arrogant, affluent, domineering leaders. Consecration can thus be a petard that can hoist the leaders by their own rhetoric. A revived insignation inspires movements of religious reformation, renaissance, and revival.

European history presents many examples of symbolic cleansing and redesignation. The Renaissance reverted to the symbols of Greek antiquity, and interpreted them as a source of inspiration for a regime that discerned divine harmony in the universe. Reform movements internal to the Catholic Church appealed to its symbols of origin and their emotional associations. The Reformation literally smashed many of the symbols associated with the Catholic regime, rejecting material symbols in order to focus on the sacred Word. Examples of desecration in the context of modern, secular societies are more likely to involve challenges to religious symbols by groups opposed to the religious regime as whole, or to religion in general. A profound emotional challenge is often involved. A recent example occurred when the Danish journal *Jyllands-Posten* published caricatures of the Prophet Muhammad. These pictures had a highly different emotional significance for Danish Christian readers and for Muslim readers in Denmark and around the world (Riis 2007). For the publisher and those who supported the publication, the cartoons were legitimated by reference to freedom of expression. Secular Danes who may have become oblivious to the emotive force of religious symbols nevertheless reacted with strong emotion against demonstrators who burned the *Dannebrog*— the Danish national flag, by legend sent direct from heaven.

Dialectical feedbacks

The discussion above points out six types of one-sided dialectical relations. The imbalances that result can reinforce one another in various ways within an emotional regime. As one side of a dialectical process becomes dominant, this often has an influence on other processes. Two forms of feedback seem particularly important, one giving rise to emotional enthusiasm and passion, the other to boredom and tedium (Fig. 4).

Religious enthusiasm often occurs when religious symbols appeal in an especially forceful manner to human agents (ultra-subjectification). This may happen in the context of a charismatic leader and/or collective movement, such as a revival or a rally, that inspires a peak of emotional intensity. Those who relate to the symbols in a staid, composed manner are classified as 'lukewarm' or deviant. As true believers collectively express the emotional appeal, they are grasped and impassioned by it (externalization), and it becomes infectious and possessing (internalization). Their emotional state becomes a guiding motif for their whole life, pushing to one side other considerations (Weber noticed that the divine calling of a 'prophet' sets aside all common standards, whether traditions or calculated reasons).

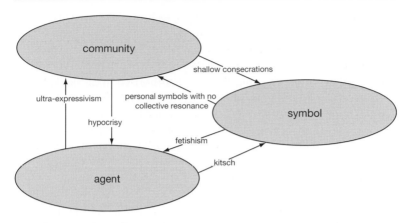

Figure 4 One-sided dialectics

Concerns about propriety may be swept aside as emotionally charged agents feel compelled to express their feelings. For outsiders, such passion is often interpreted as hysteria, madness, or fanaticism.

Such a state of enthusiasm is rarely long-lasting. A religious community may experience such a 'revival' for a time, whereupon its members revert to their everyday chores and common sense. Expressive rituals may function as an outlet for suppressed emotions that have accumulated through everyday life. In special cases, however, religious passion does not revert to the calm of everyday life. This usually points to special circumstances, in restricted communities, or situations of social change, crisis, and upheaval. Millenarianism provides a good example (Cohn 1972). The expectation of an imminent end of the world gives rise to an intense state of expectation, excitement, and anxiety. Everyday life can be set aside, and accepted standards become irrelevant. People start to act with an intensity that enhances their emotional experiences and amplifies their actions. They may sacrifice their belongings as a demonstration of detachment from material interests. They may leave their family and abandon their status. They may punish themselves as flagellants, accept death as martyrs, or destroy others as religious warriors.

Eruptions of millennial passion often occur when forms of social and emotional control are slackened. England under the conditions of Civil War is an obvious example. As the social and political world was 'turned upside down', a plethora of religious enthusiasms broke out

(Hill 1980). Religious and social protests went much further than the Puritan, let alone the establishment, fraction found acceptable. Religious dissent was often based around networks of small groups inspired by itinerant preachers and vagrant prophets rather than by established congregations under the guidance of an authorized minister. 'Ecstasies were everyday occurrences, prophecies were uttered on all hands, millennial hopes were rife throughout the population' (Cohn 1972: 288). Many passionately believed that the day of the Lord was imminent, and that the current order would soon pass away. The famous Ranter Abiezer Coppe (1619–72) describes how he was converted from a life of 'Zeal, Devotion, and exceeding strictness of life and conversation' to 'joy unspeakable' when he heard 'a most strong, glorious voyce' speak of 'the spirits of just men made perfect' (Cohn 1972: 316, 320). Coppe dedicated himself to 'the Eternall God, who am Universall love, and whose service is perfect freedome, and pure Libertinism' (Cohn 1972: 324). Among sects like the Ranters, human standards of sin, and associated feelings of shame and guilt, ceased to apply, and universal love became the rule of life, inspiring a commitment to primitive communism: 'The true communion amongst men is to have all things common and to call nothing one hath one's own' (Hill 1980: 212). Coppe was eventually sent to prison and ended by recanting— as did many other dissenters. In retrospect, he described his ranting as a state of 'being mad drunk'. This retrospective reflection was quite common. The former Ranter Joseph Salmon recalled that he 'walked in unknown paths, and became a madman, a fool among men', subject to 'a principle of mad zeal' (Hill 1980: 283).

If combined and reinforcing processes of strong subjectification and externalization, perhaps leading to new consecrations, are characteristic of religious enthusiasm, the reverse cycle of emotional dispassion— Whitehouse's 'tedium effect'—may begin with the belief that religious symbols are human products that express emotions in an artificial, superficial, or manipulative manner (ultra-objectivism). Because sacred symbols are used and abused by humans for many purposes, they may eventually become tainted by their misuse. For example, begging often appeals to religious sentiments, as in Buddhist cultures, but when it becomes a profession it may lead to a suspicion that the religious proclamations are merely instrumental. Similarly, as masterpieces of religious art are copied cheaply for profit, they may turn into kitsch. Such obvious cases of ultra-objectification lead to an emotional dissonance as appeals are made to the highest religious emotions with reference to symbols that have been discredited. The result may be an emotional disharmony that is annoying, irritating, and eventually infuriating. It disturbs the sense of a pure emotional message and hinders subjectification. With an ultra-objectified stance, the agent becomes emotionally alienated from the symbol, which becomes a mere object that can be dismissed without any remorse. When a community takes such a stance collectively, it leads to a policy of iconoclasm. A campaign of iconoclasm is often followed up by an effort at internalization and new consecrations: from the perspective of the regime and its leaders, it is not enough to reject the old symbols; it is also necessary to correct and guide peoples' religious emotions in correspondence with new norms. Former emotional outbursts need to be tempered and regulated. However, this policy of control and tempering can in turn lead to hypocrisy. People start to go through the motions of religious compliance, without feeling what they profess, and the newly consecrated objects fail to move people.

An analysis of one-sided dialectics also raises questions about what factors hinder feedback in particular cases. For example, internalization can be blocked because the emotional standards of the community are undefined or vague, or because individuals are unwilling to follow the authority of the community and its leaders. Externalization can be blocked because people do not have opportunities to express religious emotions, or are directly hindered from doing so. And subjectification can be hindered when religious symbols fail to evoke appropriate emotions—for instance, because of changing cultural fashions and styles of domestic arrangement.

Other forms of feedback and adjustment in relation to dialectical imbalances may produce other outcomes, including religious reforms. In some cases, a growing tedium may lead to emotional adjustment, or the emergence of an emotional regime that is entirely different from the one maintained by the existing elite. For instance, the Danish revivals of the eighteenth and nineteenth centuries expressed a protest against the dull, unemotional regime of the rationalistic state church of the absolutist monarchy, and gave rise to a movement of reform that was soon split between two alternatives: one stressing light and joyous emotion inspired by N. F. S. Grundtvig and one stressing more solemn feeling organized by the Home Mission (Riis 1987). The Grundtvigian movement eventually become predominant in the Danish folk church.

The balance of emotional dialectics is often related to issues of power. Religious authorities may appeal to an ideally balanced emotional regime in order to suppress dissonant voices, or support a consecration. Hypocrisy emerges as a community enforces norms in a coercive manner. An uncontrolled enthusiasm erupts as agents try to express suppressed emotions without coordination. A common reason for the decline of a religious community is that its members start to feel bored by its symbols, rituals, and so-called celebrations. Such a situation prompts questions not only about the nature of the emotional regime and its repertoire, but how it is established and applied. This directs us to the distribution of power and its legitimacy. Dialectical relations become one-sided if the emotional programme set by an elite does not correspond with the emotional experiences of its members. Furthermore, if the emotional programme of the community does not relate to regimes in a wider society—for example, by sustaining, supplementing, or correcting—we can expect tensions and dissonances to arise.

In assessing dialectical imbalances in an emotional regime, it is always important to consider the regime in relation to its wider social and cultural contexts. In a religiously homogeneous society, there is no need to distinguish between the religious community and the larger society. However, in a heterogeneous society, religious communities may form subcultures with specific emotional regimes. A community may thus present an emotional regime that would appear to be unbalanced if looked at in isolation. However, when the analysis is extended, the regime can be seen to be one of several, which may be linked, nested, or related in some other way—and which may be mutually compatible or incompatible. In many societies members of a religious community are not able to live entirely within it, but their lives are subject to several emotional regimes. Analysis must, therefore, take into account when and how a regime is actualized (for instance, when do agents notice that they enter or leave the regime of a religious community?). Furthermore, we must analyse how a religious regime relates to other emotional regimes, which may be regarded as competitive or supplementary or compartmentalized.

Conclusion

The previous chapter proposed a model of a balanced emotional regime; this chapter shows how such a model also allows us to analyse empirical cases where the dialectical relations are unbalanced.

Unbalanced regimes can lead to more extreme emotions, either in the sense of intense emotional outbursts, collective or private, or in the sense of tempered or even absent emotions. Using this model, it is possible to analyse such extremes, which are typically avoided in social research that focuses on social coherence and 'function'.

Since our conceptual model contains three dialectical relations, we have identified six possible kinds of imbalance that can occur, with consequences for religious emotions. First, the community may predominate over the emotional lives of its members, demanding that they suppress their private feelings and merge into the common emotional life of the community. Second, the community becomes a stage upon which members express their innermost feelings. Third, the religious symbols contain an emotional message that is regarded as obligatory for the community, an unchangeable tradition and truth. Fourth, the community actively seeks, selects, and appoints religious symbols according to what seems to function for its emotional programme. Fifth, religious symbols are regarded by individuals as human constructions that may be selected, used, and discarded at will. Sixth, religious symbols are regarded by individuals as containing an inner force that compels emotions and is beyond human agency and control. By considering these types of relations we have been able to analyse extreme religious emotions: mortification, expressivism, symbolic inspiration, iconoclasm, kitsch, and fetishism.

The chapter also highlights two kinds of feedback that can reinforce imbalances within an emotional regime. One involves a process of emotional enthusiasm, and the other one of emotional tedium. The establishment of a new religious movement or a religious revival may originate with a charismatic person who communicates an emotionally charged inspiration through encounter with religious symbols, which leads to actions that inspire a whole community, whereby the whole community becomes influenced by the symbols. An opposite process of emotional tedium may begin with a community feeling bound to inherited symbols, which members regard as mere objects, with the result that authorities have to impress a regime derived from these symbols upon members, and members relate to these in a manner that merely conforms with the imposed regime. Since this process lacks feedbacks from subjectification of symbols and externalization of feelings towards them, the result is habitual behaviour that conforms with the regime but lacks emotional vitality.

None of the processes illustrated here, or in the previous chapter, is mechanical or deterministic. Since human agents are involved, feedbacks and dialectics involve choices, altered commitments, resistances, and rebellions. Emotional relations do not 'naturally' tend towards a state of balance and social harmony (as in a functionalist, coherence model of society), nor towards a state of conflict and dissolution (as in a conflict model). The scheme we propose is open to both possibilities, and provides the sensitizing concepts for making sense of either.

This chapter and the preceding one focus upon the inner emotional dynamics of religious communities. The latter are, of course, not insulated from wider society. The invigoration or extinction of religious emotions also depends upon the larger social context. This theme is taken up in the next chapter, and developed in relation to late modern societies in the one that follows.

5

The Power of Religious Emotion

To speak of power is to speak of the capacity to make a difference in the world. If emotions are considered only as private, subjective impressions, they hardly seem relevant to that—which explains why the topic of emotion is so often ignored in discussions of power. But, once the concept of emotion is broadened to take account of emotion as feeling, sensation, evaluation, motivation, and relational stance, its 'potency' becomes clearer. As that which moves people and inhibits them, as that which helps to bind and coordinate social groups, to attach them to some symbolic objects and repulse them from others, emotions are relevant. Of course, a comprehensive analysis of power involves much more than an investigation of emotion—the capacity of individuals and groups to act is affected by a whole range of factors, including material resources and forms of social organization—but emotions have a place. This chapter contributes by expanding the discussion of religious emotion in the previous chapters to show how it relates to the issue of power. Following the approach developed so far, we frame the analysis in terms of emotional regimes, and hence in terms of personal power, social power, and symbolic power.

Approaches to power and emotion

The German for power, *Macht*, the finite form of the verb 'to make' or 'to do', captures an important part of what is meant by power. Latin captures even more by marking the distinction between exercised power, *potestas*, and potential power, *potentia*, as does French with *pouvoir* and *puissance*. The distinction between exercised and potential power is important, because power can be held in reserve (as a resource) without being actively exercised, and can have effects as a mere potential (Scott 2001; Sayer 2004). If we are thinking only of individual (agential) or social power, we can define it as the capacity to act, but if we are thinking also of symbolic power, broader terms like the capacity to 'do' or 'effect' something may be more appropriate.

There are many different approaches to power. A major sociological tradition of analysis, influenced by the work of Weber, stresses the rational agency of actors—paradigmatically an individual or a state—as they pursue their own interests at the expense of others, and impose their will (e.g. Lasswell and Kaplan 1950). Some make the account tighter by suggesting that the intention of an actor must be taken into account: persons and organizations can be said to be powerful not merely when they cause some effect, but when they bring about an *intended* effect. This may be achieved either by action or by inaction, by act or by omission. For example, omitting an issue from an agenda, refusing to discuss something, or failing to respond to another's demands may be as powerful as more active intervention (what Lukes (1974) refers to as the 'second dimension' of power; see also Wrong 1967–8). A more strenuous definition takes into account the *interests* of the agent, whether perceived or real (Lukes's 'third dimension' of power; see also Dowding 1996). Thus some theorists suggest that an actor is truly powerful only when he or she intentionally brings about effects that further his or her real interests.

A corollary of the last point is that power can be exercised invisibly and manipulatively by influencing how people understand the world and their place and goals within it. People can be *manipulated* by the powerful to make apparently free decisions that are based on mistaken beliefs about their real options and deepest interests. Foucault's work has introduced into the discussion greater attention to the discursive aspects of power, whereby experts and specialist discourses shape, constrain, and distort the very basis on which people understand and act (Scott 2001). Here, however, the focus shifts away from the rational agent and the canalization of power, to 'discursive formations' and everyday interpersonal encounters that incorporate individuals into formations of power by shaping and 'disciplining' them as subjects (e.g. Foucault 1979b). Central to Foucault's argument is the belief that modern discipline arose as an aspect of the construction of systems of expertise. Scientific disciplines and professions and their discourses established systems of knowledge to govern whole populations (e.g. Foucault 1980).

Despite their diversity, what these approaches have in common is a stress on rational action that tends to render emotion invisible. Foucault's work is a partial exception. Although he focuses on knowledge and discourse, the body and practice, his account—particularly in later works—is potentially fruitful for an exploration of the emotional dimensions of power. By focusing on power not just as the force of agential imposition, but as inherent in social relations, Foucault's approach can converge with one aspect of the relational approach we are advocating. Above all, it helps draw attention to power working through social interactions that structure action. Thus Foucault (1982: 220) describes power as:

A total structure of actions brought to bear upon possible actions: it incites, it induces, it seduces, it makes easier or more difficult: in the extreme it constrains or forbids absolutely; it is nevertheless always a way of acting upon and acting subject or acting subjects by virtue of their acting or being capable of action. A set of actions upon other actions.

As Burkitt (2002) points out, incitement, induction, or seduction would not be possible if human relations were not charged with emotion. In order to be incited, one must be angered; to be seduced, a structure of actions must converge with an emotional programme; to induce there must be a meshing with hopes, loves, and commitments. Thus violence or struggle does not necessarily define power: 'instead its defining element is the modes or strategies of action that structure the possible field of action of others' (Burkitt 2002: 165).

There is also the potential to take emotion seriously in approaches that focus not on dominating forms of agential power that work through coercion and manipulation (what Poggi (2001) calls the 'bloody-minded' approach to power), but on power as persuasion. Scott (2001) refers to this as the 'second stream' of power studies, which emphasize 'signification' (the power of knowledge and expertise) and 'legitimation'. This approach 'embeds persuasive influence into larger and more complex structures of commitment, loyalty, and trust, using means of information and communication' (Scott 2001: 17). It takes account of what Weber called structures of domination 'by order of authority' and what Giddens has called 'authoritative domination', and of Talcott Parsons's emphasis on the importance of shared norms and value commitments in society. Although none of these writers give much explicit attention to emotion—preferring to see values and value commitment as a rational matter—it is not a huge stretch to see how the focus on power as persuasive can be enriched through more explicit attention to the role of emotion.

Such attention is starting to be evident, above all, in the literature on social movements (for overviews, see Godwin et al. 2001, 2007). The fact that 'movements' are defined by shared identity and programmes of action, by 'motion' rather than rationally structured organization, indicates why they lend themselves to such analysis. And, because they challenge established structures of power, they work through persuasion, pressure, and protest (della Porta and Diani 1990). Nevertheless, it is only recently that emotion has begun to be taken seriously. Early theories of 'collective behaviour' (Smelser 1963) saw social movements as fired by irruptions of irrational emotion in response to strains in the social system—neuroses, crazes, manias, panics. In reaction, later studies tended to focus on the rational dimensions of such collective action, stressing interests, mobilization of resources, and the structure of political opportunities (e.g. McCarthy and Zald 1977). By focusing more on the importance of shared identity and solidarity, and the mobilization of symbolic resources (e.g. Melucci 1996), more recent work has opened the way for taking emotion seriously. Shared memories and experiences, rituals, shared narratives, and symbols have all begun to enter into the discussion (e.g. Fernandez 2000). Moreover, there is a new awareness of the need to consider not only the dynamics of social movements themselves, but relations between movement culture and wider cultures (Williams 2007). Building on such work, Goodwin, Jasper, and Polletta (2007) draw attention to a number of emerging themes that chime with the approach we develop here, including: the importance of affective bonds—including trust, affection, solidarity—for movements and their sense of shared identity (and opposition to 'outsiders'); the significance of moods and motivation—whether it be a mood of enthusiasm, hopeful confidence, or grim determination (concomitantly, loss of morale may be devastating); the significance of 'moral emotions'—such as compassion on the part of humanitarian movements and protest groups, disgust and outrage at perceived injustices. Although these authors do not consider the idea of analysing movements' emotional regimes, they move towards it by noting that movements may have different emotion and display rules, and that elites and members often reflect upon which emotions to display and how, in order to maximize their power and effectiveness with different constituencies.

A relational approach

We propose the concept of an emotional regime as a useful organizing framework for thinking about emotion and power. The idea of emotional norms and standards sanctioned and enforced by social and symbolic means is integral to the concept. Moreover, it recognizes that not all members of a community or movement necessarily sing from the same emotional hymn sheet. More typically, we have suggested, regimes have differentiated programmes in which different 'parts' are taken by different actors, thereby reflecting and reinforcing power relations, including inequalities of power. The concept is also able to help frame discussions of relations between a particular regime and other regimes, including means of emotional boundary reinforcement. Finally, and most importantly, the concept of an emotional regime makes possible an analysis of dialectical relations between agential, social, and symbolic power.

To see what is at stake, we can begin by considering the sociological approach to power and emotion of Theodore Kemper (1978) already introduced in Chapter 1. Kemper's account views status and power as structural *stimuli* whose exercise gives rise to a predictable range of individual emotional *responses*. Even if we remain confined to the broadly individualist and behaviourist approach that this enshrines, we should note that a given stimulus is likely to have different impacts on people whose sensibilities have been schooled in different ways, and who occupy different social positions. The implications of this are developed by Barbalet (1998), in relation to a range of different emotions and social sectors. We can add to this analysis that power will also be interpreted differently within the context of different emotional regimes. For example, although emotions like anger have an obvious power potential for triggering action, while emotions like anxiety are associated with inhibition, the force of different emotions is often recalibrated within different regimes: for example, Westen (2007: 128–9) reports that Americans from the northern states of the USA are more likely to respond to personal insults by laughing or shrugging them off than Americans from the south, who perceive such 'attacks' as assaults on their honour and react with anger and aggression. Such emotional schooling is directly relevant to the exercise of social power, and a significant factor in the ways in which social inequalities based around class, gender, and ethnicity are produced and reproduced (e.g. Skeggs 1997 on working-class women).

But, as well as viewing power as a stimulus to which emotion is an (individual) response, it is also important to consider the more ne-glected topic of how emotions can themselves be a stimulus to ac-tion—that is, to see emotions as sources of power rather than just reactions to power. We have already stressed the active as well as the passive dimensions of emotion in relation to the work of writers such as Sartre and Solomon (Chapter 1). Our account was bound up with an appreciation of the bodily dimensions of emotion and its physiologi-cal as well as psychological 'moving' force. We presented emotions as active, relational 'stances' within the world; as means by which indi-viduals and groups actively negotiate their relational standing, as well as monitoring and reacting to their social and material-symbolic positioning.

The dialectical scheme presented in Chapters 3 and 4 allows us to go further. Rather than dwelling exclusively on either emotional action or reaction, it considers emotional power as inherent in the relations between actors, groups, and symbols. As we have already noted, all emotions, even the most personal, register and 'set' a relationship—whether with self, others, or symbols. To feel proud or ashamed, for example, is to rank oneself relative to other people or symbolic objects, and/or to one's own standards. As Spinoza (1677/2001) noticed, such feelings carry with them an empowering or disempowering force: thus 'sorrow lessens or limits a man's power of action ... joy increases or assists a man's power of action' (3.126).[1] Similarly, with feelings of pride comes an expansive energy that enables a person to act in the world with forceful confidence, and with shame may come a diminution of energy and a desire to shrink into oneself, become invisible, or act self-destructively.

---

[1] In the *Ethics* (1677/2001) Spinoza argues that emotions are related to the exercise or impediment of action. They are both the accompaniment and signal of effective action, or of its failure, and a motive force of such action. Joy, for example, makes us more inclined and able to act in the world—it increases our potential—and it is also what we feel when we have been able to carry through an action successfully. Sorrow is the opposite. It disinclines us to take any action—disempowers—and it is what we experience when our action is impeded. Spinoza believed that all emotions could be classified in terms of their link with potency or impotency—with what we might call active intervention to change relation-ships in one's favour, or submission to the power of others. For Spinoza all emotions are variations of joy and sorrow. For example, hatred is sorrow with the accompanying idea of an external cause, and shame is sorrow with the accompanying idea of some action that we imagine people blame. This view is linked to Spinoza's wider understanding of the essence of a being as lying in its endeavour to 'persevere in its own being' (3.6), to perfect itself, and increase its power of action (3.13).

Such emotions are not just episodic. They may develop into habitual dispositions, with crippling or enabling consequences. They are the product not merely of particular situations and encounters, but of individuals' positioning within social and symbolic structures. To be working class, for example, may engender a lack of confidence; such a lack of confidence militates against taking the actions that could raise one's class status; and those from higher classes will judge the lack of confidence as a sign that someone is not qualified to move outside his or her social position, thus reinforcing the status quo. Social groups also enhance or diminish their standing and emotional energy relative to one another: an in-group feels better about itself when it looks down on the out-group, and may well enhance its power in the process.

On the other hand, more equal social relations are likely to be *mutually* empowering—contrary to the zero-sum 'bloody-minded' view of power. We noted in Chapter 1 how Randall Collins (2005) uses the concept of 'emotional energy' to capture the way in which social relations may either drain participants of power, or 'charge up' that power. For Collins, social life is a 'chain' of interactions in which we are attracted to social settings that provoke positive, empowering emotions and avoid those that provoke negative, disempowering emotions. In congenial, mutually affirming encounters, all the participants find their level of enjoyment and energy enhanced. The effect is particularly pronounced for people (or symbols) who find themselves the focus of emotional energy—at a point of shared attention. The power to raise or lower emotional energy is also directly related to the number of people involved. In a negative encounter, for example, to be ridiculed and 'mobbed' by several people is more debilitating than being ridiculed by one person, and to be humiliated by a large group may be permanently traumatic. Similarly, the humiliation of a group, including a nation, by another nation, leaves permanent emotional traces, and may inhibit the power of the society and its members (as we will see below, humiliation may also provoke emotions like anger that lead to an outburst of creative or destructive activity). In positive emotional encounters the effect of numbers is also important: the attraction of performing to crowds, or of being a 'world celebrity', acknowledges the emotional multiplier effect.

Furthermore, a dialectical approach allows us to take seriously the power of culture, material objects, and symbols. Indeed, it is only by introducing emotions into the analysis that we can really make sense of symbolic power. We have noted that symbols have the power to move people—not only to feel, but to act. This is explicable in a dialectical context, in which the *relata* are constitutively affected by their interactions. Take the example of a gun: the simple fact of carrying a gun affects an actor's power not merely because of the enhanced physical capacity it affords, but because of the feeling of pride and strength it engenders. Moreover, the gun is a symbolic object freighted with cultural meanings, and capable of generating associated feelings. When it becomes the focus of strong collective emotion—as, for example, for the National Rifle Association of America (NRA) or in the setting of a militia—its power is further enhanced. Another good example is money: currency is not only symbolic of market exchange; it is symbolic of status; it is ascribed with an inherent power, and it is an object of personal and collective veneration.

Thus the power of symbolic objects seems to be directly related to the way people feel about them, as well as to the number of people who feel this way about them. Symbols that are the focus of devotion and respect, or of revulsion and disgust, have particular power, and those that have been the focus of such feeling for a long time, perhaps over many generations, have even more. As noted before, that power may be sufficient not only to inspire collective action, but to constrain the actions of powerful elites within and outside the regime. Symbols have power by representing an agenda in a concentrated form and focusing feeling towards it. By appealing to symbols, a group can hold its leaders accountable to an agenda that they are felt to have betrayed, and can trigger action and inspire devotion to a cause. Conversely, by desecrating symbols, a group can express its anger and hatred of those whose agenda is represented by those symbols, can trigger action against them, and can foster long-standing hatred and revulsion.

Power and religion

This general account of power and emotion is also applicable to religion, but, in relation to religion, certain aspects assume a heightened importance.

One important trajectory of analysis, stemming from Weber, focuses upon the ideological nature of religious power and, in particular, upon its legitimating capacity (e.g. Mann 1986; Poggi 2001). The latter is related to religion's ability to shape values and 'value-direction'. This is very different from utilitarian, self-gratifying interests subject to rational calculation. In macro-analyses of religion and social power directly influenced by Weber, Mann (1986) and Poggi (2001) consider how different kinds of social power derive from the different resources they seek to monopolize. They argue that political power is backed by physical force and the threat of force, and economic power is backed by material resources and their distribution. Both authors argue that religious power derives from religion's ability to provide, first, meaning (including ultimate metaphysical schemes of understanding and classification), second, normativity and value-direction, and, third, sacred symbols reinforced by collective sentiment that solidify and communicate meaning and value (Poggi 2001: 60–1). Having distinguished between the main forms of social power, such analysis goes on to discuss relations between them and, following Weber, to highlight the way in which each seeks to co-opt, or dominate, the others, drawing their resources into its own orbit. In this scheme, the ability of religion to provide meaning and value-direction gives it a power that is relevant to other social domains, including the political and economic. As Weber suggested, religion can inspire forms of action that are influential within economic life. Moreover, religion plays a key role in the legitimation of forms of political and social organization. Even the most brutal political regime, for example, cannot be sustained by coercion alone, but will in addition seek to legitimate itself by association with symbols, including religious symbols, which inspire admiration, assent, and loyalty.

A different trajectory of reflection on religion and power inspired by Durkheim supplements this analysis by stressing how religion serves as a space in which a society holds up a symbolic image of itself and affirms itself and its boundaries through the experience of collective effervescence. This approach draws attention to the emotional power of religion, and to its ability to generate a sense of loyalty and commitment that transcends personal interests. The role of symbols is of importance in shaping emotions, partly because of symbols' ability to communicate, evoke, and carry social emotion, and partly because of their ability to represent a form of power and inspiration that transcends the limitations of human power.

Thus religious symbols are significant in relation to power not merely as symbols, but as a particular kind of symbol. They represent a special kind of power: a higher power that transcends worldly power.

More importantly, they are experienced as placing those who give assent to them in a direct relation with such power. Many religions refer to God, gods, or divinity in terms of power and energy, terms such as *dunamis*, *mana*, *orenda*, *charisma*, or *chi*. Transcendent powers may be divine or demonic, good or evil, creating or destroying. They may need to be pacified, worshipped, revered, exorcised, or absorbed. Such powers may compel not only by force and fear, but by their beauty, moral appeal, and ability to inspire devotion. By comparison, human powers—even the power of the most powerful individuals and institutions—may be limited. Divine power, therefore, provides a standard for assessing the demands of earthly power, and relativizing its claims. As such, it has the potential to galvanize opposition to worldly powers, and to mobilize support for change. Such change may be radical, as in millenarian movements, which work for a complete overthrow of the existing unjust order of power. Or, at the opposite extreme, it may be manifest in small actions of resistance or in small steps to overcome personal misfortune or draw on supernatural assistance in negotiating the vicissitudes of life. As these examples suggest, belief in an active connection to divine power is itself no guarantee of effective action (which requires many additional resources), but may be an important trigger, stimulus, and sustaining inspiration for such action.

Many religions hedge divine power with prohibitions. People who draw too close to it, or abuse it, may be empowered, overpowered, or destroyed. Some are considered better qualified or engage closely with sacred power, including evil powers. Many communities designate elites to mediate such power, including a hereditary or ordained priesthood, mystics, shamans, or diviners. In addition, figures like prophets may claim such power, even though a community does not at first accept it. Their special relation with transcendent power empowers them in the eyes of others, and allows them to claim special status and privileges.

Thus a Durkheimian approach draws attention both to the way in which religion empowers a social group and draws a distinction between the sacred and the profane. What this approach neglects, however, are both the internal differentiations of power within religious groups, and the relations between such groups and others. It is misleading to suggest that certain sorts of social interaction are inherently energizing for all participants, since their ability to empower depends upon the different emotional possibilities for those who participate within a particular regime. The effect of tightly bounded emotional regimes is not always socially consolidating. Harshly regulated emotional regimes may lead to emotional tensions and dissonances among members, and build up of emotional energies that can be harnessed for change. A group that feels oppressed by a religious emotional regime may call for internal reform, or may be motivated to leave the parent group, form a schismatic group, or take up an anti-religious stance.

As our dialectical approach shows, although religious emotional regimes may be able to control the expression of emotion, they find it harder to control what people feel subjectively, and emotions may seed resistance and change if they are mobilized and integrated into wider social and symbolic formations that are experienced as more meaningful and inspiring. All social groups must regulate and coordinate the emotions of their members to some degree, and use both social and symbolic means to do so. For social harmony to ensue, it is unlikely that anyone could be permitted to express exactly how they feel. Yet some members of the group will have greater power than others to define how all should feel. As we will argue in the next chapter when we look at religious emotions in late modern societies, many members of contemporary societies expect their feelings to be taken as seriously as the next person's. They may well resent having some authority, including a religious authority, telling them how to feel—even if it is in God's name. This sets up fundamental emotional tensions and leads to an imbalance in dialectics.

Balanced dialectical relations and power

The approach we are proposing suggests that the power of a religious group is likely to be heightened when emotional dialectics are in balance, reinforcing one another. Individual participants are in solidarity with one another and with the group as a whole. Their feelings are amplified by being reflected in the feelings of other participants. Whether metaphorically or literally, everyone is dancing to the same tune, their bodies, thoughts, and feelings echoing and reinforcing one another. Feelings are experienced as authentically personal, not as externally imposed. There is harmony between the group and its leaders: they are all parts of the same whole, participating in the same experience. The experience is not amorphous, but structured by consecrated symbols that provide the focus of attention, contemplation, devotion, feeling, and action. Because participants feel equally strongly about their focus of devotion, their sense of harmony and kinship with their fellows is heightened; they are united by common inspiration and commitment. Although religious emotions are intensified in collective settings, we have seen that they occur in a range of other settings, including domestic ones, and are strongest when reinforced across a range of social domains. We have noted how individuals objectify and subjectify religious emotions in a wide variety of ways, including by devotion to a holy book, a personal shrine, a set of rosary beads, an icon, a devotional image, music, rhyme, and song. When dialectical processes are in harmony, personal objectifications have a strong relationship back to the group and its consecrated symbols: the 'private' experience vivifies the collective experience, reinforces and reaffirms it, and feeds its emotional energy. Thus, for example, a Hindu woman alone in front of a shrine may experience renewed calm and hope in relation to the household deity; she communicates this experience to her family and friends; it links her back in memory to her mother, aunts, and grandmothers; the experience is reinforced in a public festival and procession; the latter serves to reinforce the emotions felt in private. Thereby she may feel reassured, affirmed, part of something larger than herself, and gain in confidence and power.

In such ideal-typical situations of dialectical balance, each 'node' is empowered by being brought into relation with the other: each is able to 'move' to a greater extent than would otherwise be possible; hence each is empowered. This is clearly true of the group and its leaders, whose power is enhanced and reinforced by means of emotionally charged gatherings focused on evocative symbols. The power of a particular religion to focus, communicate, contain, and transform powerful emotions—from grief and mourning in the face of tragedy to joyful optimism in relation to birth and new life—lends that religion wider social power. As we have seen, such power is enhanced by the number and status of those who participate, and by the group's antiquity and connection with past generations. But it is the ability to generate and manage strong, symbolically focused, personal, and collective emotion on which a religion's power depends in the present (alongside other power resources, of course, including economic, political, and even military ones).

The role of symbols in this process is vital. Despite the example of charismatic power, discussed later in this chapter, it is difficult for human beings—even religious leaders—to inspire the awe, obedience, and unquestioning submission that can be evoked by contemplation of an omnipotent, morally perfect, eternal, and infallible being. Symbols do not suffer from the same limitations as humans. They transcend the human condition, and are not subject to its limitations. They are immaterial, having a reality that transcends their material forms. Once consecrated, religious symbols bind the emotional regime of a group, and cannot easily be separated from it. By the same token, they accrue enormous power, including power *over* the group, its leaders, and members. In the right context, the most powerful of all sacred symbols are the monotheistic Gods. Their power is related to the emotions of terror, awe, and surrender that they may evoke, and to counterbalancing feelings of joy, assurance, security, and power that come from knowledge of their protection and blessing. As we have argued, such symbols help individuals, groups, and nations gain a sense of control and meaning in life, while helping to sacralize their agendas.

The power of a religious community and its symbols is related to the empowerment of its members. Faith that one has 'almighty' power on one's side is likely to generate assurance and confidence as well as fear and trembling. The believer feels she is acting not just for herself, but in the name of Allah, under the protection of Mary, or with the inspiration of Ram. As Durkheim (1912/2001: 157) notices: 'A god is not only an authority to which we submit...it is also a force that supports our own. The man who has obeyed his god, and therefore believes he is on his side, approaches the world with confidence and the feeling of accumulated energy.' Such experience in a collective religious setting can transform everyday feelings of insecurity, uncertainty, hesitation, inferiority, caution, and lack of confidence into emotions that prompt actions by enhancing feelings of being approved, inspired, and protected by higher power. By way of emotive connection with a group and its symbols, individuals become capable of feelings and actions of which they would be incapable on their own.

Unbalanced relations and power

Situations where emotional dialectics become unbalanced within a religious group or community also have power implications, because these imbalances often involve asymmetries in which one element subjects another (and power relations are, as the term suggests, *relative*). The most importance instances are those in which personal emotions are overridden by the group and its symbols, and the opposite, some-times reactive, situation in which individual emotions contradict and override the collective agenda.

To begin with the first case, emotional regimes of religious groups can overwhelm the individual feelings of participants, or a particular category of participants. This is most likely when dialectics are tipped towards strong internalization and consecration. Then emotional stan-dards are powerfully imposed. Far from appearing merely human, required emotions seem to be sacred and non-negotiable; they may be represented as the will of God, the command of the Prophet, or part of the ordained order of things. Those who express inappropriate emo-tions risk not only earthly happiness, but other-worldly salvation, enlightenment, and social incorporation. Compared with the author-ized emotions, the feelings of individuals count for little or nothing. They will attract little or no interest within the community, and no provision will be made for emotional expressions that include an element of individual spontaneity.

There are many accounts of this form of emotional overpowering in autobiography and fiction, usually from the point of view of those hostile to religion as a consequence of their own experiences—for example, Edmund Gosse's *Father and Son*, James Joyce's *Dubliners*, or Jeanette Winterson's *Oranges are not the Only Fruit*. The latter, for example, presents a semi-autobiographical story of how a young girl's 'inappropriate' feelings of love and desire for another girl are condemned by the Christian sect to which she and her family belong, and interpreted as demon possession. The narrative comes to a climax with the attempt by religious leaders to cast out the demons by tying down the girl and terrorizing her. Like many similar narratives, this story reveals how individuals in such a situation try hard to make feelings and behaviour conform with the required norms, and how failure results in feelings of sin, guilt, shame, and confusion—which may be followed by angry rebellion.

Rituals of exorcism are an important means by which many religions name, control, and 'cast out' emotions that clash with their emotional programme. Such rituals may invoke evil spirits, the Devil, ghosts, witches, and so on—all of whom represent, in part, the forbidden emotions. Another strategy is to use rituals and markers of exclusion which sever connection with those whose emotional non-conformity threatens an emotional regime. Such rituals aim to restore the emotional harmony of a group, both by signalling which emotions are forbidden, and reuniting the community in common purpose against the 'deviant'—who is either restored with the correct emotions in place, or socially excluded. In modern societies, religions may adopt different symbolic framings and practices of control and banishment, including those which borrow from medical, scientific, and therapeutic discourses. In many American Evangelical circles, for example, 'Biblical Counselling' is used to 'treat' a range of emotions which disrupt the emotional programme, including the sorrows and resentments of divorcees, and the 'sinful impulses' of homosexuals.

Processes of consecration and internalization can also be used to support the power of dominant groups within religious communities, who may claim that they are acting not for themselves but on behalf of the divine, or for the good of the group as a whole. Emotional regimes that differentiate sharply between the emotions permissible for different categories of devotee can serve the interest of elites. So too can practices that require 'lay' members to submit themselves to the discipline of religious professionals—as, for example, in confession. Sometimes such power imbalances reinforce inequalities that are also marked in other social domains—as, for example, in relation to gender difference. For example, some religious emotional regimes authorize an emotional scale for men that supports feelings of pride, confidence, and warrior-like ferocity, while promoting a scale for women that emphasizes love, care, chastity, humility, and self-sacrifice. Women shaped by such an emotional regime are unlikely to be able to confront masculine domination directly, lacking as they do the emotional triggers, value-direction, emotional resources, and legitimation to do so.

Turning to the opposite case, the power balance can also tip towards individuals within a religious community. As we will see in the next chapter, the characteristically high valuation that modern societies place on self-expression, individual freedom, equality, and democratic participation conflicts with forms of religion that place more value on the emotional coherence of the group than the emotional satisfaction of the individual. Here internalization becomes less important than externalization, and consecrations become less important than personal and collective symbols that are experienced as personally meaningful.

Such a 'tilt' in religious emotion is not, however, something exclusively modern. All the major world religions have mystical traditions that have some parallels. Many draw a distinction between a 'higher path' of inner-focused mysticism or 'spirituality', and a 'lower way' that makes more use of 'externals' (rituals, symbols, group practices). The former is often reserved for religious virtuosi, who may attain considerable power within the religion, and in wider society—like Buddhist monks in Thailand and Burma. Nevertheless, in those forms of mysticism that find acceptance within a wider religious community, some acceptance of the sacred symbols of the tradition is normally required.

A distinction can be drawn between religions that are subjectively focused in the sense that they pay *attention* to the inner, emotional states of the individual (what we earlier referred to as 'emotionally explicit'), and those that not only pay attention but give significant *authority* to those states. Many forms of monasticism exemplify the former tendency of attending to, but not necessarily legitimating, individual subjective experience. Buddhist monasticism, for example, offers various means of training the body and mind in forms of meditation that give the individual access to subjective states, and greater control over them. Similarly, some Christian contemplative traditions, like those inspired by the *Spiritual Exercises* of Ignatius, revolve around solitary introspection and guided meditation. In neither of these, however, are the individual's inner emotional states regarded as overridingly authoritative. Some states—like those of anger and hatred—are regarded as negative emotions that must be destroyed by way of a range of guided techniques. In the case of Ignatian spirituality, for example, the *Exercises* help shape an emotional life focused around passionate loyalty to Jesus Christ, and willingness to sacrifice all in his service.

This is different from forms of spirituality, including much contemporary spirituality, which not only offer techniques to engender greater subjective self-awareness, but authorize and sacralize subjective life (Heelas and Woodhead 2005). Although they often draw from existing spiritual traditions, they do not train individuals to conform their inner lives to pre-existing emotional programmes, but cultivate a subjectively focused spirituality based around validation of people's unique inner lives. Such spirituality has close links with those modern therapeutic procedures that are premised on the conviction that personal emotions are reliable guides, but go further by sacralizing personal feelings and intuitions as the authoritative voice of an inner spiritual guide or 'god within'.

Both forms of spirituality empower their adherents *as individuals*, albeit in somewhat different ways. Monastic traditions of 'spirituality' train an elite whose power rests on their claim to closer contact with the sacred, or a higher degree of enlightenment, than 'lay' members of the religion. In terms of power they consequently attain not only self-control by way of their emotional disciplining, but power within their own religious group and, if that group is authoritative within wider society, within society as well. Modern, individualized forms of spiri-tuality, which are not necessarily linked to a single religious group, and which do not often have great social legitimacy, are more likely to offer power over the self and within personal relationship than power over others. The role they play in fostering greater 'emotional management' and control is explicitly advertised (Sointu and Woodhead 2008).

Even the most highly individualized forms of contemporary spiritu-ality may, however, converge in a common emotional programme that is exemplified by respected figures within a religious network, and captured by a canon of some widely revered symbolic objects and texts (Aupers and Houtman 2006). Contemporary 'mind, body, and spirit' or 'holistic' spirituality, for example, has an emotional scale in which notes of calm assertiveness, self-acceptance, self-confidence, peaceableness, gentleness, tranquil joy, and loving compassion are prominent. It is related to a range of symbols that include natural objects such as rocks, crystals, and flowers, statues of the meditating or smiling Buddha, of goddesses, and of a mother and child. By con-trast, neo-Pagan Goddess feminism is more often characterized by an emotional scale that has some overlaps, but also includes notes of anger, rage, fury, sexual desire, and a fierce but compassionate striving for justice. Correspondingly, its consecrated symbols include the god-dess Kali and other warrior goddesses, the labrys (double-headed axe), and ancient fertility symbols. Such goddess spirituality explicitly sup-ports women's empowerment and political action against what are perceived to be oppressive, patriarchal structures (Salomonsen 2001; Rountree 2004; Woodhead 2007).

The category of 'magic' has also been used to capture a range of practices and experiences of a highly individualistic kind. For Durk-heim (1912/2001), magic tips the balance so far away from the col-lective and its symbols and towards the individual that it ceases to classify as a form of religion. As we have noted, the contemporary revival of magic, within the broad frame of neo-paganism, does indeed exemplify a practice that is often focused on altering individual 'con-sciousness'—particularly feelings—often with the explicit aim of per-sonal empowerment (Berger 2005). As Mauss (1902/2006) pointed out, however, magic in traditional societies retains a relation with social groups, since the power of the magician depends in large part upon the confidence, hopes, fears, and expectations invested in him or her by those affected by his magical practice—whether for good or ill.[2] Moreover, traditional magic often retains a close connection to consecrated objects of a powerful religion, which are used for magical purposes. Contemporary magic also works with a delimited range of sacred objects, and emotions associated with those objects are manipulated by the magic-worker to effect change.[3]

Charismatic power

Whereas Durkheim highlights the process whereby the group impassions and empowers the individual, Weber's discussion of charismatic power draws attention to the way in which the individual can impassion and empower the group. The emotive gifts (charisma) of some individuals are so great that they seem to set them apart from others. Those who possess such power seem able to get their way without encountering resistance; those who encounter them fall under their spell and are 'charmed' to such an extent that they rush to do their bidding. The charismatic individual seems emotionally charged; he or she immediately catches the attention and provokes strong feelings. Being in the presence of such a person is experienced as personally empowering.

As Weber points out, however, charismatic power is not so much a gift of the individual, as a giftlike exchange between individual and social group. Like beauty, charisma is in the eye of the beholder. Moreover, it requires support and training, and depends upon the proper social setting and 'props'. The way in which people react depends upon their emotive standards and cultural background.

---

[2] 'When the people gather around a magician and he withdraws into his private world, it may seem at this moment that their participation is also withdrawn, but in fact it is more real than ever at this point because it is society's presence which gives him the confidence to become possessed and permits him to come out of this state in order that he may perform his magic' (Mauss 1902/2006: 165). Also: 'Throughout the course of history magic has provoked states of collective sentiment, from which it derives stimulus and fresh vigour' (Mauss 1902/2006: 169).

[3] Some modern magical practice, like much Wicca, is self-conscious about the fact that it works on the level of emotional transformation (even when practitioners believe that magic also works on other levels simultaneously). Thus Starhawk (1979: 37) calls magic 'the art of transforming consciousness at will'.

Reactions may differ even within a single group, with some reacting positively and others negatively. The charismatic actor amplifies the positive reactions, while those who react negatively tend to retract, leaving only the enthusiasts. Once someone has been ascribed with charismatic power, disciples seek an affirmation for what they feel, and feel gratified when they find it. In some extreme situations, positive feedback can occur in a group surrounding a charismatic leader, which may accelerate into frenzy or ecstasy.

For Weber, charisma is the starting point of prophetic religious movements as well as many political movements. He distinguishes charismatic leadership, and the power to which it is related, from bureaucratic and traditional authority. The latter binds a leader by memory and precedence, while bureaucratic or 'rational' power binds a leader by laws, rules, and procedures.[4] Since charismatic authority may contradict and trump that of tradition or legal-bureaucratic rationality, it has revolutionary power in epochs dominated by these other modes of authority. Weber indicates that charisma is the typical starting point of prophetic religious movements and political uprisings. Marx stressed how religions could express a sense of powerlessness, despair, and day-dreaming; Weber's concept of charisma points out that religion can also inspire a sense of empowerment and extreme action. By forming an affective bond, inspired by a leader ascribed with charisma, members of a religious group dare to break with tradition and everyday rationality. By acting as a collective committed to its leader, the group may be able to confront the dominant power in society. More rarely, charismatic authority may co-exist alongside the other forms of authority, and there may even be complementary relations between them—including within religious communities (Miller 2002). However, a charismatic leader has to reconfirm his (or her) status continually, and the bonds of charisma easily slacken and fail.

---

[4] Weber's broad theme is the establishment and domination in the Western world of a purposive rationality (*Zweckrationalität*), which is based on instrumental calculation of means for a given end. Such 'rational' acts are contrasted with irrational acts, such as those based on acute emotions such as rage, enjoyment, or devotion. Acts based on religious beliefs tend to follow a special type of rationality, which Weber labels 'value-rationality', since they pursue a single-minded aim in a systematic and predictable manner. However, religious acts can also be emotionally charged, according to Weber. This is especially noticeable with prophetical ecstasy (Max Weber, *Die Wirtschaftsethik der Weltreligionen*, S. 1860. Digitale Bibliothek Band 58: Max Weber, S. 7663 (vgl. Weber-RS Bd. 3, S. 303–4)). A reflexive sublimation of affective action may lead in the direction of value-rationality or, possibly, purposive rationality.

The charismatic character recedes as such movements gain mass character. Eventually, the original charisma becomes routinized, and it is transferred either to the leader's successors or to an institution.

Appropriations of religious emotional power

The emotional power of religion can be harnessed by other institutions, which then impacts back on the religion in question. The most well-recognized example is the way in which political power has regularly sought religious legitimation throughout the course of history. Tocqueville (1835, 1840/1988: 287) explained the process as one in which religion and politics seek some degree of harmonization: 'Every religion has some political opinion linked to it by affinity. The spirit of man, left to follow its bent, will regulate political society and the City of God in uniform fashion; it will, if I dare to put it so, seek to *harmonise* earth with heaven.'[5] This process is not only cognitive, but emotional. If, for example, a religion can engender feelings of respect, obedience, and reverence among a population, then some of those feelings may be transferable to a political leader—as, for example, when a religious leader anoints a monarch in the presence of religious symbols. It is even more empowering for political leaders or programmes if they can appropriate religious symbols, and the emotions they evoke, more directly. Thus a political leader may wear religious insignia, pray and invoke a deity, or erect buildings dedicated to the gods. Conversely, however, religious disapproval and denunciation can assist in undermining political power.

The rise and success of modern empires and nations often involved the harnessing of religious symbols and commitments to evoke appropriate emotions of devotion, service, and sacrifice towards the empire or nation state, and to evoke feelings of hostility, contempt, or condescension towards other peoples and nations. Religious symbols could be turned into imperial or national symbols, and the sentiments they evoked could be directed towards earthly rather than heavenly homelands. Even secular nationalisms have attempted to appropriate typically religious means of emotional inspiration, including by

---

[5] For more reflections on the relation between religion and politics in the modern context, see the readings in Woodhead and Heelas (2000: 214–63).

inventing new sacred symbols, ritual processions, and even sacred calendars and festivals (Llobera 1994; Burleigh 2006, 2007). Religious ideas of sacred election and manifest destiny have inspired many imperial and national projects, including the 'new' nations of Israel and the United States of America (Longley 2002). Sometimes selected narratives, symbols, and sentiments from a single historic religion are used to justify a single political programme—as, for example, by fundamentalists in India, the Middle East, and the USA today. Emotions of anger and hatred are often used to reinforce an exclusivistic and supremacist stance. At the same time, and often in the same countries, more inclusive forms of 'civil religion' appropriate a different set of religious symbols, loosen their connection with a single historic religion and its leaders, and weave these symbols into narratives, rituals, and celebrations that evoke less aggressive and more solidaristic emotions like love, solidarity, liberty, and service (Bellah 1967).

Thus religious sentiments do not necessarily support political hierarchy and unequal distributions of power. Tocqueville, for example, argued that American Christianity was an indispensable support of democracy in the USA. Not only did clergy support political doctrines of equality and liberty by presenting them, often in contexts of prayer and worship, as God's will, but Christianity shaped the 'habits of the heart' of the American people (Tocqueville 1835, 1840/1988: 288–90, 287). Even by regulating piety within the domestic setting, Tocqueville believed that religion helped regulate the state, by instilling emotions of calm, peaceableness, restraint, a love of order, a sense of duty, a spirit of self-sacrificial care, and temperance. Religion, then, although it never intervenes directly in the government of American society, should be considered 'as the first of their political institutions, for although it did not give them the taste for liberty, it singularly facilitates their use thereof' (Tocqueville 1835, 1840/1988: 292).

Religious emotion can also be relevant for formations of economic power. For Marx, religion served as an 'opiate', which masked or compensated for the harshness of working life, and so inhibited political protest and change. E. P. Thompson (1972) developed this analysis with his account of the way in which Methodism in Britain generated emotions in its followers that were powerful enough to divert anger and dissipate revolutionary sentiment. Weber suggested that ascetic Protestant Christianity actively promoted and supported the accumulation and investment of wealth. His account suggests that this was the result, in part, of emotional regimes that associated thrift and hard work with the confident assurance of salvation, and that linked guilt, shame, and fear to indolence, concupiscence, and display. In late capitalist societies, some forms of Christianity continue to place ethical and emotional strictures on the personal consumption and display of wealth and associated inequalities. Equally important, however, are new forms of 'prosperity religion', which associate material prosperity with divine blessing, and associate emotions of joy and blessed assurance with consumption and display rather than charity and thrift.

Given that social inequalities are produced and reproduced across a range of social domains (Walby 2009), it is clear that the ways in which religious emotions support political, economic, and other forms of social power can and have reinforced forms of social inequality. For example, religions may defuse the feelings of anger that could be provoked by undertaking demeaning forms of labour, by teaching that these should be treated as forms of devotion or penance, to be undertaken with joy and acceptance. By presenting certain racial, class, or gender characteristics as divinely ordained, they may inculcate a sense of humility and dutifulness. By stigmatizing certain forms of sexuality or sexual behaviour, they may inculcate shame and guilt among whole categories of people, with corresponding power implications. Equally significant can be the proscription of certain emotions among certain categories of people—such as anger among the oppressed, or resentment among the poor.

On the other hand, religious emotions can help to subvert existing constellations of social power. They do so, for example, where a religious group serves as an emotional enclave, in which the expression of emotions proscribed in other social domains can take collective form and be recognized and honoured. A good example is furnished by slave religion in the USA, where men and women would meet in secret to express their rage and grief, and to experience comfort, consolation, and a renewal of hope (Raboteau 1978). Elements of such an emotional repertoire can still be experienced in Pentecostal churches serving the poor in parts of America today. In certain circumstances such emotional catharsis and consolation can be transformed into a spring of widespread resistance and protest, as, for example, in the civil-rights movement. Martin Luther King was, famously, able to harness religious emotions of righteous anger and grief, hope and deliverance, and turn them to this-worldly, political ends and demands. At the same time, he was able to appeal to Christian sentiments of patience, peaceableness, and forgiveness in order to orchestrate non-violent protest. Other religious groups, both Christian and Muslim, invoked different emotions in order to mobilize violent rather than peaceful protest against existing conditions.

Decoupling of religious and other forms of social power

The power of religion may be maximized when its emotional regime is supported by balanced dialectical processes *and* reinforced by compatible emotional regimes in other social domains. This approximates to a monolithic system with a single emotional regime. But religion can flourish in more diverse, competitive, and pluralistic situations, including ones in which it provides emotional alternatives to other spheres of society. Its power then resides in its ability to provide a space for the cultivation and expression of feelings not permitted elsewhere—whether of solidarity and hope in the midst of grindingly hard conditions; calmness and relaxation in the midst of the multiple demands of a capitalist economy; or righteous anger and indignation in conditions that are perceived to undermine a group's values and identity.

The power of a religious community may be enhanced when it offers emotional resources that help life both inside and outside the religious community, but is diminished when it offers less emotional satisfaction than other spheres of social existence, or clashes unhelpfully with other emotional regimes. For example, modern forms of primary and secondary education may foster feelings of self-worth that are found to be incompatible with the guilt and humility that traditional church services engender (a sense of guilt that is compounded by living a lifestyle that clashes with the church's moral teachings). Raves, clubbing, music festivals, and intense leisure pursuits may generate feelings of excitement, joy, freedom, confidence, and solidarity, by contrast with which religious gatherings seem dull, boring, and depressing. Or an emotional programme associated with masculinity and centred around confidence, strength, pride, and self-determination may prove incompatible with the 'effeminacy' of a religious regime that exalts kindness, mildness, and loving service to others. Issues of power are never far from the surface in these emotional clashes. Some have to do with access to power on the part of a previously marginal group whose marginality was reinforced by religion. Others have more to do with shifts in structural power, as when capitalism demands more of its workers, or consumerism takes over more of life, or a welfare regime impacts on social relations.

Although the close integration of emotional regimes in religious and other domains of society can temporarily enhance the power of all parties, it also renders religion vulnerable to decline in the others. There is a clear illustration of this in the way in which religious regimes that support particular forms of nationalist or other political sentiment often decline along with the latter. The decline of state churches in Europe, of national Catholic churches allied with monarchial regimes, of imperial religion in China, and of imposed colonial forms of religion can all be explained in this way.[6] The same process sees certain religio-political symbols lose their emotional power, or even become de-sacralized and rejected. They may be replaced by new objectifications and insignations—the flowers and teddy bears at the heart of the mourning for Princess Diana, for example. By an analogous process, forms of religion that support local class and gender hierarchies are abandoned by economic migrants who travel to growing cities to start new lives—whether the nineteenth-century peasants who left their religion at the Gare du Nord according to Halévy, Brazilian migrants who move to the city and join Pentecostal churches, or Chinese women who leave the village to seek work and new social relations in the town.

Simultaneously, new forms of religion, or new interpretations of old religions, arise to support the emotional lives of the migrants who traverse the globe in response to the arbitrary flows of global capitalism. In the alien societies to which they travel, religion often serves as the only social arena in which they can establish an emotional regime appropriate to their past, present, and hoped-for futures. Old symbols are often abandoned or renewed and reinterpreted, their emotional force changing in the process. In the context of European societies, for example, the Muslim *hijab*, *jilbab*, *niqab*, and *burqa* may still evoke modesty, humility, and devotion, but such forms of traditional dress also come to symbolize religious pride, personal confidence, and individual freedom on the part of the middle-class Muslim women who adopt it in growing numbers. With migration to a new, late modern context, symbols change their emotional associations and power implications.

---

[6] The same can happen to 'sacred' secularism and its symbols, as we see in the Islamic revival in Turkey after Kemalism, in Indonesia after Pancasila, with the BJP after Congress power, in Iraq after Baathism, and in Iran after 'Shahism' (Riis 2008).

Conclusion

This chapter completes the development of our general analytical scheme. Chapter 3 presented dialectically balanced regimes, and this chapter shows how social, symbolic, and personal power may support and augment one another. Chapter 4 presented broken dialectical regimes, and this chapter shows how such regimes are characterized by imbalances of power. An extreme form of the latter involves an elite that dictates the emotional programme of religion by reference to consecrated symbols, irrespective of the feelings and devotional objects of participants. Another extreme form involves spontaneous emotional outbursts of anger that may be organized into coherent forms of protest and rebellion. This chapter has also broadened the discussion of religious emotion by considering emotional regimes not only according to their internal emotional dynamics, but in their relations with emotional regimes in other parts of society. It has discussed examples of both complementarity and dissonance between emotional regimes in religious and other spheres of society, and considered how religious emotion can both legitimate other forms of power, and be undermined by them. These topics are particularly relevant for late modern societies, given their highly differentiated social structure, and the diversity of their emotional regimes. This is the subject of the next chapter, which shifts attention from abstract models and concrete but scattered examples to our own social world, and asks what happens when we apply the analysis developed above to the emotional situation we ourselves inhabit.

6

Religious Emotion in Late Modern Society, and Culture

The three central topics of interest in this chapter—religion, emotion, and late modern society—are all the subject of extensive academic debate, but have not been brought together. We aim to contribute by showing how the approach developed in the preceding chapters can shed light on religious emotion in the late modern context. A key theme of our analysis is that relations between social groups, their participants, and symbols are typically out of balance, and that this has destabilizing consequences for some religious emotional regimes, particularly those of historic forms of once 'mainstream' religion, most notably Christianity. The widespread destabilization and deregulation of religious emotion does not, however, mean that the late modern environment is inhospitable for religion: while it renders certain forms of emotional regime unsustainable, it opens up new possibilties for others.

The social context of emotional life

Because late modern society can be characterized in many ways, it is useful to begin with a short summary of features that are particularly salient for our discussion of religious emotion.[1]

---

[1] Modernization theory is foundational to the sociological enterprise (Lee and Newby 1983), and the sociological debate about modernization has basic consequences for sociology of religion, as demonstrated by Beckford (1989). As Beckford (1989) also points out, sociology of religion has remained tied to models of industrial society, when it would be more illuminating for the study of contemporary religion to pay attention to theoretical perspective on late modern (or 'advanced industrial') society.

First and foremost, late modern society is complex and polycentric, with highly differentiated social spheres, domains or fields, each with its own characteristic and often mutually conflicting logics and characteristics.[2] Moreover, these spheres themselves are multi-layered: technologically, late modern society has agrarian and industrial as well as new computer and communication technologies; geographically, it interconnects the world by way of globalized networks of communication and transportation; demographically, it has low reproduction figures and an ageing profile, along with minority immigrant communities with the opposite characteristics; economically, it is characterized by an unprecedented general affluence, which allows priority to be given to values and enterprises that go beyond the servicing of basic material needs. In the economic sphere, a large proportion of the workforce is employed in knowledge and service industries relative to that engaged in production of food and material goods. But there is also growing economic inequality. Capitalism with a strong orientation towards consumption is dominant in the economic sphere, and, in terms of economic ideology, a free market 'neo-liberal' programme competes with a social-democratic, regulated market model. Politically, late modern societies are characterized by democratic polities that control society primarily, but not exclusively, through legal and bureaucratic regulations. This whole constellation of features can be classified as 'late modern'. Cultural aspects will be considered in the next section, but it is important to note at the outset that some scholars would include cultural features in their characterization, including a continuing 'modern project' oriented around human rights and equality, and an ideal of progress towards these ideals that tends to emphasize the superiority of Western culture. Others would point to individualization and a stress on autonomy as characteristic of late modern self-understanding—or at least to that of privileged groups within it.

---

[2] We use social 'sphere' or 'domain' as synonyms referring to a broad sector (or 'subsystem') of society with its own set of values and aims, and a functional approach to further them. We also think of these spheres as related to a particular form of social power (economic, coercive, cultural, etc.). A sphere can be analysed empirically as a 'field' or constellation of positions that relate to the setting, production, and distribution of values and resources. Each position in a field is characterized by its access to resources (or 'capital'), which influences the production and distribution of the specific values. Social spheres become legitimated and obtain status as relatively autonomous subsystems, which pursue a set of accepted values by means that are regarded as necessary. Thus our analysis combines systems theory and field theory with a broadly Weberian approach.

This implies that society is not subject to domination by one social domain and its power elite—for example, an economic system or a single political party. Individuals are subject to several social domains and their internal and external power struggles. They experience different constraints and opportunities in relation to socialization, education, employment, citizenship, parenthood, healthcare, social welfare, and so on. Individuals are differentiated by their varied opportunities for empowerment within different spheres, and by their struggles for status and recognition within them. This situation opens a new range of options for late modern individuals, albeit varied by gender, ethnicity, class, religion, and physical ability.

Diversity is increased by virtue of intensified forms of globalization, including new flows of migration. New groups and identities challenge established ones, and local elites may be undermined by appeals to more dispersed forms of authority. Social relations now reach beyond the boundaries of the nation state. Politically, nation states are interwoven in supra-national networks. Economically, international corporations and global flows of capital disperse more settled forms of local and national employment relation. New media enhance the speed of communication and help establish new communities of interest across the world. Late modern societies are increasingly interdependent, but this does not mean that they necessarily converge structurally or culturally. The idea that Western societies are at the leading edge of modernization, pursuing a trajectory that all societies must travel, is challenged by the idea that human society has itself become polycentric, and that diverse pathways of development with their own integrity should coexist, rather than being subordinated to a single programme of modernization imposed by powerful national and 'imperial' institutions (Eisenstadt 1987; Wagner 2008). New models of 'multiculturalism' are also proposed at the national level, where they compete with more monocultural defences of civil identity.

Such polycentrism and diversity influences a second key feature— namely, a pluralization of meaning and authority, and a growing reflexivity. Because individuals experience several often incompatible spheres of social life, with their accompanying sets of values and 'habits of the heart', they are forced to become aware of the range of possible values, commitments, moral projects, choices, and identities open to them, and to make choices between them. Sometimes the value systems that individuals experience in different spheres of their life are profoundly incompatible. For example, a middle-class mother may have to conform to an ethos of competitive individualism in the workplace, and care and self-sacrifice in the home. This value pluralism is accentuated by diminished respect for tradition and the past (Heelas et al. 1996), and by the plethora of lifestyles advertised in a commercial culture and mediated by new media of communication. It becomes almost impossible to be unselfconscious about who we are and how we live. It is hard to be emotionally spontaneous when one is aware that there is a plurality of emotional programmes that commend different norms. It may be necessary to hold inner conversations, considering whether and how one 'should' feel in a certain situation, and whether and how one's emotional expression may be received by others. This leads to the 'reflexivity' emphasized by Giddens (1991) and Beck and Beck-Gernsheim (2002). It is accentuated by the increasing realm of personal choice and growing responsibility placed on individuals. Even if the expansion of choice is illusory, or confined to trivial or difficult choices, it does not diminish the reality of individual encounter with diverse spheres of meaning and value, different lifestyles and cultures, and the imperative to make choices—however constrained. This leads to heightened reflexivity: we are aware there are different options, whether or not they are open to us. While theories of individualization that posit a turn to 'the self' and the authority of personal choices may be chiefly applicable to affluent, middle-class males, there is nevertheless a widespread suspicion and distrust of 'higher' authorities and a desire to shape one's own life in one's own way.

Thus a third important feature is a disenchantment with many spheres of late modern life that is related to the way in which polycentric spheres, and institutions within them, often pursue their own goals irrespective of moral considerations and social and ecological costs and risks. The theme of individuals faced by impersonal systems is common in social theory—as in Riesman's picture (1965) of atomized, alienating society, Foucault's account of internalized forms of social alienation (e.g. Foucault 1979a), or Habermas's account (1981) of the colonization of the 'life world' of human relations by the logic of dominant systems. However, this is not simply a matter of rationalization and captivity in an 'iron cage' of impersonal, bureaucratic norms. Rather, there is a double pressure, from impersonal norms pursued by autopoietic spheres, on the one hand, and from growing demands for authentic self-expression, on the other. Whereas social relations in modern societies were shaped by the demands of industrial society, late modern societies are characterized by their relatively privileged position within the increasingly global division of labour, whereby a large proportion of the workforce is occupied with information, service, and other 'post-industrial' functions (Bell 1973; Kumar 1978). Many jobs now call for a demanding combination of independence and flexible sociability, as well as technical expertise and adherence to regulations (Boltanski and Chiapello 2005). Ironically, however, while there is a new demand for emotional skill and self-development (Inglehart 1990) and a proliferation of therapeutic and self-help practices (Illouz 2007) to assist this, the 'expressive' self (Taylor 1989, 1991) remains subject to manifold regulations. Moreover, the premium placed on emotional fulfilment heightens disappointment when the authentic self is not respected or even recognized by self-interested and impersonal institutions and elites—whether politicians, capitalists, or the media (Taylor 1991).

One effect of these combined forces and tensions is to undermine powerful, socially extensive, and long-lasting emotional regimes, along with their ability to regulate personal emotions throughout society and bring them into a common patterning and harmony. Emotional life in late modern contexts is simultaneously regulated and unleashed, and emotional fulfilment is both demanded and restricted. As we will argue here, this leads to an increasingly subdued and self-conscious emotionality (with outbursts of spontaneity and intensity), a high valuation of the emotionally 'cool' and controlled (with a longing for greater authenticity and openness), and a strong attachment to, and quest for, people, institutions, and symbols to which it is possible to give wholehearted and trusting commitment (despite growing cynicism and distrust).

The cultural context of emotional life

If we turn to the cultural dimensions of late modern societies, many postmodern analyses characterize the contemporary situation in terms of a loss of faith in foundational schemes and an incredulity towards metanarratives (Lyotard 1979). Signs float free from traditional locations and referents and take on an unregulated variety of new associations. Processes of globalization involve the transfer of symbols and narratives to new environments in which they may carry different emotional associations from those they had in the regimes in which they originated. Variety stimulates more variety, and new tokens of cultural communication enlarge the pool of symbolic resources. In a culture in which symbolic objects are transferred, copied, reshaped, and mixed, established relations between signs and social groups dissolve. Personal reaction to symbols becomes increasingly important as a criterion of value and meaningfulness. If an object seems impotent to evoke appropriate emotions, it may be replaced with alternatives drawn freely from other cultural and historical contexts.

There are two very different assessments of this 'postmodern condition'. For the first, culture is becoming fragmented, superficial, and commercialized. For Baudrillard (1998), for example, it is constituted by an all-encompassing flow of fascinating stimulations and images. The result is a communicative saturation that overwhelms the consciousness and discrimination of subjects. According to Featherstone (2007: 27), 'consumer culture uses images, signs and symbolic goods which summon up dreams, desires and fantasies which suggest romantic authenticity and emotional fulfilment in narcissistically pleasing oneself, instead of others'. Parallel ideas can be found in Ritzer's ideas (2000) about the Macdonalization of society and Baumann's description of postmodern consumerism (in Woodhead and Heelas 2000: 340–1).

The second assessment of the same condition emphasizes, by contrast, new opportunity, freedom, and possibilities of enchantment. It welcomes what it sees as a dissolution of the boundaries between 'high' and 'low' culture, and argues that, as culture becomes more open, pluriform, personal, and reflexive, it is better able to support the playful self-construction of multiple identities. Thus Lash (1990), for example, identifies a shift towards a postmodern 'figural' stance to cultural objects, which is integral to the 'aestheticization of everyday life' and the erosion of cultural boundaries. The postmodern is marked by a bricolage that juxtaposes previously unconnected signs, and a self-conscious and creative intertextuality. Stylistically it involves the freeing and creative blurring of boundaries of genre, style, and history.

If we consider these themes in relation to a concrete example—the changing position of religious symbols in European cultures—it is possible to see that each one has some truth, but not the whole truth.[3] In these societies, Christian symbols maintained a cultural monopoly

---

[3] Sociology has presented a wealth of studies on the usage of symbols in late modern society. For instance, socio-semiotics has demonstrated how symbols can be interpreted and deciphered in relation to their social context (such as Fairclough 2003), and cultural

that lasted until the latter part of the twentieth century in many countries. Although Christian symbols had been in competition with secular symbols for some time, particularly those related to nationhood and ethnicity, in many instances there was still no sharp disjunction. In the UK and Denmark, for example, national flags still carried the symbol of the cross, and national celebrations such as the anointing of the monarch, or the commemoration of the dead and of national triumphs and disasters, continued to employ Christian imagery (and still do). Such symbolism also remained powerful at the local level, whether in civic parades, holidays and festivals such as Easter, Harvest, and Christmas, the ceremonies and symbolism of schools, or in local and civic churches. At the personal level too, key rites of passage continued to be celebrated according to Christian rites, crosses marked the graves of loved ones, and people decorated their homes with Christian images and regulated the rhythm of week and day, of feast and fast, of joy and sorrow, according to Christian tradition. In other words, Christian myths, narratives, and symbols were pervasive within the culture, and bound up with dominant social institutions and structures of power. To take a single instance, in the later nineteenth and early twentieth century, paternalistic Christian symbolism—centred around a sovereign but benevolent Father God—was echoed in the figure of the King, the squire or local dignitary, the factory owner or responsible employer, the local policeman, the clergyman, the schoolmaster, and the father of a family (Woodhead 2004).

From the 1960s onwards, however, this Christian cultural monopoly was decisively challenged and lost. Although still influential, Christian cultural influence now has to compete with both secular and 'multicultural' competitors. The postmodern narrative of deregulation and variety holds true. But should it be counted as gain or loss? What this concrete example shows is that there are gains *and* losses, and that an overall assessment depends very much on point of view and interests. Christianity was tightly bound up with the social hierarchy and its legitimation. Therefore it is no surprise that the cultural and sexual 'revolution' of the 1960s often took Christianity, the Church, and the clergyman as key symbols of oppression or repression, and found in

---

sociology has presented a wealth of studies on the influence and usage of symbols (e.g. Archer 1996; Featherstone 2007). However, these studies pay little attention to religious symbols. The focus of cultural sociology is more often secular high culture or popular commercialized culture.

'eastern' forms and figures of spirituality more fitting symbols for spiritual life and rebellion against the established order as a whole (McLeod 2007). As Brown (2001, 2006) argues, post-1950s secularization involved, among other things, the rejection by many women of a model of chaste, modest, and subordinate femininity, and the paternalism with which it was linked. The shift to a postmodern condition of deregulated symbols and narratives was bound up with changing distributions of power and changing social structures: the fusion of high and popular culture challenges established elites, including the religious elite. Losses include the loss of solidarity; of the ability to respond to common experiences (say, an experience of bereavement) with common symbols and formulae (say, the Lord's Prayer); the resource of a common culture that can be drawn upon in creative works of art and literature without the necessity for explanation or introduction; the ease and simplicity of communication within a common symbolic code; the solidity and sanctity of a code that is so well established as to appear natural or God-given (a 'sacred canopy'), with a consequent power to order common and personal sentiment. Gains include a deregulation that sets individuals free from a cultural and social order that might undermine their interests and trap them in forms of representation that render them invisible or subjugated; the loosening of the grip of elites over 'cultural capital' and an expansion of cultural creativity and appreciation of a broader range of cultural products; a blurring of socio-cultural boundaries and markers and with it a greater tolerance of difference; new opportunities to propose and affirm cultural symbols and tailor them to the interests of the individual and groups, including for the purposes of self-definition against imposed stereotypes; diverse cultural projects in a vibrant civil society.

Overall, the impression of increased personal freedom is not merely an illusion, and the commercialization of culture does not eviscerate symbols of all significance. Most members of late modern societies live with a relative affluence, which makes possible a new form of lifestyle in which goods are purchased as markers of a personal lifestyle and 'authenticity' as well as markers of status. Though traditional religious symbols may fail to evoke emotion, individuals may construct their own personally meaningful cultural packages from a wealth of resources on offer, including music, films, and other entertainments. Commercialized dream worlds are often inspired by religious traditions and have parallel mythic functions, though the new myths do not refer to any specific community as the source of an obligatory set of values. Individuals are not just passive recipients or victims of cultural manipulation, but active consumers and co-producers of postmodern culture. They select and reinterpret symbols according to their own preferences, and are increasingly reflective about cultural symbols: each generation is more skilled than the next at debunking emotional appeals from the state and the market, and individuals are often conscious of the efforts to manipulate them. Nor does the constant symbolic bombardment mean that people relate to all of the symbols all of the time. An 'over-supply' of cultural goods does not necessarily lead to cultural dissonance or dissolution, but increases the pressure to filter cultural items as irrelevant, trash, kitsch, or 'noise'.

Thus the multiform culture of a polycentric society in a globalizing world allows a new breadth of choice. It allows individuals to adopt an ironic distance to symbols that refer to emotional regimes they find unacceptable, and to create informal social networks in which elective cultural symbols nevertheless have a shared significance, and continue to serve purposes of demarcation, inclusion, exclusion, and objectification of shared values. Considerable effort may be made to ensure that such symbols do not overwhelm or crush personal emotional experience, but augment and amplify it in a balanced dialectical relation. Not surprisingly, it is common to encounter consecrated symbols that themselves stand for individual freedom and the power of spontaneous emotional expression. Many charismatic figures, both real and mythic, of late modern society symbolize authenticity, the strength to resist social pressures, and the ability to 'be themselves'.

Nevertheless, once everyone becomes a sophisticated interpreter of culture and a 'demythologizer', the power of symbols to relate individuals and groups directly to sacred power inevitably diminishes (Lyon 2000; Bellah and Tipton 2006). The iconic ability of some symbols actually to present the reality—and the corresponding emotional impress—of that which they represent is compromised. The 'machinery' behind the objects that elicit emotion is more exposed—as in numerous films from *The Wizard of Oz* to Ingmar Bergson's *Fanny and Alexander*, in which a Godlike figure is revealed to be a human creation. This makes it more difficult for symbols to bring the sacred into people's lives, as does the lack of reinforcement by a shared community of 'believers'. The power of emotional regimes diminishes, particularly their extensive power. They may retain their ability to structure the emotional programme of groups and communities (including transnational communities), but not that of society as a whole. Fewer common symbols remain 'live' in the culture, and the emotional structure of life loses complexity. Thus 'happiness' becomes a widely accepted emotional goal, and a sign of emotional 'success'. More complex harmonies of feeling, which set the standards for a range of both positive and negative emotions and associated symbols, lose their general relevance. In their place, individuals put together their own packages of emotional resources, which may include personally meaningful images, objects, films, stories, and music. Rather than submitting to an existing regime, men and women learn to 'self-medicate' emotionally from the vast range of cultural products on offer.

Changing configurations of religion

The late modern situation involves not only religious decline but transformations of religion, both of which are significant for emotional life. There are many challenges to established forms of religion. The capitalist agenda of late modernity stresses material values and progress, whereas the major religious traditions stress spiritual values (which may involve acting against one's own economic self-interest) and tradition. The churches' historic social functions—including law, education, and welfare—are increasingly ascribed to autopoietic institutions that operate by their own logic and exclude religious considerations. Many societies have also used political means to restrict the impact of religion: some make a constitutional separation between state and religion, some pursue anti-religious secularism and install a state-worshipping ideology, and some reduce the impact of religious organizations by policies of institutional differentiation and legislation protecting both freedom of and freedom from religion.

However, the complex functions of late modern institutions call for some reorganization of social domains and some cooperation between them in order to obtain symbiotic advantages. In the last few decades this restructuring has led to an invitation to religion (now understood pluralistically, rather than as just a national church) to re-enter institutional spheres from which it had previously been excluded, including healthcare, education, development work abroad, and contribution to social cohesion. However, the new role of religion is as a competitor alongside others for state contracts, and as a short-term contractual partner. It does not regain its role as a supervising moral authority, and its power of critique is curtailed. For instance, religion is not allowed to interfere with the wider healthcare regime, but it can provide services within it, offer guidance on the treatment of different ethnic and religious groups, and offer spiritual care to the dying (Middlemiss Lé Mon 2009).

Simmel (1917/1976) pointed out a tendency that has become ever more visible in late modern society—namely, the rejection of fixed forms of religious life. The new religiosity consists of 'wholly formless mysticism', which 'marks the historical moment when inner life can no longer be accommodated in the forms it has occupied hitherto' (in Woodhead and Heelas 2000: 349). In more recent sociology of religion this analysis was developed by Thomas Luckmann, who observed that:

The sacred cosmos of modern industrial societies no longer has one oblig-atory hierarchy, and it is no longer articulated as a consistent thematic whole... The assortment of religious representations... is not internalized by potential customers as a whole. The 'autonomous' customer selects, instead, certain religious themes from the available assortment and builds them into a somewhat precarious system of 'ultimate significance'. (Wood-head and Heelas 2000: 468)

In the proliferation of more individualized and expressive forms of spirituality, symbols from high and low culture and from different cultures are mixed up, and traditional religious symbols are reconfi-gured accordingly. Sacred and secular symbols are presented in new constellations. While historic forms of church religion recede, new types of religion emerge that are dominated not by the consecrations of higher authority, but by the promptings of personal experience and conviction (Heelas and Woodhead 2005). Religious elites find it harder to filter out the secular from the sacred and to control the use and interpretation of sacred symbols.

Thus late modern societies offer a new set of opportunities and restrictions for religion. The national churches of Europe, both Catho-lic and Protestant, suffer most, as their religio-cultural monopoly with-in their own territories is challenged by new religious as well as secular competitors, their entanglements with ethno-national symbols and social elites become a liability in the face of social change, and their civic and national functions are challenged by globalization and trans-national commitments. On the other hand, the polycentric organiza-tion of social power and the inability of states to dominate the market or control global civil society offer new opportunities to those forms of religion that are able to creep back into domains like healthcare, education, and leisure; to commercialize their products; or to enter into casual partnerships with the state. The destabilization of any one religion's ability to control sacred symbols and narratives leads not only to the collapse of a unified sacred canopy, but to the proliferation of symbolic options, to a revitalization of the spiritual quest on the part of many individuals, and to a revitalization of religion's role in providing social and symbolic support for minorities rather than majorities.

Emotion in late modern society

As we noted in Chapter 1, sociological theories about emotion in modern societies bifurcate into one narrative concerning a rationalized, unemotional society organized by formal procedures, and a contrasting account that highlights the triumph of manifold emotional expressivism.

The first narrative follows Weber's theme of purposive rationalization and the adaptation to the functional requirements of a modern social system. Freud's theme of the repression of subconscious forces by civilizational pressures is a further influence. We can trace this approach in several forms, including David Riesman's *The Lonely Crowd* (1965), Norbert Elias's study of *The Civilizing Process* (1978), George Lukacs's study (1923) of reification under capitalism, and Foucault's work on the institutionalization and internalization of disciplinary processes (for example, *Discipline and Punish* (1979b)). According to this line of argument, instrumentalism in the scientific sphere, utilitarianism in the economic sphere, and bureaucratization in the political sphere lead to the suppression of emotion or a lack of emotional profundity. A recent variation on this theme is found in Mestrovic's thesis (1997) about the post-emotional society. Post-emotionalism refers to a tendency for emotionally charged collective representations to be abstracted from their cultural contexts and then manipulated in artificially contrived contexts. Various groups become the reference point for synthetically created quasi-emotions: audiences for mass media become voyeuristic consumers of second-hand emotions; citizens are involved in a public discourse that is staged by public-relations professionals and spin doctors who sell their campaigns by engendering synthetic emotions; the culture industry manipulates vicarious and conspicuous 'dead' emotions from a nostalgic tradition as objects to be consumed. Thus emotions are displaced, misplaced, manipulated, and eviscerated: anger becomes indignation, envy becomes craving, hate becomes malice, loving becomes liking, caritas becomes tolerance, and sorrow becomes upset and discomfort. Emotional display is rehearsed with a peer group in mind, and the post-emotional type becomes incapable of reacting spontaneously to the present event.[4]

The second narrative points instead to the personal autonomy, consumer freedom, cultural pluralism, and therapeutic turn that lead to an unprecedented explosion of emotionality in modern and late modern societies. According to Inglehart (1990), influenced by Maslow, an affluent society frees individuals—or at least the privileged within it—to devote a great deal of energy to the cultivation of their own emotional lives and identities. The 'turn to the self' and personal emotions, whose cultural roots can be traced to Romanticism, involves a casting-off of ascriptive status and fixed roles (Taylor 1989). Individuals are encouraged to probe their true, inner feelings and to express their emotions in a creative, playful manner, forming uniquely personal identities in the process. If one expression does not work, it is possible to experiment with different options. Such emotional self-construction is aided and encouraged by an explosion of therapeutic and self-help literature. The late modern profusion of cultural resources, breakdown of cultural consensus, and pressures for autonomy and self-realization increase the pressure to achieve emotional prosperity, whose markers are happiness and well-being. Equally, emotional suffering is publicly paraded and discussed in a new 'confessional' mode exemplified by chat shows, confessional novels, and autobiographical accounts of emotionally traumatic childhoods. Emotional consumers also display a thirst for new sensations, for being thrilled, horrified, disgusted, fascinated, enthralled, and uplifted. Pets and children are cherished for their emotional spontaneity.

These apparently contradictory narratives tell us something important about emotion in late modern societies. One way of reconciling

---

[4] Beckford (2003) is critical of Mestrovic's reduction of religion to a simulacrum of 'real' religion in his vision of post-emotional society. However, Beckford (2003: 204–5) thinks that it is correct to the extent to which emotion is shaped by interests and forces associated with consumerism and public relations. The production and merchandizing of emotions is a major industry, and a commercialized bombardment of emotional stimuli may lead to a superficial and artificial emotionality, which is often directed towards fictive persons rather than real human persons.

them is by referring them to different chronological stages: the first to modern, industrial society, and the second to late modern, advanced industrial society. But, according to our analysis of contemporary society as multi-layered, it is even better to regard them as coexistent in the present social situation. In addition, the different narratives should be interpreted as applying to different spheres of a polycentric and highly differentiated society. One way of doing this is to locate the rational, emotionally 'cool', tendency in the public sphere, and the emotionally hot, expressive tendency in the 'life world' or 'private' sphere. Such a move may also identify the former with masculinity and the latter with femininity, and may regard the two spheres either as complementary (e.g. Parsons 1977) or contradictory (e.g. Bellah et al. 1985). While there is some value in this approach, particularly in identifying the unequal distribution and reward of emotional labour between the sexes, we favour a more polycentric analysis, which recognizes the cross-pressures towards warm expressivism and cool rationality in all spheres of society, and which is open to empirical exploration of how they interplay and compete in different settings. Each sphere in society, and its manifold institutional instantiations, have their own characteristic emotional programmes, which may favour the rational or the expressive, or which—more commonly—will allocate different possibilities to different actors.

In everyday life an agent encounters a series of different emotional programmes and regimes, which may support or supplement one another, or generate emotional tensions and dissonance. Family and primary schooling may support expressive tendencies that encourage emotional self-development. In employment individuals are subject to a range of very different work regimes that may support or contradict the emotional programmes into which they have been socialized. There is, for example, a major tension between emotional regimes that stress competitive individualism and those that emphasize love and care for others. People are not entirely free to choose their attachment to social spheres or their role in them, and in some cases people are bound to perform their roles as hypocrites. In their leisure time, however, some individuals are free to identify with organizations and activities whose emotional programmes they find resonant, and that are complementary with their emotional convictions and needs. Agents typically have some choice of affiliation, which includes their job, and most organizations depend on active support from their subjects, and thus on whether its emotional regime is meaningful.

185

Thus members of late modern societies are subject to a series of emotional stimulations and regulations in their everyday lives, which may be experienced as numbing and dissonant, but also allows for some choice and creativity, particularly for those who enjoy class, gender, and ethnic privilege.

At the same time that 'public' spheres of late modern society become at least superficially more 'emotionalized'—that is, more attentive to the feelings of those who inhabit them—so 'private' life becomes more subject to pressures of emotional regulation and standardization (Illouz 2007). Private life is not simply a 'back stage' of intimate relations in which mutual self-disclosure can be performed. The 'private' sphere has never been without rules, roles, and regimes. It can, for example, be a sphere of hard emotional labour, particularly for women and care workers (Hochschild 1989). Moreover, as intimate relations become disembedded from structures of obligation, kinship, and wider social association and subject to greater personal control, so the pressures to conform to standards set by emotional 'experts', commercial products, and powerful cultural symbols become stronger. 'Lifestyles' are measured against those of celebrities and peers, informed by self-help guidance, and made subject to therapeutic guidance. Reflexive monitoring may even extend to dreams and suppressed desires. A plethora of legal and illegal pharmaceuticals help those who cannot measure up to required emotional standards to temper and regulate their moods.

One important result is a greater emotional reflexivity and critical self-awareness that can often lead to a subduing and blunting of emotion. 'Hot' expressions of strong emotion are generally frowned upon, especially in the workplace, in most public places, and even in the family. They are confined to very limited, controlled spheres—like sports events, and pubs and clubs. As Stearns (1994) argues, the late emotional style is 'cool', not 'hot'. In a clear break from the greater emotionality of the Victorian period, Stearns finds a gradual 'cooling' of emotion from the 1920s onwards. It is now high status to be cool, and embarrassing and low status to be hot (although a few powerful people, including male managers and sportsmen, are exempted). A blunting is evident in the sense that the emotional repertoire of late modernity becomes very limited. A crude distinction is routinely drawn between 'positive' and 'negative' emotions, and of the former happiness is considered by far the most important. This overemphasis on the importance of happiness is massively reinforced by consumerism, since products are sold with promises of joy and satisfaction. Rather than viewing a positive emotion as a fitting and truthful emotion (which in certain circumstances means anger, rage, disappointment, shame, guilt, fear, and even depression), there is a widespread sense that anything other than happiness is a problem that requires some form of treatment. Likewise, negative feelings are often lumped together as 'stress' (which may actually mean anything from anxiety to ennui to lack of confidence, to dejection and accidie—to draw on the richer vocabulary of past times). Sensitivity to the variation of emotion and to the need for harmonies and contrasts fades, as does ability to discriminate between different emotions, and appreciation of the importance of a trained sensibility.

This is not to say that late modern society is 'post-emotional' in the sense that emotions are absent or superficial or universally degraded. There is certainly both a subduing and a blunting of emotion. But there are also spheres and pockets of 'enchantment' and meaningful emotions, sometimes in unlikely places (Bennett 2001; Watson 2006). And there is a lively and widespread desire for greater emotional openness, honesty, and richness—associated with a longing for meaningful systems of value and dependable moral communities. Thus the contemporary context leads to a dispersed series of searches for emotional authenticity that can go in many directions and draw on many resources.

It is this situation that can be further analysed in terms of our scheme of tilted emotional dialectics, both within and outside religious regimes. Processes of emotional internalization and externalization, of subjectification and objectification, and of consecration and insignation can still be observed, but they are often one-sided, reflecting the disjuncture between society and agents, and between collective symbols and personally meaningful objects. This context forms a fertile ground for fetishism, shamanism, expressivism, hypocrisy, iconoclasm, and kitsch. Many forms of established religion struggle to overcome these pressures, and the religious field as a whole is characterized by change and diversification in the face of new emotional expectations and demands.

Empty religious symbols and dazzling material objects

In late modern societies symbolic objects are still created and appreciated for their emotional value and connection with personal emotional programmes, but the balance is tilted towards objectifying personal commitments and emotions. Rather than mutually interpreting and shaping one another, personal feelings become the measure and standard by which sacred objects are judged. Consumers choose, design, purchase, and shape objects that they experience as emotionally affecting, rather than subjecting themselves to the influence of religious symbols and conforming their emotional lives to the agenda they embody. Popular symbols with which previous generations might have had profound relationships—such as the sacred heart of Jesus, a statue of Mary, a poster of Vishnu—are more likely to be treated as kitsch, and religious paintings and sculptures will be presented for aesthetic and historical contemplation in museums and galleries.

The loosening of a balanced dialectical relationship between human agents and symbolic objects was noticed by Simmel, who commented on the widening gulf between the modern culture of 'things' and personal culture: 'the vast, intricate sophisticated culture of things, of institutions, of objectified ideas, robs the individual of any consistent inner relationship with culture as a whole, and casts him back again on his own resources' (quoted in Woodhead and Heelas 2000: 372). Gehlen expands on this view, referring to a cultural situation characterized by a flood of stimuli that overtax our capacity for emotional response: 'Emotional reactions can no longer be invested in an external world which has become so reified and deprived of symbolic undertones' (quoted in Woodhead and Heelas 2000: 373; see also Gergen 2000). In this view, the dialectic between agent and object breaks down completely, and individuals become unable to react emotionally to a world of ever-changing stimulation.

We prefer to emphasize how late modern men and women become their own cultural experts and interpreters—demythologizers who can debunk 'naive' uses of religious symbols, but gather around themselves objects that echo and reinforce their own emotional programmes (Campbell 1987). Emotionally charged symbols are likely to be emotionally assessed rather than treated unquestioningly as effective channels or sacraments of transcendent power. In previous centuries depictions of the devil provoked many people to struggle against his lurking and threatening presence, manifest in temptations, evil deeds, and misfortunes. Now diabolic images are more likely to be regarded as interesting depictions of negative human emotions, or as cynical attempts by religious elites to control the masses. They are skilfully orchestrated in horror movies with the express intention of provoking fear, dread, and thrill.

The capitalist backdrop to this altered relation to objects is clearly important. As Marx emphasized, the restless movement of capitalist production disrupts stable and long-lasting attachments, while inducing desire for an endless succession of material goods. Such goods may become sacred objects in their own right—'fetishes' that we imbue with supernatural power over us—but that are in reality merely human products. But their power is unlikely to be as long-lasting and life-shaping as that of the divinities of the historic religions, since the logic of capitalism demands that we become bewitched by an endless succession of dazzling objects that promise to provide emotional satisfaction and fulfil our relations with ourselves and others. Religious objects, which demand life-long devotion, but promise eternal salvation, have less place in this scheme.

Far from extruding religion and religious symbols, however, capitalist enterprises appropriate and utilize them. In commerce, entertainment, and tourism, religious themes endlessly emerge and re-emerge. Many people watch movies in which religion and magic are prominent, listen to sacred music, and visit temples, cathedrals, and holy sites. They read books that present a magical, sacred universe. Some of these are designed for children, such as the magical world of Harry Potter; some are written for adults, such as the *Lord of the Rings*, *The DaVinci Code*, and a good deal of sci-fi. Indeed, many of the most widely appreciated movies and novels of late modern culture pursue religious themes, but these themes are usually pursued in a manner that does not fit into any orthodoxy of the world religions (Marsh 1998).When orthodox religion is presented, it is often as an adversary of the free mind.

As well as coming at religion 'from the outside', capitalism also comes 'from the inside', in the rise of 'prosperity religion'—that is, forms of religion that are themselves shaped by the logic of capitalism (Lyon 2000). An example that is often given is New Age spirituality, whose symbols, products, and practices are put on sale, and whose teachings often promise to equip the consumer with skills that will enhance their performance in the workplace and enable them to achieve prosperity of body, mind, and spirit (Carrette and King 2004). A clearer and more important example is prosperity-focused evangelical Christianity (Bellah and Tipton 2006).

The pervasiveness of religious themes and symbols in late modern culture does not, however, indicate a revival of religion. People may use religion as a source of entertainment and therapy, of emotional

189

stimulation and self-medication. They do not confuse the religious or magic universes of the books or films with 'reality', and do not feel a moral commitment to their programme. Religious symbols are useful in constructing emotional journeys and sensations that present an alternative to the 'real' world. This 'as-if-world' presents utopias and dystopias that form templates for comparing features of the everyday world and the known social system. If people commit themselves too fully to such imaginaries, they are seen as sad, odd, or mad. Children as well as adults play along in 'as-if' games, because the myths and rituals involved—such as those surrounding Santa Claus—evoke fond memories and good feelings. It is natural to transfer this 'as-if' stance to the grand religious 'myths'. Thus many people in Europe express scepticism about Jesus and the basic dogmas of Christianity, but embrace church rituals for the most important events in life—birth, marriage, and death. They may not believe in what the symbols point to, but they understand the value of the emotions that are evoked by the symbols. The mythical 'as-if-worlds' do not convince because of their seeming realism but because they evoke genuine emotions, in a way that non-religious alternatives fail to do.

Religious symbols, including the established Christian symbols of Western culture, now have many competitors. The global reach of late modern culture allows it to draw on themes from past and present world cultures. For most of European history the only real alternative to Christian symbolism was that of classical mythology (a sharp boundary being drawn with Islamic culture, despite its pressing presence). Now symbols from the whole human religious history appear not just in the media but in the local environment, as migration makes 'the other' the neighbour. In this symbolically plural context, individuals may chose to embrace a single symbolic system, and to draw sharp boundaries against the incursion of symbols from other religious or secular sources. This is now an option both for threatened majority religions, and for minority religions, as we discuss below. A very different option is to assemble a spiritual package that incorporates a range of symbols drawn from diverse religious traditions. This does not necessarily imply an arbitrary and superficial stance towards religious symbols, but the meaning ascribed to the latter is, of course, not the same as when religious regimes operated as monopolistic authorities. The authority of the symbols now lies in their impact on the lives and emotions of those who recognize them, rather than in their conformity with a community's regime. As we obtain an insight in the autobiographical meaning of the symbols, their seemingly vulgar or ironic forms may turn out to mirror a more profound message about a person's life story, stance towards life, and basic values.

Although there is a tendency in symbolic analysis to focus on practices most typical of a cultural and intellectual elite, and hence to notice those that stress self-determination and reflect a breadth of personal choice, it is important to note that there are also religious symbols in late modern culture that support a more fatalistic view of life. Lucky charms are widely used, and may provide a sense of hope in the face of poor social odds. By igniting hope and halting despair, such symbols can be effective in a seemingly magic way (especially when socially reinforced through conversation and encouragement). They can empower individuals to take a chance, to persevere despite weariness, to perform beyond one's confidence, and to make use of the sudden unexpected possibility. Lucky charms, talismans, crystals, horoscopes, even tattoos may have such a character. For the majority, which has little probability of winning in the market economy, such symbols can be sustaining, comforting, and encouraging. Further research is likely to show their importance even in social spheres that are supposedly the most rational and emotionally cool—from the world of banking, to that of political calculation. In a supposedly rational society, 'superstition' is widespread, even in settings that are supposed to be most firmly based on rational norms.

Thus the differentiation and complexity of social domains in late modern society is echoed in cultural diversity. The collapse of an integrated social order goes along with the collapse of an integrating cultural system or 'sacred canopy', which covers the whole of society (and in which Christian symbols had a central place). Sacred symbols are no longer taken seriously according to their consecrated reference. This does not mean they are regarded as meaningless or empty, but that they are treated as personally meaningful created objects. Nevertheless, religious symbols can still carry subtle and intimate emotional messages. Despite being regarded as a contingent product, they may still carry a special emotional message for those who relate to them. Even 'kitsch' religious objects can privately provide comfort and nostalgia, or inspire hope, love, and happiness; but they also have to compete with a plethora of alternative 'secular' goods and symbols.

Multiple consecrations and fragile insignations

We have pointed out the difference between a coordinated social-symbolic system and its emotional regime, and a polycentric society based on independent fields of social life each with its own emotional regime. In the latter, each field strives to expand and consolidate its power, including by establishing collective symbols, but the many different attempts and symbolic consecrations compete and undermine one another and the emotional allegiances they seek to win. This is tied to a structural disjunction of the religious community from other spheres of society. Contradiction also arises between the plethora of polycentric attempts at consecration, and sets of inherited cultural symbols that communicate emotional allegiances and consolidate social bonds. The struggle for consecration is a struggle between different attempted legitimations of power, but its end result is a shift towards 'ultra-insignation' in late modern societies, in which collective emotions become bound to symbols and objects that are not approved by social and religious elites or bounded religious communities or society as a whole. Though they may fleetingly evoke powerful and highly expressive emotion, without the support of social power and a firm institutionalization, such insignation usually proves transient and unable to provoke lasting social change (though there are some successful and durable examples, including, for example, some of the music of the 1960s, which lit up and reflected a complex of feeling centred around a clear set of anti-authoritarian values, and which continues to evoke powerful sentiments to this day).

Consecration refers to a collective's elevation of symbols to a sacred status, and/or its endorsement by a religious elite. Far from abandoning attempts at consecration, late modern society is characterized by an expansion of symbolic production and efforts by different elites to consecrate symbols. Established religious symbols are now subject to competition from many directions. Symbols that are successfully consecrated by a community, group, or organization form a reminder about its past and its purpose. As such, they are resources for both legitimation and critique. A political party, bank, or football club has its logos, mission statements, brands, sacred sites, and emblematic figures—and may demand as much devotion and obedience as an organized religion (Hochschild 1997). However, the emotional power of these symbols is easily compromised not only by the competition between them, but when their wider, sometimes cynical purposes become clear, when there is a clash between practice and the values the symbols represent, or when they are subject to frequent change and manipulation, through rebranding exercises and management overhauls.

To establish a powerful collective symbol involves both an economic and an emotional investment by an organization or institution. Members of late modern society are constant targets for appeals for consecration, from governments, corporations, and cultural organizations— including religious communities. Huge sums are paid to advertisement and marketing agencies and public-relations consultants in order to win 'share of mind' or, better, 'share of feeling'. Secular symbols often achieve a power that religious ones cannot emulate, as is evident in legal systems that hesitate over charges of blasphemy against religious symbols, but vigorously pursue cases concerning commercial symbols, whether Golden Arches, Mickey Mouse, or Barbie. One of the most powerful consecrations of all is that of money, which circulates in purely symbolic forms (Cowley 2006).

In the midst of multiple consecrations, the line between religious and secular symbols may become blurred. Religious symbols become disconnected from their context, and used as instruments for corporate aims. In the process, what Hervieu-Léger (2000) calls the 'chain of memory' may be broken, and with it the power of a symbol to convince and compel, even in its traditional religious setting. Thus Michelangelo's depiction of the creation is used as an advertisement for jeans, and Da Vinci's *Last Supper* is restaged in numerous ironic group portraits. A religious symbol is traditionally consecrated by a society or community in a particular historical situation, and affiliated with other symbols that express its emotional programme. When such a symbol is dissociated from this context, some of its emotional associations can be transferred. A symbol can be consecrated as a reference to one part of a complex emotional programme, but it no longer presents the whole programme.

When a religious symbol is plucked from its context in this way, it changes its associative meaning. Its original meaning can be profaned and reversed, or it can be amplified in a particular direction. To take the Christian cross as an example, its meaning has shifted over time and in different uses. For the earliest Christian communities it symbolized victory over death and the power of God, but by medieval times it focused attention upon a suffering God. During the crusades it became a symbol of chivalry, and in the context of European wars it became a symbol for valour in battle or loyalty to the monarchy or the state. Nazi propaganda twisted it into a Swastika, related to a pagan Sun-sign, which became a quasi-religious focal point for emotional attachment to the Führer and the German Volk. In the contemporary context the cross becomes a fashion accessory, particularly associated with the 'Gothic', and hence still carrying some resonance of death. Its failure to mesh with an emotional culture that prefers to stress joy, happiness, excitement, and gaiety hinders its use as a commercial symbol, as does its continuing place in collective Western memory, and the reverence that many people still feel for it. However, such associations make both the cross and the figure of Jesus a popular image for artists, who may still be able to attract attention by using these images in ways that shock and offend by placing them in settings that contradict the reverence some people still feel for them.

In the face of such unregulated symbolic creativity, religious groups and communities adopt a range of positions. One obvious consequence is that many close-knit religious communities based around face-to-face association and tight emotional regimes are weakened, and looser networks of more distanciated religious association come into being—often across national boundaries. If members have only a sporadic connection to an organizational core, they can form interpersonal networks that share a programme based around expressed symbols that are found to be collectively meaningful. They make a common reference to a set of religious symbols that have a profound emotional significance across borders. The distinction between insiders and outsiders may come to be based on whether these symbols have an emotional resonance. To carry a religious symbol, such as a headscarf, a turban, a hairstyle, or a cross, may signify allegiance to a religious emotional regime in a world where people would otherwise be strangers to one another. In a society based on loose networks and overt signs, this is a hint to like-minded people about a shared emotional programme, shared value commitments, and hence a shared belonging.

A different response is for established religious communities to try to reassert their symbolic boundaries, and to repel incursions. This option has, for example, been pursued by the Roman Catholic Church under Pope John Paul II and Pope Benedict XVI. Differences between both New Age spirituality and Islam have been highlighted, and the uniqueness of Catholic sacraments reasserted. Historically, however, centrally controlled religious communities like the Roman Catholic Church develop by incorporating and consecrating spontaneous insignations—as in the process of incorporation of mendicant orders, or the beatification of popular saints. There is a danger in the present situation that the dialectic will tilt towards ultra-consecration, and that collective symbols will lose their connection with the emotional lives of the faithful.

However hard some religious communities try to preserve and guard their symbolic repertoire and emotional regime, the programme of even the most conservative groups changes over time, and responds to wider emotional developments. When a symbol emerges that carries a strong emotional message in a surprising way in a community, its leaders are pressed to interpret it as corresponding with the community's programme and to consecrate it. When a symbol has been consecrated by the leaders of a community, they have a vested interest in maintaining its status. Conversely, when symbols no longer 'fit' the emotional programme of the members of a community, there is a strong pressure on the leadership to discard or downplay them, and to change its emotional programme. Thus, historic Christian symbols illustrate themes such as evil, temptation, sin, fear of hell, and diabolic power. But such themes clash with a contemporary emotional agenda that places more stress on love, forgiveness, mercy, compassion, peace, and joy. Such unfitting symbols become a source of embarrassment and emotional discrepancy. They can be dismissed, reinterpreted, recontextualized, or sent to a museum. The religious community is confronted with the choice of either clinging to the original emotional regime in opposition to prevalent emotional trends, or adapting to the emotional values expressed by many of its members.

National churches that attempt to serve the majority have special problems in this regard, since their emotional symbolism is inherited from the past, but is called upon to serve a diverse and very different present. The leadership is challenged to select and recontextualize its symbols, but the task is complicated. There is a difference between symbols and ritual that have ceased to have emotional significance (like some of the saints), and those that have come to be offensive (like hell and damnation and prayers to destroy enemies). Moreover, some parts of the community may react differently to them from other parts. And there is the option of reconfirming traditional symbols in a confrontation with the predominant values of society and their symbolization. For instance, symbols that stress the humble poverty of early Christians or the world renunciation of the Buddha can form a source of critique against the hedonism, materialism, and cynicism of capitalist society. However, national churches also have duties to the whole society. Public demonstrations of religious emotions are still required at some public events, such as a shipwreck or a terrorist bombing. Religious emotions are evoked when human intervention seems insufficient, and when the emotional reference must therefore be extra-human. As they continue to try to cater for the whole of society, such churches also have to take account of the way in which popular practices change—for example, in the growth of new practices surrounding death, including new symbolic memorializations of the deceased (a new form of 'ancestor worship'). There is a constant tension in religious history between popular practices, which stay close to emotional stresses, loves and demands of everyday life, and the demands of religious elites, who attempt to conform everyday life and emotions to a higher pattern, like that symbolized by the life of Jesus. In the late modern society, those forms of religion that are able to sacralize and stabilize the everyday life experience of men and women and satisfy their emotional needs fare better than those that attempt to impose an emotional regime that overrides popular feeling.

Thus our claim is that, although society still consecrates sacred symbols, and although many sacred symbols are still able to evoke powerful collective emotions, these processes are increasingly disconnected. The result is that collective symbols with intensive and extensive emotional resonance fade in significance. A whole society can no longer be mobilized around the symbol of a cross, or a flag, or a leader, but late modern societies are still subject to strong collective moods and dramatic outbursts of emotion, often focused around a particular symbolic event. These are not, however, closely tied to established consecrations and structures of collective feeling, and fall away as quickly as they arise. Collective emotion becomes the statement of the moment. Without consecration it does not unite individuals around a common purpose. Even an intense insignation will fade if it is not renewed across time and lifetimes, and if it is not backed by social power.

To illustrate these points, it is interesting to reconsider the story of Princess Diana.[5] The British monarchy is legitimated by its affiliation with the established religion, and associated with the inherited

---

[5] For earlier treatments, see Kear and Steinberg (1999); Richards et al. (1999); Walter (1999).

emotional regime of the Church of England. It is not the present emotional regime of the Church, but its historical symbolic forms and emotional associations, that legitimate the monarchy. Its symbols and ritual practices support emotions of respect, deference to authority and society, humility, and emotional self-control and self-sacrifice. To start with, Diana was able to appeal by being depicted in the symbolic clothing of an innocent and beautiful princess. The real person disappeared behind tales of girls who win their princes because of their beauty and kindness. To the extent that Cinderella fairy tales belong to a feudal era and its emotional regime, this proved compatible with the regime of the monarchy. In the contemporary context the princess myth blended with other dreams about fame, and being the subject of public adoration. It forms a part of what Bourdieu (1974) describes as an ideology of charisma. A princess story of today parallels stories about a young talent who wins the audition, enthrals the public, overcomes adversity and opposition, and becomes famous and rich. Eventually, a whole mythology grew up from the scattered popular images, a public profile of the dream princess, which did not correspond with the actual person, but which supported a highly popular emotional programme.

As in many similar cases of public idols, this led to role stress and nervous breakdowns. They were at first an embarrassment, because they broke up the dream role, but they were eventually integrated in a more complex fairy tale. Diana's heartache and personal struggles proved that she was just an ordinary and fragile person, whose ability to overcome made her more extraordinary, and whose identification with the 'outcaste', and ability to symbolize and overcome the hurts suffered by many at the hand of a cold and distant 'higher authority' made her an even more resonant symbol. However, the monarchy was increasingly unable to solve the contradiction between its own emotional regime and the emotional programme behind the wounded but triumphant princess image. With the divorce of Diana, the tale of the stiff court that was unable to accept the natural, spontaneous, beautiful princess flourished. The image of the rejected princess thereby became a symbol for marginalized people who felt badly treated and rejected by 'the powers that be'. She was even ascribed with a religious view that corresponded with popular spirituality, a religion of the heart. In the last years of her life she had articulated religious views that were close to New Age and distanced from Anglican orthodoxy.

The basic tenet focused on affective, engaged, reciprocated love—a loving kindness directed to all needy human beings, self and others (Woodhead 1999).

The tragic death of Diana, haunted to death by paparazzi who trailed a good story about a romantic affair with an Arab multimillionaire, led to an outburst of strong emotions. Anger was directed against the paparazzi and cynical editors for a short while. Admirers of Diana were angered that the Queen followed the court's emotional regime and withheld grief in public. The Prime Minister, on the other hand, was able to resonate and amplify the common emotion in his public reaction to the tragedy. The Church of England was successful in blending its traditional symbols and emotional regime and a romantic, modern, populist one: Elton John sang 'Candle in the Wind' in the nave of Westminster Cathedral. Thousands of people demonstrated their feelings for their image of the deceased princess. Emotions that were normally private were displayed in public, and these acts sustained and amplified one another. But it is the aftermath of the death that is the most revealing of our theme of fragile collective symbols. To some extent a 'cult' has developed around the symbol of Diana. Sensing this possibility, her family insisted that she be buried in a private and inaccessible place, so that her tomb did not become the focus of veneration. But alternative sites of popular appeal were consecrated: the Diana memorial in Hyde Park, near the monuments to Victoria and Albert, and the shrine to Diana and Dodi in the basement of the Harrods store. Her main memorial does not depict her as a person: it is abstract, water in stone, in correspondence with ecological spiritual symbolism. You can watch people visit the site and show reverence or enjoyment. To some extent Diana has become a saint without a church, but the image of Princess Diana has not been institutionalized and consecrated by religious or political powers. It is an individualized cult, whose power lies in its ability to focus certain feelings. As such it is scattered and disorganized, with no regular ritual occasions, and little collective aspect, and no official patronage by powerful social institutions (unlike, say, the cult to the fallen heroes of war). Its ability to sustain itself over time and across generations is limited, as is its impact on the values and wider emotional regimes of society. Diana's religion of the heart may resonate emotionally with many individuals, but is unlikely to have extensive or lasting collective emotional power.

Weakened internalization and strengthened externalization

Moving to the final tension and disconnection, we can note how late modern society calls for a high level of emotional self-awareness and engenders high expectations for emotional fulfilment, while also setting strict parameters about how, where, and by whom emotion can be expressed and acted upon. The workplace calls for both emotional reflexivity and the subordination of feelings to the demands of functional rationality. The intimate sphere and the worlds of leisure and entertainment give opportunities for emotional expression, but even here emotion is regulated by therapeutic norms and popular expectations. A confessional culture exists in uneasy relationship with a culture that celebrates success, hard work, and masculine rationality. Cool emotionality has come to have more prestige and social acceptability than 'hot' expressions.

These tensions mean that there is a strong demand not only for emotional freedom, but for emotional recognition. When personal feelings are ignored or trampled on in the course of daily life, a demand arises for an equal and opposite confirmation of one's emotions. Individuals are somewhat free to express how they feel in privacy, and to select music and books and charismatic figures that confirm and symbolize their feelings. But these cannot completely substitute for social confirmation of feeling. Such emotional recognition may be offered by intimate relationships, or purchased from medical, therapeutic, and well-being practitioners—whose numbers are burgeoning.

Religion is also an important arena in late modern societies in which individuals may express their 'innermost' emotions in one-to-one and collective settings, often without charge. There is nothing new about this function, which was also performed by institutions like the confessional, forms of ritual healing, shamanism, ceremonies for the dead, and so on. What is distinctive of the contemporary setting, however, is that the dialectical relation between emotional externalization and internalization tend to tilt towards the former. Where confessional practice, for example, was not merely about self-expression, but about self-examination in relation to established norms of feeling and behaviour, such practice is now experienced as intrusive, repressive, and restrictive. The religious arena is expected to allow for individual emotional expressions, while integrating them into a communal emotional regime that does not restrict personal freedom or trample on individual sensibility.

This creates a particular difficulty for religions that seek to uphold comprehensive emotional regimes under the leadership of religious elites. The difficulty is compounded by the sheer variety of emotional regimes characteristic of polycentric, pluralistic, and multi-layered societies. No longer, for example, are Christian sensibilities upheld not only in church but in schools, the workplace, the built environment, and the culture as a whole. Even religions that succeed in establishing strong emotional regimes for their members recognize that it may be hard for them to maintain the religious emotional programme in their daily lives.

Modern democratic citizens find the strict regimes of the Puritans, the Jesuits, or even the Victorians repulsive. State institutions that try to establish tight regimes, such as prisons or psychiatric institutions, are subject to democratic critique. Efforts to continue strict regimes in religious communities are regarded as even more bizarre. If the programme does not adapt to the members, they experience it as irrelevant, boring, or embarrassing. A recurrent theme among individuals who disaffiliated from conservative Protestant communities in southern Norway is their inability to connect with an emotional regime that emphasized notes of guilt, shame, sinfulness, and repentance (Repstad 2008). It becomes increasingly difficult to sustain an emotional regime based around the symbols of a strict deity judging a sinful humanity. Even conservative theologians are pressed to adapt their regimes to the values and emotions that predominate in democratic society, and even the strictest religious regimes are modified and loosened to make some accommodation to the changed emotional environment.

Religious leaders who resist such change are, in any case, likely to be confronted by it in their own congregations. An attempt may be made to uphold an entire emotional programme, but individual members will select from it; an attempt may be made to coordinate emotional expressions, but participants behave in ways that are often unpredictable and unmanageable. An open emotional regime based on loose internalization and strong externalization can trigger emotions that are very strong, but are not stable, unified, or capable of constituting an enduring resource. While a closely directed religious performance is likely to be experienced as habitual and boring, more expressive and spontaneous events contain surprises that may be hard for a community and its leaders to contain. Change may come about in the first instance through a conflict over symbols: apparently trivial moves like taking down a statue, replacing hard pews, or changing the colours of the walls actually prepare the way for significant emotional and relational shifts.

Thus widespread social values in late modern society point to an emotional programme that excludes some of the themes that were prevalent in former religious regimes. Democratic-minded members expect an emotional regime to be subject to choice and consent, not based around blind submission to an authority based on tradition and ascribed status. Most people assume that they have a voice in establishing the emotional programme and that it must adapt to their own wishes. They do not regard their emotional needs as selfish indulgence that must be tempered and reformed by the regime.

In the face of this challenge, many historic churches scale down their emotional programmes, and loosen the enforcement of their regimes. This happens, for instance, as Easter becomes a celebration of resurrection, new birth, spring, and renewal with little reference to the cross, the tomb, and the descent into hell. A narrower, light emotional scale is easier to internalize semi-spontaneously: it is easier to be joyful together without direction, than to shift from sinfulness to joy, and to harmonize a more complex emotional repertoire. A consequence of such emotional simplification is that emotions of despair, grief, anger, guilt, and sorrow may no longer be addressed by the religious community. For example, the emotional programme of funerals may allow controlled expressions of grief, but not the expression of emotional conflict, anger, and confusion. When such collective expressions are encountered in other religious systems and societies, they may be dismissed as exaggerated, inappropriate, and embarrassing. The basic task of dealing with emotional conflicts is left to the individual to solve in his or her own way, since the community cannot provide a collective solution by integration into a consistent emotional regime. Emotions that find no collective recognition may be reinterpreted as personal problems, to be treated by therapy or a pill. The social recognition of emotional distress is delegated to specialists such as medical doctors, psychologists, and social workers, who cannot support their clients for life, or for free.

One effect of the loosening of religious emotional regimes is that religious emotions, and their associated symbols, may float free of religious communities—often into the embrace of the market. Occasions such as Thanksgiving, Halloween, Mother's Day, and Valentine's Day have become entirely separated from their religious origins. They lodge in the general culture, because they allow people to express basic social emotions such as gratitude to parents, solidarity with kin, confirmation of national pride, love of intimates, and protection from fear. In societies where social networks have become more fluid and extended, there is still a need for expressing such emotions, but they cannot be confined to a religious community.

Faced with the danger of the decomposition of an entire emotional programme, some religious communities take steps to maintain a tight emotional regime. This generally implies a policy of encapsulation, whereby the distinctiveness of an emotional programme and its associated symbols is highlighted and protected. For example, a religious community may contrast the true freedom, love, and peace within the community with the artificial happiness, drunkenness, lust, and hypocrisy outside. Fundamentalisms of various hues exemplify this option, and produce simplified codes of conduct that can be rigorously maintained (they are distinctively modern phenomena). Such regimes demarcate, control, and banish improper emotions, and cultivate a delimited set of feelings. In the USA, for example, fundamentalist Christian groups retreat into subcultures where education, entertainment, leisure, and even work can be controlled by religious standards. Religious sects, ghettos, and 'cults' may also serve as what Palmer (1994) calls 'cocoons' within which emotions that are not generally acceptable in society can be experimented with and cultivated.

Another religious response to the challenges of late modernity is to reinvent the form of religious community. The clearest example is the mega-church, a new type of religious organization that has proved successful, not only in America, Europe, and Australasia, but in Latin America and Asia. Such churches combine a regular mass gathering of hundreds or thousands of people in collective worship, with weekly small group meetings (bible studies, prayer groups, youth groups, counselling groups, special interest groups, and so on). This allows them to combine extremely powerful orchestrations of mass emotion, with a setting that is perfectly designed for the expression of personal emotion, including emotional traumas (Wuthnow 1996; Brasher 2001). It also serves to combine a universal emotional regime with a set of nested options tailored to members in particular life situations (abused wives, married homosexuals, elderly people, cancer survivors, teens, and so on). The effect is to encourage 'specialisms' within the emotional programme, and subdivide its scale into distinct parts that can be comfortably internalized by distinct emotional interest groups. This embrace of the late modern bias towards emotional externalization is also exemplified by the growth of new forms of spirituality. Within the religious field, spirituality institutionalizes the turn towards personal emotional exploration and expression. Its characteristic forms are the one-to-one encounter between a spiritual practitioner and a client, the small group that is structured in such a way that the emotions of all its members can be expressed and recognized, and the loose network that joins such individuals and groups in national and transnational linkages (Woodhead 2010). The group, its leaders, and its symbols are viewed as resources that are useful only insofar as they enable the individual to pursue his or her spiritual journey more effectively.

More and more religious communities use emotions purposively as part of their mission. Barker (1984) illustrates this in her discussion of the 'love bombing' of the Moonies, or the 'flirty fishing' of the Family, while Tipton (1982) shows how a range of different emotional styles were employed by religious groups that came to serve as havens for refugees from the sixties counter-culture. Even mainstream forms of religion have begun to use emotional motivations in their appeal to potential members, whether in Protestant Bible camps or at Catholic youth events. It has also become common for religious-minded Americans who move to a new locality to go 'church shopping', a process in which they test out whether they can find a community with whom they experience an emotional match. From the 'supply side', American churches have been quicker than European ones to assess their emotional offerings, and adjust them to ensure they are attractive to potential recruits.

To sum up: in the late modern context we can observe a general trend whereby religion becomes more explicitly focused upon the emotional demands of its 'users', and takes steps to ensure that its emotional programme is appropriate to those it wishes to recruit or retain. Processes of internalization, like those of consecration, may be reined back, or at least presented in a way that makes them appear responsive to members' emotional sensibilities. This necessity makes it harder for religious communities to impose strict emotional regimes, unless they opt for some form of encapsulation. As a result, we can observe a gradual diminution of emotional transcendence, as emotional programmes come to revolve not only around symbols of transcendent divinity, but around the routines, demands, and sensibilities of everyday life. This does not mean that religion's ability to foster social change through emotional persuasion and seduction diminishes, but that its power resides not so much in its ability to mobilize large numbers (even a whole nation) around collective symbols, but in its ability to give symbolic and social expression to the sensibilities and passions of particular groups, and minorities, within society. Thus religion may serve as a vehicle for recognition and expression of the values, emotions, and self-definition of, say, an ethnic Muslim population in an inhospitable cultural climate, or of middle-aged women struggling to articulate their frustrations, desires, and hopes for greater recognition and empowerment in a society experienced as both sexist and ageist, or of eco-pagan groups uniting across national boundaries in their struggles to establish new emotional programmes based around reverence for the natural world, anxiety about its destruction, and hope for its future.

Conclusion

This chapter has focused on features and tensions of late modern society and culture that have consequences for emotional life. We have highlighted the ways in which different domains of a polycentric society pursue their values self-referentially and sustain emotional regimes that are mutually incompatible; contradictions of value between different domains lead to emotional dissonances (for instance, between respect for human dignity, and corporate pursuit of profit) and to increased reflexivity; a growing diversity of symbols introduces new potentials for emotional pluralism and choice; high levels of sophistication in interpreting and manipulating emotions and symbols lead to widespread 'demythologization'. Many individuals find their lives dispersed between competing symbolic and social systems, while seeking a unified and consistent biography. Each of the social domains calls for full commitment and emotional surrender, while agents seek autonomy, freedom, and personal fulfilment. The polycentric powers try to legitimate themselves by operations of consecration that challenge and relativize established traditional symbols. The different social domains pursue their own logics and render human beings instrumental, while individuals increasingly understand themselves as autonomous beings of unique value.

This situation presents religion with new opportunities as well as difficult challenges. The religious field is reconfigured. Established connections with political power and social hierarchy become liabilities, and symbols of these connections become museum pieces. Rather than simply retreating into a narrow private sphere, however, religion insinuates itself into new social spaces and takes on new functions. It enters into global civil society, for example, in the shape of eco-spirituality and various fundamentalisms, it enters into new instrumental patnerships with the state, it takes on new roles in education, healthcare, and the leisure industry—and so on. On a global scale, the 'world religions', and revived forms of indigenous religion, are revitalized as vehicles for consolidating various forms of collective identity, pursuing different value agendas, and contesting with one another and with secular forms of power (though we cannot pursue these themes, it is interesting to note how a study of religious emotion points towards them).

This complex context is reflected back in changes in the form of religious emotion in late modern societies. Most importantly, we see a series of imbalances in the dialectics of religious emotions. First, there is a tilt towards objectification, in which religious symbols are valued for their emotional impact rather than as effective connections with divine power. Second, the multiple consecrations of symbols by a huge range of organizations loosens mutually-constitutive relations between collective symbols and social emotion, while collective emotions surrounding popular symbols rise and fall spontaneously, but remain fragile without institutional support. Finally, religious authorities' ability to control emotions and give them lasting social form diminishes as the balance tips towards uninhibited externalization.

If we take into account these characteristics of religious emotion, religion in late modern societies has open to it a range of possibilities, with different emotional consequences:

1. it can adapt to the wider emotional situation by suppressing unacceptable parts of its emotional scale and offering only those for which there is an emotional demand. This means that it is left to individuals to assemble their own harmonized emotional programme from a range of cultural sources, of which religion is just one;

2. it can deal directly and explicitly with the emotional states and requirements of individuals, and offer either limited therapeutic interventions, or more encompassing emotional regimes that promise an alternative to the contradictions of everyday life;

3. it can encapsulate itself to provide an internally consistent and encompassing emotional regime that offers a sharp alternative to the emotional orderings of wider society;

4. it can confront the social and cultural sources of emotional dissonance, offer critique, and propose social reform.

The first two options address the issues at agency level, the third at group level, and the fourth at societal level. While religious reform movements follow the last option, and some sects and minority religions follow the third, denominations that have adapted to religious pluralism in late modern society generally follow the first strategy. Alternative forms of spirituality exemplify the second option. By taking religious emotions seriously, it is, therefore, possible to gain an interesting perspective on the issue of how and why religion is accepted, rejected, or transformed in the context of late modern societies.

Conclusion

There has been an understandable reluctance among academics to take emotion seriously. Feelings seem somehow too subjective, too slippery, too unscientific. Even religion, that most passionate of commitments, has been studied as if it were simply a matter of belief and ritual practice. This book has tried to break down barriers that inhibit studies of emotion in general, and religious emotion in particular, and offer a sociological framework within which it can be rehabilitated in scholarly investigation.

One of the main barriers to taking emotion seriously—a 'rationalism' that sets objective scientific knowledge against subjective matters of feeling—is being undermined. We have emphasized the challenge presented by new approaches to cognition that recognize bodily, sensory, and emotional engagement as foundational to human understanding. The result is not a denigration of reason and an elevation of emotion, but a refusal to hypostasize them and set them against one another. This has cleared the way for a renewed interest in the study of emotion in many fields. In international relations, for example, the significance of emotions such as fear, terror, solidarity, and trust has become a central focus of interest; in recent political campaigns experts on emotion have been called upon to help script candidates' campaigns; in economics, the significance of collective sentiments such as confidence and 'irrational exuberance', and countervailing distrust and 'depression', is starting to be appreciated. More generally, a model of human beings as rational actors living by cost–benefit calculation is losing credibility as an adequate account of social action.

These developments have not, however, entirely abolished the difficulty of studying emotion, nor lessened the hesitation that many feel in entering this territory. Much social research continues to regard emotions as residuals or as inner states. To move beyond this impasse, we have developed a framework for the sociological study of emotion in general, and religious emotion in particular. Ironically, the sociology of religion—which has been particularly slow to catch up with the growing interest in emotion—also has some of the most important resources for constructing such a framework. A central task of this book has been to take stock of resources from the formative period in the scientific study of religion, relate them to more recent work from across a range of disciplines, and allow them to inform a coherent and synthesizing approach.

A framework for making sense of religious emotion

Our starting point is the recognition that emotions are always related to somebody and to something. Instead of trying to isolate elusive 'primary' emotions located in the inner depths of the psyche, we direct attention to structures of feeling that are integral to the situations in which they arise. Emotions relate the self to society, to cultural symbols, and to the self itself—or some combination of these. Emotion is not a 'thing' but an embodied stance within the world. This means that it is open to observation through its manifestations in action, social structures, and cultural symbols. When we enter into a social setting, we quickly discern its emotional 'atmosphere' by noting these different signs. Normally we make this assessment quickly and informally, in a way that is barely conscious. Our proposal is that this can be formalized according to a scheme that lays bare its separate elements and provides a framework for analysing their interrelations.

These relations have a connection and mutual influence. That which is related is changed by the relation. Thus various emotions are evoked, amplified, modified, or extinguished through their connections. We have suggested that these relations can be either reciprocal or one-sided. In the former, relations between agents, society, and symbols are reinforced through correspondence between emotionally laden symbols, the community's collective emotions, and the personal feelings of individual members. An 'emotional programme' is the outcome of a coordinated emotional pattern that structures the emotive life of participants and the social whole, and an 'emotional regime' enforces these norms. For those involved, collective symbols relate seamlessly to the emotions that the community expresses and the members internalize. These dynamics can be disrupted, however, when relations become one-sided or unbalanced. Then clashes or hiatuses between the group, its members, and its symbols bring its separate relational elements into sharper contrast.

Emotional ordering is not static, but is constantly produced and reproduced in the lives of societies and their members. Both connections and disconnections of self, society, and symbols express and embody different balances of power. Such power embraces both exercised and potential impact, and both relations of domination and mutual empowerment. Emotional life can be imagined as a field of forces in which energies are charged or released. How a person or group feels affects its capacity to act, and the power of a community to shape and coordinate feelings may lend it wider social power. Observation of the feelings of different sections of a community, how they are differentiated from one another, who sets the emotional rules, and who enforces them, reveals a great deal about power relations more generally.

Using this framework, we can make better sense of religious emotion. Contrary to existing approaches, which try to identify some essentially religious emotion like awe, we argue that religious emotions are simply those emotions that are integral to religious communities and their sacred symbols. As such, religious emotion can include any conceivable feeling, from tender love to violent hatred and disgust. The authorities in a religious community focus attention on a certain set of coordinated feelings, whose status is confirmed through the social and ritual life of the group and in its symbols. Thereby, the community establishes an emotional regime in terms of which its members learn to identify some emotions as legitimate and prescribed, and others as forbidden or distracting.

It is characteristic of religious emotional regimes to present their programmes as embodying a more profound sensibility, which relates to an 'alternate ordering' of reality. Religion offers to order emotional lives in accordance with this foundational pattern, and provide perspective on everyday feelings. Religions shape sensibility by reconfiguring it around worldly and spiritual relationships. To feel appropriately is to participate in a more perfect ordering of relations than that which pertains in everyday life. To be religious is not only to ponder on the foundations of human life, but to unite or reconcile oneself with the design incorporated in those foundations. This lends religious emotion the characteristic of providing anchorage for meaning and moral identity, and a reference point for mundane interactions and choices. Religions characteristically inculcate long-lasting moods and motivations that provide a general orientation towards life and death. As such they reach deep into human identity, both personal and collective, and cannot be easily changed or discarded.

Religious emotion in late modern societies

Because it is insufficient to focus solely on intra-group dynamics of religious emotion, our scheme broadens out to encompass relations with other surrounding, competing, or encompassing emotional regimes. Our aim as sociologists is to make sense of religious emotion in late modern societies like our own, which are constituted by a multiplicity of distinct social domains, each bound up with their own emotional regimes.

Our approach distances us from theoretical meta-narratives that highlight a single emotional characteristic of late modernity. These include the narrative of postmodernism that posits a superficially emotionalized society saturated with attempts to manipulate feeling; the liberal narrative that discerns continued modernization carried by rationalized control of human passions; and the romantic expressivism that celebrates freedom from emotional bonds that inhibit emotional authenticity. The effect of our interest in the internal dynamics of emotional regimes, and their interrelations with other regimes, is to generate a more complex picture of the emotional life of late modern societies, which brings to light the tensions, contradictions, and reinforcing alliances generated by the multiplicity of emotional regimes embedded in different social domains.

To live in late modern societies is to live *across* many different social domains, and to experience resulting emotional cross-pressures. There are differences in the intensity of the emotional contradictions that different categories of social actors experience: generally speaking, the most privileged members of a society will experience least contradictions, since different spheres reflect their emotional programme more consistently. Nevertheless, it is common for an individual to play different emotional roles in the workplace, in leisure activities, and in a family setting. Emotions prescribed in a religious setting may be different again. This may result in emotional fragmentation and confusion; but there are also strategies for avoiding this. One such strategy privileges a certain emotional patterning as true and authentic, and merely 'acts out' required emotions in other emotional domains. This may lead to charges of hypocrisy, but can equally be seen as a flexible and adept 'fitting-in' to the demands of diverse and shifting regimes. Identity may remain intact, unless other emotional regimes clash so strongly that confrontation becomes inevitable—as, for example, when members of a religious minority feel their identity to be under threat in a secular society.

The experience of inhabiting varied and often incompatible emotional regimes leads to a heightened emotional reflexivity. This is likely to be greatest in the case of those who make the most stretching transitions across different domains, including those who are in some way marginal to a dominant culture and find themselves caught between several powerful but very different emotional worlds. Such people have no choice but to reflect on their feelings, and to become self-conscious about the ways in which they express them. They risk losing a sense of how they 'really' feel and who they truly are. On the other hand, the creative construction of 'hyphenated' emotional identities can also lead to emotional flexibility and sensitivity and the forging of new emotional patterns—and hence to social change. This is especially true when individuals can join together in order to explore and reinforce a new emotional programme, creating and appropriating cultural symbols in the process. Otherwise the burden is cast on the single individual, and presented as an individual problem of personal adjustment, which society supports only with self-help manuals, expensive therapy, or drugs.

This combination of inescapable diversity, points of tension, and consequent reflexivity is reinforced by the vibrant multiplicity of cultural goods and symbols in late capitalist societies. Signs rapidly appear and disappear, engendering novelty and new combinations. One result is to diminish the social power of symbols, and to undermine their capacity to bind an entire society and stabilize an encompassing emotional regime at societal level. Another is to give individuals and groups a new freedom to select symbols that are meaningful for them and that support their own emotional programmes. Thus the balance tends to shift from consecrated, traditional symbols that shape and constrain personal feelings, to freely chosen symbols whose authority rests on their ability to express individual, small-group, or globally networked sensibilities. Symbols are still consecrated in late modern societies, with increasing frequency and urgency. But distrust of their calculated uses by political elites, public relations and marketing industries, and the media undermines their power to compel. Individuals may still form deep and powerful, even fetishistic, attachments to certain symbols, but, without sustained collective reinforcement and repetition, such attachments often prove fleeting and emotionally unsustaining. Regular repetition and circulation of symbols, combined with collective reinforcement, result in a more lasting power, and even a sacred status.

The main way in which religions maintain emotional currency in late modern societies at a national level is by performing residual functions of a civil religion, such as dealing with collective tragedy, suffering, and death. This highlights a gap in the emotional market that has not yet been satisfactorily filled by non-religious competitors: the late modern stress on happiness as the emotional lodestone means that there is little coordinated interest in producing cultural or social resources for dealing with grief and despair. By contrast, traditional religions have historic programmes for expressing and regulating an entire range of emotions and, in some, notes of sorrow, guilt, pain, and repentance are strong, and are inculcated as valuable in their own right, especially in ascetic traditions. Such an emphasis struggles to make headway in modern societies, except when a tear in the emotional fabric needs to be repaired.

Given this clash between traditional religious and late modern sensibilities, historic churches tend to downplay those parts of their emotional programme that clash too violently with wider emotional preferences. Humility, guilt, and meekness become minor notes in an emotional scale, and traditional symbols and practices associated with them are downplayed. By contrast, those elements that chime with contemporary sensibilities are heightened. The result may be a weakening of the overall regime, whose integrity is disrupted and whose ability to structure the individual life course, as well as the patterning of time and space, is diminished. Religious symbols become part of a nostalgia trip, a heritage industry, or a museum exhibit.

However, it is also possible for new versions of a religion to develop that are more closely fitted with the emotional programmes of other social domains—not only by accommodating, but by criticizing and ameliorating them. The most successful examples worldwide are the upsurge of revivalist forms of Islam and of charismatic Christianity since the 1970s. The latter rejects what it sees as emotionally 'luke-warm' and 'hypocritical' churches in favour of an emotionally intense and joyful form of religion with a particular appeal to the marginalized. In affluent societies, charismatic–evangelical religion sometimes moves so far towards accommodation of the emotional programme of capitalism that it turns into a prosperity religion—which also means an emotional prosperity religion—in which happiness and worldly success are celebrated as signs of God's blessing.

A further option for religions in the late modern context is to sustain an emotional regime, even though it clashes with wider morals and mores, through some degree of social encapsulation. Members shelter under the 'sacred canopy' of the group and minimize emotional clashes with wider regimes. This option is characteristic of Christian fundamentalism, a distinctively modern form of religion that has been most successful where it has been able to establish its own subcultures with separate schools, colleges, and media channels. A different example is provided by minority religions in Western societies established by recent immigration, which may shelter a pre-existing emotional regime in the case of a first generation, but which allow later generations to develop complex forms of emotional identity that have continuities and differences with the surrounding culture as well as with transnational religious and cultural networks.

The emotional conditions of late modernity also allow the growth of new forms of 'spirituality' whose refusal to appropriate the label of 'religion' indicates the difference they wish to maintain. They are characterized by a one-sided tilt towards the authority of subjective emotional experience over against that of socially imposed programmes. Their social forms are likely to be those of loose networks and occasional gatherings, but with a core of small-group membership in settings that are open to individual emotional expression and exploration. Powerful, demanding consecrated symbols are also rejected in favour of more freely chosen and personally resonant symbols. Such symbols still have the power to become a focus of shared commitment with motivational force, as we see in the growing significance of ecologically focused groups and networks that challenge emotional programmes associated with competitive individualism.

This emotionally inflected perspective on religion in late modern society has implications for the ongoing debate on secularization and sacralization, showing that both can occur simultaneously. Some established versions of religion recede, in part because they are unable to adapt to the emotional challenges of late modern life. Simultaneously, other versions find a niche for their emotional programme among the complex of emotional regimes in late modern societies. New embodiments of the sacred are continually emerging. Many are not accepted as seriously or fully religious, especially from the perspective of the historic world religions and political establishments. At the same time, individuals are increasingly subject to influences from a broad and varied set of religious symbolic appeals, which refer to emotional programmes that are limited in scope and may be combined in manifold ways. Religious symbols with emotional appeal remain omnipresent, but are detached from their socio-religious contexts. This does not mean that they lose their emotional appeal, but that they are disconnected from the programme to which they once belonged. For some people, sacred space becomes a backstage where they can withdraw from the role plays of public front stages, or a space rich with emotional possibilities in which they can develop new sets of emotional standards when other social domains are found to be emotionally meaningless or constraining.

As such, religion continues to offer the possibility of repattering emotional life and social relations. In late modern societies religions become institutions with one emotional programme among many others, and find themselves competing with other programmes that offer meaningful emotional possibilities. However, religion retains some special character. It remains a space within society where individuals can gather to affirm anchoring moral commitments and associated emotional dispositions, sometimes in opposition to competing emotional regimes. Historic forms of religion are able to link people, not only across different geographical spaces, but down the generations. They have access to a reservoir of powerful symbols, and retain the capacity to activate some and deactivate others in relation to the emerging emotional imperatives of an age.

Significance

We end by highlighting three areas in which we hope this book can make a contribution, both within and beyond the sociology of religion. First, it is a provocation to take emotion more seriously in the study of religion in general. Second, it offers an expanded dialectical approach that encompasses relations between agents, social structure, *and* cultural symbols, and that thereby encourages a rapprochement between social scientific and humanistic studies. Third, it supports a methodological approach characterized by a combination of methods.

There is much to be gained in the study of religion in general by taking emotion more seriously. A religion is not only a particular way of understanding the world, but a way of seeing it, feeling it, and taking a stance within it—both personally and collectively. It is a matter of sensibility. To neglect religious emotion is therefore to leave out something vital. We make no claim that religion is essentially emotional, or that other dimensions have less importance. Nor do we propose that a study of religious emotion should take place independently of other aspects. The point is not to study separate 'components' of religion in splendid isolation from one another, but to enrich understanding of each one by bringing them into a more integral relation with one another. A concept like 'belief', for example, can be illuminated by taking its emotive and performative aspects more seriously, rather than by considering them in parallel.

What a sociological study of religion has to gain from the approach we advocate is an expansion of its normal horizons to encompass, not only social relations, but symbolic ones. Our conceptual framework holds together, not only agents and structures, but agents, structures, and symbols. To try to study religion without taking seriously its own scheme of signification, its sacred codes, its God(s) and scriptures, its legal, theological, and aesthetic traditions, is to adopt the narrow view that only immediate human relations can shape social action. This neglects the influence of the past, of symbols, of material settings. Attention to the dynamics of religious emotion broadens a narrow social perspective. Individuals and societies are moved and motivated, not only by human relations, but by love for God or an ancestor, fear of an evil spirit, remembrance of a memorialized past, devotion to a sacred landscape, and expectation of a collectively imagined future.

This approach suggests that the sociology of religion has special potential as an arena of mutual inspiration between humanistic approaches to the study of religion and culture, on the one hand, and general sociology, on the other. Social research can learn from the humanities, including studies of religion, which have a long tradition of analysing emotive symbols in art, music, and poetry in relation to their specific historical and cultural settings. An interchange can also help the humanities in their analyses of the relevance of social context for the emotive functioning of symbols. As this book hopes to show, the sociology of religion can be enriched by engagement, not only with anthropology and cultural sociology, but with religious studies, theology, scriptural exegesis, archaeology, and historical studies. The emotional force and meaning of symbols derives not just from their embeddedness in a particular community and its power structures, but from their relation to other symbols and to a historical tradition. The sociological study of religious emotion is enriched by knowledge about the wider cultural code in which a symbol is embedded, and by familiarity with traditions of theological, legal, and scriptural exegesis. Such knowledge allows the researcher better to understand an emotional regime, and where and how its members may deviate from it. When a devotee speaks of 'love', the sociologist must be able to understand what that means in the context of a particular religious and cultural setting, rather than attempting to interpret by observing social relations alone, or by assuming that it refers to some universal inner experience.

This book also raises a more specific challenge to sociology and other disciplines—namely, to deepen understanding of the varied emotional regimes of late modern society, and illuminate the relations between them. Advances in this area will not only further our understanding of emotion, but assist general sociology in connecting a multitude of dispersed studies of separated fields of social life. The study of religious emotion should not be neglected, as it has been by sociology of emotions to date. Social life still includes confrontation with love, grief, sex, death, meaninglessness, and other basic existential themes addressed and informed by religion. Secularization has not advanced so far that all traces of religious influence have been erased from emotional life, nor all traces of its symbols wiped clean. Theories that regard religious emotions as no more than a means by which disciplinary powers enslave their subjects neglect their potential to inspire resistance, collective solidarity, and social change.

As for the methodological implications of the scheme proposed here, we suggest that the study of religious emotions requires not some special method, but a combination of existing methods that are capable of illuminating the various dimensions of emotional life. It involves trained sensitivity to the atmosphere of a social gathering, disciplined attention to the body language of individual participants, analyses of the emotional significance of texts and symbols, and a social-structural analysis of the establishment and enforcement of an emotional regime. There are well-established methods for each of these aims, such as participant observation, socio-semiotics, and analyses of symbolic hegemony. In the appendix we discuss these in more detail, and the ways in which they can be combined in order to illuminate the emotive interactions between groups, individuals, and symbols.

It should be emphasized that this book is only a first step in reviving and consolidating interest in religious emotion. We have offered a framework for further study. Our focus has been general: on religious *emotion* rather than on specific *emotions* in particular contexts. The detailed and demanding work of exploring and identifying such emotions in late modern contexts, and drawing out their wider social and symbolic significance, remains. Nevertheless, our own empirical research on religion forms the starting point of this book, since it fired our enthusiasm for taking the emotional dimension of religion seriously in the first place, and intensified our frustration at not having a framework in which we could do so. It was through immersion in religious communities that we came to realize just how much there was to be gained from taking this neglected topic more seriously, and how much was lost by neglecting it. Far from this being an esoteric new departure, we suspect that many other scholars involved in researching religion, values, and culture have at least a tacit knowledge of how much we depend upon emotional focus and understanding in the research process. What we have attempted to do in this volume is bring this 'subjugated knowledge' into the light of critical discussion, and supply it with a more robust rationale and *modus operandi*.

Emotions are vital for social life. They are not a trivial matter, as anyone who has been in love, witnessed an act of bravery, or felt ashamed knows. Symbols can inspire whole societies in acts of courage, cruelty, or revenge. They may link us to the past with pride or shame, and to the future with hope or despair. Emotions are integral to morals and meaning: they move, motivate, and inhibit. The study of religious emotion, of what a society and its members feel to be most sacred, offers a royal road into these territories.

STUDYING RELIGIOUS EMOTION: METHOD AND PRACTICE

This appendix addresses the practical issue of how to study religious emotion. Although the preceding analysis of religious emotion has drawn on observations and studies that supply some empirical foundation, much more extensive and coordinated research effort is needed. Here we offer some methodological reflections on what such research might involve, and how some of the claims we have made could be investigated further.

We do not propose a certified method with universal application, since particular studies need to be linked to their distinctive research questions, theoretical perspectives, and the resources available. Moreover, the theoretical approach to religious emotion developed in this book calls, not for a single method, but for a combination of methods. We have argued that emotions emerge in the interrelations of selves, societies, and symbols. Consequently, not one but several methods of research are called for, in order to do justice to the different aspects and dimensions of emotional life.

There is a practical background as well as a practical aim to what follows.[1] Our suggestions relate to our own successes and frustrations as we have tried to study religious emotions using various tools from the social science 'toolkit' (Riis 2005). They probably reveal more about what we think we should have done than what we actually did. We hope they will inspire others to go further.

The stance of the researcher

Emotions are not tangible objects that we can measure. We have to rely on observing emotional acts and symbols and rely on the reports people give. Emotions are embodied by human agents and interpreted by them, and we

---

[1] Although the discussion that follows is inspired by a wide literature on methodology in social research, we have tried to keep references to a minimum. Where possible we have tried to make reference to the literature by way of good textbooks that are widely available. We also mention a few other titles and articles that we have found particularly helpful. The overall aim of the appendix is to provide a *practical* resource for research.

must reinterpret their interpretations. It is often helpful to seek information about what prompts them, and what they refer to. It is insufficient merely to present self-reported sensations. But it also seems impossible to feel as an insider while simultaneously analysing how one feels: to stop and ask yourself what you really feel is to stop the affective flow.

Social research on emotion seems to call for a special stance. It is impossible to gain immediate, reliable access to what participants in a social situation are feeling: we are not socialized as they are, and we do not operate within exactly the same framework of memories and cultural resources. Thus a directly emphatic, intuitive understanding is out of reach. But an analytically focused approach carries the opposite danger of distancing too much from the emotional aspect of a situation. This recalls Evans-Pritchard's quotation (1965: 121) from Schmidt: 'There is but too much danger that the other (the non-believer) will talk of religion as a blind man might of colours, or one totally devoid of ear, of a beautiful musical composition.' Moreover, in trying to control our own emotional reactions, and separate ourselves from emotional interactions, we also risk distorting the 'data'. In a fieldwork situation, for example, participants notice if there is a distanced observer, and this may affect the whole emotional tone.

A solution to this basic dilemma is to evolve a dual stance. On the one hand, the researcher is anchored in and responsible to a community of researchers, and, on the other hand, the researcher tries to grasp the emotions of a community, of its symbols and its individual members. In practice, this means approaching the study at first with a naive, almost childlike openness and empathy, in order to tune into the basic emotional themes. This does not imply that it is possible to make preconceptual observations, but rather that concepts can be employed in an open, flexible, and provisional way. This makes it possible to develop an analytical view gradually, in interaction with emotional themes encountered. Thus empathetic participation and analysis in research on emotions will often take place sequentially, not simultaneously. Emotion research involves what might be called a critical emotional empathy.[2]

To observe and identify emotions calls for a special tuning and training. This involves skill in interpreting both verbal and non-verbal embodied emotional 'codes'. It is such high-level skill that it probably requires particular kinds of socialization and social skill as a prerequisite for further training. It requires emotional sensitivity, a mix of confidence and humility, an openness and empathy towards informants that does not compromise their emotional expression, as well as skill in identifying and articulating moods and emotions,

---

[2] Empathy may be a useful source, but it is not a method and it should not be confused with Weber's *verstehen* (1968), which is an analytical tool that posits motivational patterns as ideal types in order to explain regular patterns of social action.

and detaching one's own feelings and projections sufficiently. Such skill can never be wholly detached from the researcher's background and biography. In any case, in order to understand and analyse emotions, it is essential that there is some correspondence with the observer's own emotional memories and discourses—in order that recognition and the process of 'translation' can begin to take place (Lutz 1986). The skill of sensing and sharing emotions is indispensable, yet fallible—as we know from everyday life. As researchers, we can test and refine our 'intuitions' in the same dialogical manner that we use in everyday life. We can check our interpretations with other people, other studies, and informants themselves.[3]

Basic questions need to be posed in emotion research, and we must assume that our own feelings do not necessarily coincide with those we study. We may recognize some patterns from our own experience of life, but we need to check our interpretation. There is a constant need for translation between two sets of emotional concepts, the theoretical language of the research community and the practical language of the researched. If a researcher is considering an emotional regime with which he or she is not familiar, it will be necessary to understand the emotional scale of that regime by relating it to scales with which he or she (and potential readers) are more familiar, and presenting it in terms of similarities and differences—as Lutz does, for example, in explaining how Ifaluk *song* overlaps with and differs from Western 'anger'. It is also important not to bring too much or too little to the interpretation. On the one hand, it is necessary to avoid overinterpreting emotions by referring to abstract theories that assume that emotions are predictable reactions to certain social or symbolic stimuli, and, on the other hand, it is important not to underinterpret emotions by deconstructing them into singular empirical observations and thereby missing the processes of which they are part, and the contexts that shape their meaning.

It is important to remember that emotions do not have to be meaningful in a cognitive sense. Emotional actors cannot be expected to put into exact words what they feel, and their failure to do so does not imply a lack of feeling. As we emphasized in Chapter 1, emotions are not 'things', and emotional experience is continuous, complex, and multivalent. To name it is already to alter and 'fix' it and affects the emotional experience itself. Similarly, the research process itself, including a process of questioning, impacts directly on the emotions involved, and it is always necessary to take account of this.

Often this approach involves raising questions about seeming banalities. The researcher may have to take the stance of an annoying idiot as he or she

---

[3] This has parallels with a 'double hermeneutical' approach that seeks to understand the 'frames of meaning' implied by human acts in terms not only of concepts applied by the researcher, but of those employed by the human subjects (Giddens 1987; Sayer 1992).

questions people about what seems obvious and self-evident to them. They may think it obvious, for example, that the image of this saint makes them feel protected, while that one makes them feel watched and ashamed, that the funeral service made them enraged, or that the marriage made them a mixture of sad and happy and hopeful and nostalgic. Emotional questioning may seem awkward, infantile, or stupid, and respondents may react with surprise or embarrassment or confusion.

Being a 'cultural outsider' can allow one to ask the 'dumb questions'. But having some knowledge as a 'cultural insider' can also be advantageous in researching emotion. Sharing features of common culture can sensitize one to cultural nuances. Again the dual stance is important. As well as having some of the knowledge of an insider (or striving to attain it, not least by learning about the cultural codes and history of a community), it is also important to remain anchored in the research community outside. A good researcher is one with informants, yet not one of them. This helps in recognizing implicit moods and meanings and rendering them explicit for analysis.

The question of whether a researcher's own emotional frameworks, knowledge, and commitments help or hinder the research process, and whether they can or should be eliminated or controlled, is also important, though it raises epistemological issues beyond the scope of this discussion. Looking only at some practical aspects of the issue, we can acknowledge that passionate feeling, whether approving or disapproving, towards an informant is likely to inhibit an open-minded investigation. However, it is impossible to eliminate the values and emotions implicit in the identification of problems considered worthy of investigation, the construction of hypotheses, and the selection of solutions to problems that are considered worthy of acceptance. Not only is the 'ideal of dispassionate enquiry an impossible dream' (Jaggar 1989: 163), but the role of emotion in the construction of knowledge is not invariably deleterious. This does not call for the elimination of emotion from the research process, but awareness of one's emotional responses in a situation, and critical reflection on how they help and hinder enquiry (Kleinman and Copp 1993). Again, a double stance is helpful, as the researcher can address these worries about whether an emotional engagement leads to a bias to the research community.

The usefulness, even the indispensability, of emotion in research is the subject of Renato Rosaldo's 'Grief and a Headhunter's Rage' (1989). His observation is that it was not until the death of his wife in tragic circumstances that he came to understand the cultural practice of headhunting among the Ilongot, though he had studied it for many years. His point is not that the researcher should attribute his own experiences to research subjects, but that 'Ilongot anger and my own overlap, rather like two circles, partially overlaid and partially separate' and help to interpret one another (1989: 11). Moreover, Rosaldo suggests that his use of personal experience 'serves as a vehicle for making the quality and intensity of the rage in Ilongot grief more readily accessible to readers than certain more detached modes of composition' (1989: 11).[4]

Using the Standard Sociological Toolbox

We do not mean to imply that emotion research is mainly a matter of intuitive connection. As our theoretical framework makes clear, emotion research is equally and inseparably a matter of observing how people relate to symbols, and to one another, not only at the micro-level but also in groups, communities, and networks. It is also about sensing a collective mood and its variations, and noticing how it comes into being, fluctuates, is sustained, and dies away. This involves noticing which objects and symbols have emotional significance, whether in a domestic setting or a more public one, and how that significance varies over time, and by class, gender, and age. It implies a sensitivity to the resonance for different groups of collective symbols, and to their relation with wider emotional programmes and cultural codes. It requires attention to power relations, and noticing who has the authority to set an emotional tone, police an emotional regime, and offer sanctions and rewards. It may involve participating not only in positive experiences of solidarity and effervescence, but in uncomfortable situations of conflict—indeed the latter can be extremely revealing of deeply felt commitments (Beckford 1985).

The social sciences have developed a toolbox of methods that are widely used in its different branches, including the sociology of religion (Bryman 1996; Riis 2009). The standard toolbox provides methods for studying emotion in relation to each of the three foci we have identified (agents, society, and symbols), but some reservations and caveats are needed as we discuss their relevance to this field.

In investigating individual religious emotions, interviews and surveys are obvious tools to employ. They depend upon self-report by informants. Our experience is that these methods, though potentially useful, have to overcome many difficulties. For one thing, many people are not very self-aware of their feelings, and, even if they are, they may not be able or willing to articulate them. Skills may vary widely, including by class, gender, and ethnicity, and also vary in relation to different kinds of religious affiliation. For example, we found that elderly ladies in mainstream Christian congregations are generally much more reluctant to talk about personal feelings than participants in alternative spirituality. In general, forms of religion that encourage a high level of personal expressivism are—not surprisingly—easier to research using these methods.

---

[4] This issue is also explored by psychosocial literature in terms of how far researchers 'project' or 'transfer' their feelings onto their subjects, and vice versa, and under what circumstances this helps and hinders research (e.g. Savage 2004).

There is also the issue of how reliable people are in reporting their feeling, and how much their report is influenced by the manner in which the information is gathered. The process of questioning may be more fruitful if it takes place in the course of long-term engagement and trust, and if it can be pursued piecemeal in situations that naturally lend themselves to discussion of certain feelings. As Obeyesekere (1981: 10) says: 'I almost never interview informants "cold". I treat the initial interview as merely a prelude to later ones . . . one must have time to nurture friendships and time for reflection . . . in several cases I found that information supplied in the initial interviews was contradicted in later ones.' There is often a naivety in imagining that people should want to disclose personal information to strangers and anonymous researchers, or that, when asked to do so, they will answer truthfully. To reveal how one feels is to expose oneself; there have to be good reasons to want to do so. The question of what an informant has to gain and so lose is always relevant, and is crucial in assessing not just the ethical aspects of the research (avoiding exploitation of informants, for example), but its likely chances of success and reliability.

Personal interviews may be most useful as a method for illuminating how persons with a nuanced emotional vocabulary recall emotions, classify them, and associate them with religion. They may not give information about 'deep-deep' emotional experience (Gubrium and Holstein 1997)—even if such a thing were possible—but they at least give access to culturally accepted emotional standards and (related) personal rationalizations (Giddens 1976/1993).

By revealing the norms of an emotional regime, interviews can therefore supply the data for what the historians Stearns and Stearns (1985) call 'emotionology'. They regard the traces of emotional life left in written documents as an adequate subject for historical research on emotions in culture and society, though not for accessing personal emotions *per se*. As Gubrium and Holstein (1997: 74) write: 'Do we have any evidence of emotion other than its expressions? Can researchers give us access to "real" emotion simply by re-presenting or re-enacting subjects' *expressions* of these emotions? Do emotions exist apart from culturally available modes of expression?' Attempts to employ brain-scanning to bypass these problems are not a full solution, and can create new problems of their own. It is not possible to read off information about what a person is 'really' feeling (in any detail) from neurological information alone, and a great deal of reading-in must also be involved. A charge in the brain is not an emotion. Moreover, abstracting a person from normal social and symbolic-material conditions does not reveal a 'pure' emotional state, but a very particular and unusual one. This does not mean that we should reject such tools, but instead that we must recognize their serious limitations.

Surveys employ simple, standardized indicators to provide a snapshot of a sociological landscape. As indicated by the very word 'survey', such studies offer breadth rather than depth. (The distinction between qualitative and quantitative may be less helpful than that between extensive-standardized and intensive-open methods, see Sayer 1992; Riis 2001.) Questionnaires often touch on emotional themes, especially in the form of attitudinal items (Riis 2009). However, since religious emotions are complex, it is questionable whether they can be adequately 'measured' by a few simple items (Cicourel 1964; Sayer 1992). The surveys we looked at that asked about religious emotion were not able to provide much useful information, though well-designed items might be able to test some very general claims. The reservations we have raised about interviews also apply to questionnaire responses, and the difficulty of building trust and establishing a fruitful context of interaction is much greater. However, these are difficulties to be overcome, and there have recently been some examples of surveys being used effectively in emotional research in social movements (in Goodwin et al. 2007).

We are more optimistic about the possibility of using interviews combined with situated observations. We can observe emotional expressions, notice stances adopted in social settings, and generally read emotional clues from the body as well as from what people say. By entering into people's homes, it is often possible to observe a great deal of emotions by noting their chosen and most sacred objects, and the mood they try to engender in their domestic settings. Getting people to talk about objects and places they find emotionally meaningful can be very revealing, as can asking them to speak about how they feel about designated religious spaces—or asking them to record on audio or visual media their own choice of such spaces, and their emotional reactions to them (Stanczak 2007). In sensitive long-term participant observation it is possible for skilled researchers to become part of the social relations of the situation they are investigating, and use their own position, and others' relations with them, as an integral part of the research. Experienced researchers in particular religious fields can build up expertise, make comparisons,[5] and interpret symbols, actions, and gestures appropriately. Such participant observation may make it possible to ask nuanced and appropriate questions relevant to particular situations within relational settings conducive to eliciting such information.

Researching religious symbols calls for the use of methods that may be more refined in the arts and humanities than the social sciences. Studies in religious history, art, literature, and music are beginning to contribute to the study of religious emotion (see, e.g., Corrigan 2008). Structural analysis of language and signs can also be helpful. Some forms of critical discourse analysis, for example, may be employed to illuminate relations between symbols, social settings, and power relations (e.g. Fairclough 2003), and can be extended to the religious field. As indicated throughout the book, anthropological research has already contributed a great deal of knowledge about the emotional meanings attributed to assigned symbols within particular societies. It is possible to observe which symbols are ascribed by a society with the greatest emotional

---

[5] For instance, employing small-n-analysis (Ragin 2000).

power, how those symbols are treated, what effects they have on emotions, how they fit into the wider emotional programme, and how individuals are empowered through relation to them. It is also important to observe the full material-symbolic setting of a religious rite or gathering, taking into account, not only human constructions, but the part played by natural landscapes and features (e.g. Ivakhiv 2001). A sense of the changing emotional role of symbols over time can sometimes be gleaned through oral history and archival research, and gauging this is a useful way of investigating changes in emotional regimes over time. Conflicts over material objects and symbols in religious settings are often very revealing of emotional commitments and tensions, and observation of how and why some symbols are accepted by a community, while others are rejected, can reveal a great deal about emotional programmes and balances of power.

Concerning collective emotions, and the overall emotional regime of a community, it is sometimes possible to carry out content analysis of written and spoken communications aimed at the whole community—such as sermons, official publications, and liturgical materials. Collections of religious law, and codifications of customs and prohibitions, may be relevant, but their practical interpretation and application are also important. Through careful analysis of such materials, combined with participant observation, it may be possible to identify the characteristic emotional discourse of the community, spot which emotion words are most often employed in public settings, and notice which emotions are cultivated in collective gatherings, which are rejected, and which are rendered invisible. Some religious communities even have an explicit programme, expressed in writing and/or imagery, which clearly presents some emotions as sacred and others as evil or sinful. Observation of how an emotional regime operates, who has the power to discipline, how such power operates (for example, formally or informally, with explicit or hidden sanctions, in public or private), and what emotional expressions and roles are allowed to different members of a community is highly salient.

The collective mood generated by different religious gatherings is always of interest to the empirical researcher. We have found that it is helpful to arrive well in advance of the start of religious events, and to observe the 'warm-up' routines and preparations—how the scene is set, what 'props' are used, how participants are rehearsed, how religious leaders prepare for their roles, and so on. It is also useful to stay behind after a gathering, noticing how emotional expressions change, people come out of role, social relations are resumed. As we have emphasized throughout, it is not a question of discerning a single emotional note in a religious community or gathering, but of noticing the entire emotional scale, the sequencing of emotions, the tensions that are created and resolved, the 'rhythm' of emotional highs and lows, the harmonies and disharmonies. Cinematic and drama analysis can be useful here, since there are interesting analogies between religion, theatre, and film.

Appendix

As we have emphasized, collective emotions are not simply aggregations of individual emotions, and there is, therefore, a need for research of emotional relations, not only at micro-level, but at meso-level and macro-level.[6] We have discussed both of the former, but research at societal level may require some additional methods. Research on civil religion, for example, may use discourse analysis, analysis of media events and stories, analysis of political speeches, and observation of events captured on film and television, alongside research on related symbols and rituals (Bellah 1967). Interactions among several agents lead to the formation of structures that contain potentials beyond the capacity of the individual agents. When large numbers of individuals are involved, a critical mass can be reached that triggers special emotions, with quantitative accumulation leading to qualitative changes. We ought, therefore, to observe emotional thresholds: the points at which collective moods change dramatically. For instance, below a certain number a religious gathering that strives to produce feelings of joy and celebration is just embarrassing and depressing. Conversely, mass religious gatherings are capable of producing emotions that cannot be experienced in any other way.

Researching emotional dialectics

Although the standard sociological toolbox contains methods that can illuminate parts of our dialectical scheme, the horizon of research should include all the dialectical relations we have discussed if a more holistic analysis is attempted. It is not sufficient to study individual emotional subjectification or objectification alone, nor collective symbols, their consecration, and their emotional power, nor only a community's emotional regime and the ways it is internalized. We need methods for identifying emotional relations between religious symbols and agents, a community and its members, that community and its sacred symbols.

For example, analysis of consecration should examine how the leadership of a religious community selects, approves, designates, or rejects symbols as appropriate emotional reference points for the collective, and how this selection relates to wider intentions for the group, to existing distributions of power, and to past consecrations. Analysis of insignation might focus on the way in which symbols are proposed by members, sections, or the community as a whole. Historical analysis of how important symbolic references were established in the past is very relevant to this task, as well as analysis of which symbols lost their emotional significance and were quietly left to 'die', and which became the focus of controversy. It is also interesting to consider whether, behind the

---

[6] We therefore draw a distinction between analyses of micro-units versus structural analysis. This distinction refers to the well-known ecological fallacy (e.g. Bryman 2004: 212) and the issue of social emergence.

public presentation of consecrated symbols, there are, in practice, different symbols that are revered by many members of the group.

Researching subjectification involves investigation of the symbolic objects and settings that have a particular emotional significance—positive or negative—for informants. Individuals could be invited to discuss this topic in an interview setting, or asked to offer a commentary on religious objects and settings about which they feel deeply. The analysis is based on hermeneutics, not as a method but as a presupposition for a meaningful interpretation. Sometimes informants may be better able to communicate by non-verbal means (for example, taking a photograph, drawing a picture, moving the body), and sometimes observation of their relation to symbols may be more appropriate than lines of questioning. Processes of objectification can be studied through situated observations of how individuals create or modify symbols that serve as expressions of their religious emotions. This may involve observations of the preparations for the process as well as the act of production—whether of a style of dress or ornament, an object to be used in a ritual, a temporary statue for a procession, an icon, a food offering, and so on. It is also possible to interview people about the intention in their work, and to ask them to talk about its emotional significance, or lack of significance.

Processes of internalization can be studied by observing the behaviour of a religious community and its leaders, observing ritual processes, their preparation and outcomes, and analysing written materials and official statements from religious authorities and representatives of the community. This includes noticing how an emotional regime is presented by references to consecrated symbols, including myths with emotional motifs. We may, for instance, observe how religious leaders orchestrate a ritual, a meeting, a class—and how they are trained to do so, and train others. Material prepared for children can be revealing, sometimes expressing the emotional regime more clearly than in subtle appeals for adults. Similarly, it is useful to see how new members or initiates are trained and prepared, how those who disobey the emotional rules are treated, and what counts as transgression. Processes of externalization can be studied by field observations of how agents act and influence the communal mood of the society or community, focusing, for example, on whether emotional actions are confirmatory or challenging to the emotional regime, whether they are expressive or restrained, conforming or diverse. The aim is to decipher the emotional expressions by noticing how they fit into the emotional regime of the community. Externalizations are performed emotions, and, though it is extremely hard to judge whether they are conventional or 'authentically' felt, the question is relevant. Sometimes informants—or others who observe them—will admit to a distance between their actions and their 'real' feelings, or to the difficulty of internalizing the expected emotions. Informants who have left a community out of dissatisfaction, or are intending to do so, can be useful sources of information about emotional pressures, tensions, and dissonances.

To research dialectical relations, and imbalances within them, requires going beyond informants' reports and straightforward observations. People may experience emotional ecstasy or emotional barrenness, and they may experience emotional turmoil or discrepancy, but they do not experience 'unbalanced dialectics'. That is an analytic judgement. Actions, symbols, and regimes that seem unbalanced from the perspective we have developed here may seem perfectly natural and normal to those involved. The identification of dialectical relations demands an approach that looks for all the processes just discussed, to consider their relative force—and which, if any, are weak or absent. In order to discern both balanced and unbalanced dialectics, we need to observe both emotional expressions and the absence of such expressions in a religious community; we need to look for both religious symbols that have a clear emotional appeal and symbols that evoke no feeling or inappropriate feeling; we need to see whether emotional regimes succeed in maintaining their coherence, or whether emotional expressions are spontaneous and unregulated. However, lack of emotional expression does not by itself necessarily indicate an unbalanced relation: acts like habitual prayer before a meal, or passing by a religious symbol in haste, do not constitute reliable indicators. A better indication is provided by feelings that arise (or not) when such acts are blocked, or a symbol is removed. People set some emotional markers and fixed points in their daily lives that form a foundation for life. They may be taken for granted and hardly noticed: it is only when they are disrupted that people recognize their profound importance (a key theme of Erving Goffman's work).

With regard to emotion and power, it is important to consider who has greatest ability to affect emotions in a given situation, and who or what is the focus of collective attention. Who is closest to consecrated symbols, and most empowered by contact with them? Who is able to propose, consecrate, handle, and interpret sacred symbols? Who has most ability to stage and conduct an emotional gathering? Who is responsible for upholding an emotional regime, controlling emotions, prohibiting infringements, and rewarding appropriate emotional expressions? Power relations in contemporary religious settings can also be researched by noticing who displays pride, confidence, calmness, assertiveness, and who is more likely to exhibit reverence and deference, care and attention for others, shame and guilt. In the case of charismatic individuals, it is possible to spot that people are drawn to their presence, and emotionally energized by contact. Their emotional state may be characterized by excitement, joy, pride, confidence, and happiness as a result of relating to the charismatic leader. Interviews and conversations can also elicit some information about these areas, not only in terms of what respondents say about members of the religious community, but also in terms of who is most talked about and referred to, and in what emotional tone. Conflicts, resentments, envy, jealousy, anger, and frustration may also reveal a good deal about power relations in a religious setting.

One major methodological challenge concerns how we can investigate relations between religious emotional regimes and other emotional regimes in society. This involves macroscopic analyses of how a constellation of emotional regimes converge, compete, or confront each other, and which regimes predominate on certain issues of dispute. We may, for instance, try to investigate the constellation between religious emotional regimes and the regimes of other social institutions on certain matters of dispute, such as matters of death and bereavement or crime and punishment. Each of the regimes has an agenda for which emotions are valorized and which should be suppressed in a certain situation. They may collaborate in a scenario that ascribes emotional roles to representatives from the involved institutions. Some representatives may express grief, joy, anger, while others are supposed to keep a cool façade. The religious regimes may join the general scenario or obtain a special role—for instance, as legitimate carriers of emotional expressions on the background of neutral expressions by other institutions. Religion may furthermore voice an emotional regime that deviates from the general scenario, especially if it represents a minority section in society. The macro-analysis may also try to identify which authorities certain sections in society appeal to on emotional issues. Religion may thus legitimate certain emotions as right and proper in a certain situation. Religion may support demonstrations of anger or grief or joy. Others may instead refer to therapists or psychologists as authorities on which emotions are 'natural' in certain situations. The macro-analysis may study how religious representatives encounter representatives of the health sector in relation to matters of bereavement, or penal institutions in matters of crime, punishment, and forgiveness. Such macroscopic analyses can draw on public ritual performances, on documents codifying formal rules, on applications and responses, or focal symbols for emotional regimes, such as headscarves, crosses, black dresses, white coats, prison uniforms, or national symbols. While there are some examples of such macroscopic analyses, they have not been subject to such a refinement that a methodological paradigm has been established. This is a further challenge for future research on religious emotions.

Combining methods

As well as insisting on the need for a combination of methods in research on religious emotion, it is important to point out the necessity for thinking carefully about the manner in which methods are combined and its rationale(s). There are useful reflections on this issue in general (for example, Bryman 1996; Riis 2001; Creswell and Clark 2007; Tashakkorie and Teddlie 2009). We have already made it clear that the key rationale relates to the need to take seriously the various dimensions and dialectical relations that constitute such emotion, but there is more to be said.

Such a combination of methods can help 'triangulate' findings. As we have noted, interviews and observations alone are insufficient, as we do not know whether people's words and actions correspond with how they feel. Interviews and surveys may produce statements that are rationalizations, self-justifications, or attempts to please the interviewer. Studies of symbols in isolation cannot tell us enough about how they relate to an emotional regime, and what people feel about them. However, by combining studies of emotionally significant objects and settings, of emotive standards, emotive behaviour, emotive narratives, and personal reflection on feelings, we can obtain a more complete picture, and make cross-checks. For example, stated emotions can be compared with observed actions, and internalized emotions can be compared with externalized expressions. Thus, by using several methods, each can be checked by comparison with the results yielded by the others. Convergent or congruent findings give a more convincing support than findings based on similar methods (though they do not provide proof of the theoretical interpretation of these findings).

There is also the issue of how to sequence different methods. Our conceptual model indicates how emotional dialectics may be interrelated, but there is no fixed starting point for an integral study of religious emotions in a particular community. It is possible to start by noticing which symbols are important and what they tell us about emotional norms, and then to consider how they relate to individuals' personal practices and feelings. Or one may begin with interview and observation in people's homes, and then begin to observe the community. Then again, the research could begin with participant observation of processes of internalization and externalization in a particular ritual setting—with attention to the emotions that are corporately expressed, and who is setting emotional standards and how (this will inevitably open out to a consideration of how sacred symbols are operative, and how they relate to the objectifications that are most salient for individual members). One may also begin by considering emotional norms and symbols from the past, and then move to the present, or vice versa. There is no simple answer to the question of where to start: what is important is to take account of the specificities of the case, the practicalities and opportunities of the research, and the methodological consequences of a particular sequence of methods (for example, will it allow one to cross-refer or cross-check, will one method lead to another, or provide resources for the next, and so on).

Although our approach calls for combined methods, it is very important to point out that no one researcher or research project need encompass the whole range of possible approaches in his or her study. That choice depends on the resources that are available. More importantly, when we speak of the importance of combined methods, we have in mind the way in which different studies can be brought into relation with one another, and cross-referred to, in order to build a more complete understanding of religious emotion.

Trustworthiness and craftsmanship

Although we reject positivism and its criteria of measurement validity and reliability (in the narrow sense of obtaining the same results from repeated measurements), we cannot ignore the issue of the relationship between claims and evidence (Seale 1999). Positivism does not take account of the way in which social contexts are open systems, social agents are consciously adaptive, and social situations are rarely replicated and repeated in exactly the same forms. However, sociological theory is based on the assumption that we can discern some patterns in a study that can be at least partially replicated in other situations. Dependability can be enhanced by meticulous documentation of procedures and findings, by presenting data in a way that makes it possible for others to check one's interpretation (for example, by presenting long quotations from interview transcripts, including quotations from written materials, or making datasets available), and by intersubjective observations and intersubjective coding. It is also possible to consider 'member validation' as a possibility. This can be an ongoing feature of several methods, such as participant observation and in-depth interviews. By bringing descriptions and interpretations back to informants, it may be possible to rectify misunderstandings. Furthermore, this may provide valuable information about how the participants react to external descriptions of their emotions. However, the theoretical analysis can hardly be supported by membership validation, especially if it points to emotional mechanisms that are not recognized by the agents themselves.

The conclusion of an empirical research project is warranted by a set of findings based on methodological procedures that are generally accepted within the community of researchers referred to. Validation thus refers to whether the conclusion is adequately grounded on theoretically relevant empirical findings produced by appropriate methods. It is impossible to obtain objective measurements of religious emotions, but this does not mean that the subject is closed to scientific investigation, since the claims can be supported intersubjectively. It is a matter not of whether measurements correspond with objective standards or not, but of the adequacy of fit between interpretation of the empirical indicators and the theoretical conclusion drawn from them. In order to enhance inferential validity, we need to clarify the logic of the argument, especially the character of causal inferences. In order to enhance transferability, we need to clarify the extension of the claim, both its social reference and its thematic reference: which population of cases the claim is supposed to cover, and what thematic scope theoretical terms are meant to have. A dialectical approach provides us with useful tools for validation. It enables us to combine observations and methods in a way that allows for cross-checking of sources, and offers a foundation for interpretations of emotional regimes that cover a wide range of their aspects.

Appendix

The conceptual unfolding of the theme of religious emotions in earlier chapters has led to a practical unfolding of possible methodological approaches in this brief appendix. We have no doubt overlooked some other fruitful approaches to the study of emotion, and failed to imagine methods that may be proposed by creative researchers in the future. But even this sketch indicates that it is not a simple matter to test and refine the claims made in this book, particularly those in the final chapter. That calls for a plethora of studies by different researchers, employing a range of methods, and investigating varied aspects of religious emotion. Such work will lead to the formulation of more precise descriptions and explanations of contemporary religious emotional patterns, and advance our understanding of religion and late modern societies by integrating the neglected but crucial topic of religious emotion.

References

Abu-Lughod, Lila (1986). *Veiled Sentiments: Honor and Poetry in a Bedouin Society*. Berkeley and Los Angeles, CA: University of California Press.

Adams, Richard N. (1975). *Energy and Structure: A Theory of Social Power*. Austin, TX: University of Texas Press.

Ahmed, Sara (2004). *The Cultural Politics of Emotion*. Edinburgh: Edinburgh University Press.

Allport, Gordon W. (1950). *The Individual and his Religion*. New York: Macmillan.

Appadurai, Arjun (1986) (ed.). *The Social Life of Things: Commodities in Cultural Perspective*. Cambridge and New York: Cambridge University Press.

Archer, Margaret (1996). *Culture and Agency: The Place of Culture in Social Theory*. Cambridge: Cambridge University Press.

Archer, Margaret (1998). 'Introduction: Realism in the Social Sciences', in Margaret Archer et al. (eds), *Critical Realism: Essential Readings*. London: Routledge, 189–205.

Aristotle (1926). *The 'Art' of Rhetoric*. Cambridge, MA: Loeb Classical Library.

Aristotle (1932). *Nicomachean Ethics*. Cambridge, MA: Loeb Classical Library.

Armstrong, Karen (2007). 'A Question of Faith', interview with Madeleine Bunting, *Guardian* (Review section), 6 Oct.

Arnold, Magda B. (1960). *Emotion and Personality: Psychological Aspects*. New York: Columbia University Press.

Asad, Talal (1993). *Genealogies of Religion: Discipline and Reasons of Power in Christianity and Islam*. Baltimore, MD: Johns Hopkins University Press.

Assmann, Jan (2005). *Religion and Cultural Memory: Ten Studies*. Stanford, CA: Stanford University Press.

Astuti, Rita et al. (2007) (eds). *Questions of Anthropology*. Oxford: Berg.

Aull Davies, Charlotte (2007). *Reflexive Ethnography: A Guide to Researching Selves and Others*. ASA Research Methods. London: Routledge.

Aupers, Stef, and Dick Houtman (2006). 'Beyond the Spiritual Supermarket: The Social and Public Significance of New Age Spirituality', *Journal of Contemporary Religion*, 21/2: 201–22.

Baggley, John (1995). *Doors of Perception*. Crestwood, NY: St Vladimir's Seminary Press.

Bakhtin, Mikhail (1993). *Rabelais and his World*. Bloomington, IN: Indiana University Press, 1993.

References

Balagangadhara, S. N. (1994). *The 'Heathen in his Blindness . . . ': Asia, the West and the Dynamic of Religion*. Leiden: Brill.

Barbalet, Jack (1998). *Emotion, Social Theory and Social Structure: A Macrosociological Approach*. Cambridge: Cambridge University Press.

Barbalet, Jack (2002a) (ed.). *Emotions and Sociology*. Oxford and Malden, MA: Blackwell Publishing/Socological Review.

Barbalet, Jack (2002b). 'Introduction: Why Emotions are Crucial', in Jack Barbalet (ed.), *Emotions and Sociology*. Oxford and Malden, MA: Blackwell Publishing/ Socological Review, 1–9.

Barker, Eileen (1984). *The Making of a Moonie: Choice or Brainwashing?* Oxford: Blackwell.

Barnes, Barry (1988). *The Nature of Power*. Cambridge: Polity Press.

Bateson, Gregory (1936/1958). *Naven*. Stanford, CA: University of California Press.

Bateson, Gregory (1963). 'A Social Scientist Views the Emotions', in Peter Knapp (ed.), *Expression of the Emotions in Man*. New York: International University Press, 230–6.

Bateson, Gregory (1973). *Steps to an Ecology of Mind: Collected Essays in Anthropology, Psychiatry, Evolution and Epistemology*. St Albans: Paladin.

Baudrillard, Jean (1983). *Simulations*. New York: Semiotext(e).

Baudrillard, Jean (1998). *The Consumer Society: Myths and Structures*. London: Sage.

Beck, Aaron (1991). *Cognitive Therapy and the Emotional Disorders*. Harmondsworth: Penguin.

Beck, Ulrich, and Elisabeth Beck-Gernsheim (2002). *Individualization: Institutionalized Individualism and its Social and Political Consequences*. London: Sage.

Beckford, James (1985). *Cult Controversies: The Societal Response to New Religious Movements*. London and New York: Tavistock.

Beckford, James (1989). *Religion and Advanced Industrial Society*. London: Unwin Hyde.

Beckford, James (2003). *Social Theory and Religion*. Cambridge: Cambridge University Press.

Bell, Katherine (1997). *Ritual: Perspectives and Dimensions*. New York and Oxford: Oxford University Press.

Bell, Daniel (1973). *The Coming of Post-Industrial Society: A Venture in Social Forecasting*. New York: Basic Books.

Bellah, Robert (1967). 'Civil Religion in America', *Daedalus*, 96/1: 1–21.

Bellah, Robert, and Steven Tipton (2006). *The Robert Bellah Reader*. Durham, NC: Duke University Press.

Bellah, Robert N., Richard Madsen, William M. Sullivan, Ann Swidler, and Steven M. Tipton (1985). *Habits of the Heart: Individualism and Commitment in American Life*. Berkeley and Los Angeles: University of California Press.

Bendelow, Gillian, and Simon J. Williams (1988) (eds). *Emotions in Social Life: Critical Themes and Contemporary Issues*. London and New York: Routledge.

References

Benedict, Ruth (1935). *Patterns of Culture*. London: Routledge.

Benhabib, Seyla (1992). *Situating the Self: Gender, Community and Postmodernism in Contemporary Ethics*. London: Routledge.

Bennett, Jane (2001). *The Enchantment of Modern Life: Attachments, Crossings and Ethics*. Princeton, NJ: Princeton University Press.

Berger, Helen A. (2005) (ed.). *Witchcraft and Magic: Contemporary North America*. Philadelphia, PA: University of Pennsylvania Press.

Berger, Helen A., and Douglas Ezzy (2007). *Teenage Witches: Magical Youth and the Search for the Self*. New Brunswick, NJ: Rutgers University Press.

Berger, Peter (1967). *The Sacred Canopy*. Harmondsworth: Penguin.

Berger, Peter, and Thomas Luckmann (1966). *The Social Construction of Reality: A Treatise in the Sociology of Knowledge*. Garden City, NY: Anchor Books.

Berger, Peter, Brigitte Berger, and Hansfried Kellner (1974). *The Homeless Mind: Modernization and Consciousness*. Harmondsworth: Penguin.

Berger, Peter, Grace Davie, and Effe Fokas (2009). *Religious America, Secular Europe? A Theme and Variations*. Aldershot: Ashgate.

Beyer, Peter (2006). *Religions in Global Society*. London and New York: Routledge.

Bhaskar, Roy (1993). *Dialectic: The Pulse of Freedom*. London: Verso.

Bibby, Reginald W. (1987). *Fragmented Gods: The Poverty and Potential of Religion in Canada*. Toronto: Irwin Publishing.

Bloch, Maurice (2002). 'The Disconnection between Power and Rank as a Process', in Michael Lambek (ed.), *A Reader in the Anthropology of Religion*. Malden, MA, Oxford, and Victoria, Australia: Blackwell, 432–45.

Boltanski, Luc, and Eve Chiapello (2005). *The New Spirit of Capitalism*. London: Verso.

Bolton, Sharon (2005). *Emotion Management in the Workplace*. Basingstoke: Palgrave MacMillan.

Bolton, Sharon, and Carol Boyd (2003). 'Trolley Dolly or Skilled Emotion Manager? Moving on from Hochschild's Managed Heart', *Work, Employment and Society*, 17/2: 289–308.

Bolton, Sharon (2007) (ed.). *Dimensions of Dignity at Work*. Amsterdam: Elsevier; Oxford Butterworth-Heinemann.

Boulding, Kenneth E. (1990). *Three Faces of Power*. London: Sage.

Bourdieu, Pierre (1974). *Zur Soziologie der symbolische Formen*. Frankfurt am Main: Suhrkamp.

Bourdieu, Pierre (1977). *Outline of a Theory of Practice*. Cambridge: Cambridge University Press.

Bourdieu, Pierre (1984). *Distinction: A Social Critique of the Judgement of Taste*. London: Routledge & Kegan Paul.

Bourdieu, Pierre (1990). *The Logic of Practice*. Cambridge: Polity Press.

Bourdieu, Pierre, and Loïc Wacquant (1992). *An Invitation to Reflexive Sociology*. Cambridge: Polity Press.

Bourke, Joanna (2005). *Fear: A Cultural History*. London: Virago.

References

Bowie, Fiona (2000). *The Anthropology of Religion*. Oxford and Malden, MA: Blackwell.

Bowlby, John (1982). *Attachment and Loss*, i. *Attachment*. New York: Basic Books.

Braidotti, Rosi (2002). *Metamorphoses: Towards a Materialist Theory of Becoming*. Cambridge: Polity.

Braidotti, Rosi (2008). 'In Spite of the Times: The Postsecular Turn in Feminism', *Theory, Culture and Society*, 25/6: 1–24.

Brasher, Brenda (2001). *Give me that Online Religion*. San Francisco, CA: Jossey-Bass.

Bringsværd, Tor A. (2006) (ed.). *Inuit: Myter og Sagn fra Grønland*. Oslo: Bokklubben.

Brown, Callum (2001). *The Death of Christian Britain: Understanding Secularisation, 1800–2000*. London and New York: Routledge.

Brown, Callum (2006). *Religion and Society in Twentieth-Century Britain*. London: Longman.

Brown, Frank Burch (2008). 'Music', in John Corrigan (ed.), *The Oxford Handbook of Religion and Emotion*. Oxford: Oxford University Press, 200–22.

Bryman, Alan (1996). *Quantity and Quality in Social Research*. London: Routledge.

Bryman, Alan (2004). *Social Research Methods*. Oxford: Oxford University Press.

Budd, Malcolm (1985). *Music and the Emotions: The Philosophical Theories*. London: Routledge.

Burkitt, Ian (1997). 'Social Relationships and Emotions', *Sociology*, 31/1: 37–55.

Burkitt, Ian (2002). 'Complex Emotions: Relations, Feelings and Images in Emotional Experience', in Jack Barbalet (ed.), *Emotions and Sociology*. Oxford and Malden, MA: Blackwell Publishing/Socological Review, 151–68.

Burleigh, Michael (2006). *Earthly Powers: Religion and Politics in Europe from the Enlightenment to the Great War*. London: Harper Collins.

Burleigh, Michael (2007). *Sacred Causes: Religion and Politics from the European Dictators to Al Qaeda*. London: Harper Collins.

Calhoun, Cheshire (2003). 'Cognitive Emotions?', in Robert C. Solomon (ed.), *What is an Emotion? Classic and Contemporary Readings*. 2nd edn. New York and Oxford: Oxford University Press, 236–47.

Campbell, Colin (1987). *The Romantic Ethic and the Spirit of Modern Consumerism*. Oxford: Blackwell.

Cancian, Francesca M., and Steven L. Gordon (1988). 'Changing Emotions Norms in Marriage', *Gender and Society*, 2/3: 308–42.

Capetz, Paul E. (1998). *Christian Faith as Religion: A Study in the Theologies of Calvin and Schleiermacher*. New York: University Press of America.

Caroll, John (1977). *Puritan, Paranoid, Remissive: A Sociology of Modern Culture*. London: Routledge & Kegan Paul.

Carrette, Jeremy (2008). 'William James', in John Corrigan (ed.), *The Oxford Handbook of Religion and Emotion*. Oxford: Oxford University Press, 419–37.

Carrette, Jeremy, and Richard King (2004). *Selling Spirituality: The Silent Takeover of Religion*. London: Routledge.

Carruthers, Mary (1998). *The Craft of Thought: Meditation, Rhetoric and the Making of Images, 400–1200*. Cambridge: Cambridge University Press.

Carsten, Janet (2007) (ed.). *Ghosts of Memory: Essays on Remembrance and Relatedness*. Oxford: WileyBlackwell.

Champion, Françoise, and Danièle Hervieu-Léger (1990). *De l'émotion en religion*. Paris: Centurion.

Christian, William A. (2004). 'Provoked Religious Weeping in Early Modern Spain', in John Corrigan (ed.), *Religion and Emotion: Approaches and Interpretations*. Oxford and New York, Oxford University Press, 33–50.

Cicourel, Aaron W. (1964). *Method and Measurement in Sociology*. New York: Free Press.

Clark-King, Ellen (2004). *Theology by Heart: Women, God and the Church*. London: SCM.

Clegg, Stewart (1989). *Frameworks of Power*. London: Sage.

Cohn, Norman (1972). *The Pursuit of the Millennium*. London. Paladin.

Collins, Randall (2005). *Interaction Ritual Chains*. Princeton, NJ: Princeton University Press.

Conklin, Beth A. (2001). *Consuming Grief: Compassionate Cannibalism in an Amazonian Society*. Austin, TX: University of Texas Press.

Corrigan, John (2004) (ed.). *Religion and Emotion: Approaches and Interpretations*. Oxford: Oxford University Press.

Corrigan, John (2008) (ed.). *The Oxford Handbook of Religion and Emotion*. Oxford: Oxford University Press.

Cowan, Douglas E. (2008). 'New Religions Movements', in John Corrigan (ed.), *The Oxford Handbook of Religion and Emotion*. Oxford: Oxford University Press, 125–40.

Cowley, Catherine (2006). *The Value of Money: Ethics and the World of Finance*. Edinburgh: T&T Clark.

Creswell, John W., and Vicky L. Clark (2007). *Designing and Conducting Mixed Methods Research*. London: Sage.

Crossley, Nick (1998). 'Emotion and Communicative Action: Habermas, Linguistic Philosophy and Existentialism', in Gillian Bendelow and Simon J. Williams (eds), *Emotions in Social Life: Critical Themes and Contemporary Issues*. London and New York: Routledge, 16–38.

Csikszentmihalyi, Mihalyi (1993). 'Why We Need Things', in Stephen Lubar and W. David Kingery (eds), *History from Things: Essays on Material Culture*. Washington, DC: Smithsonian Institute Press, 20–9.

Csikszentmihalyi, Mihalyi, and Eugene Rochberg-Halton (1981). *The Meaning of Things: Domestic Symbols and the Self*. New York: Cambridge University Press.

Csordas, Thomas (1997). *The Sacred Self: A Cultural Phenomenology of Charismatic Healing*. Berkeley and Los Angeles, CA: University of California Press.

References

Cumming, Robert D. (1992). 'Role-Playing: Sartre's Transformation of Husserl's Phenomenology', in Christina Howells (ed.), *The Cambridge Companion to Sartre*. Cambridge: Cambridge University Press, 39–66.

Damasio, Antonio (2004). *Looking for Spinoza*. New edn. London: Vintage.

Damasio, Antonio (1994/2005). *Descartes' Error: Emotion, Reason, and the Human Brain*. Harmondsworth: Penguin.

Dandelion, Ben Pink (2004) (ed.). *The Creation of Quaker Theology: Insider Perspectives*. Aldershot: Ashgate.

Darwin, Charles (1872/1999). *The Expression of the Emotions in Man and Animals*. London: Fontana Press.

Davidson, Joyce, Liz Bondi, and Mick Smith (2005) (eds). *Emotional Geographies*. Aldershot: Ashgate.

Davie, Grace (2002). *Europe: The Exceptional Case: Parameters of Faith in the Modern World*. London: Darton, Longman and Todd.

De Rivera, Joseph (1992). 'Emotional Climate: Social Structure, CA, and Emotional Dynamics', in Kenneth T. Strongman (ed.), *International Review of Studies on Emotion*. New York: John Wiley and Sons, ii. 197–218.

Della Porta D., and M. Diani (1999). *Social Movements*. Oxford: Blackwell.

Delumeau, Jean (1983). *Le Péché et la Peur: Le Culpabilisation en Occident, XIII–XVIIIe siècles*. Paris: Fayard.

Delumeau, Jean (1989). *Rassurer et protéger: Le Sentiment de sécurité dans l'Occident d'autrefois*. Paris: Fayard.

Denzin, Norman (1984). *On Understanding Emotion*. San Francisco, CA, and London: Jossey-Bass.

Denzin, Norman K., and Yvonne Lincoln (2005) (eds.). *The Sage Handbook of Qualitative Research*. Thousand Oaks, CA: Sage.

De Sousa, Ronald (1989). *The Rationality of Emotion*. Cambridge, MA: MIT Press.

De Sousa, Ronald (2003). 'From the Rationality of Emotion', in Robert C. Solomon (ed.), *What is an Emotion?* 2nd edn. *Classic and Contemporary Readings*. New York and Oxford: Oxford University Press, 248–57.

Desjarlais, Robert (1992). *Body and Healing: The Aesthetics of Illness and Healing in the Nepal Himalayas*. Philadelphia, PA: University of Philadelphia Press.

Dewey, John (1983). *Human Nature and Conduct. An Introduction to Social Psychology*. Carbondale, IL: Southern Illinois University Press.

Ditmar, Helga (1992). *The Social Psychology of Material Possessions: To Have is to Be*. New York: St Martins Press.

Dixon, Thomas (2003). *From Passions to Emotions: The Creation of a Secular Psychological Category*. Cambridge: Cambridge University Press.

Douglas, Jack D., and John M. Johnson (1977) (eds). *Existential Sociology*. New York: Cambridge.

Douglas, Mary (1966). *Purity and Danger: An Analysis of Concepts of Pollution and Taboo*. London: Routledge & Kegan Paul.

Douglas, Mary (1970). *Natural Symbols: Explorations in Cosmology*. New York: Pantheon Books.

Douglas, Mary (1975). *Implicit Meanings: Essays in Anthropology*. London, Boston and Henley: Routledge & Kegan Paul.

Douglas, Mary (2003). *Natural Symbols*. 2nd edn. London: Routledge.

Dowding, Keith (1996). *Power*. Buckingham: Open University Press.

Durkheim, Émile (1895/1982). *The Rules of Sociological Method*. London: Macmillan.

Durkheim, Émile (1912/2001). *The Elementary Forms of Religious Life*. Oxford: Oxford University Press.

Ebersole, Gary L. (2004). 'The Function of Ritual Weeping Revisited: Affective Expression and Moral Discourse', in John Corrigan (ed.), *Religion and Emotion: Approaches and Interpretations*. Oxford and New York: Oxford University Press, 185–222.

Edwards, Jonathan (1957). *The Works of Jonathan Edwards*, i. *Freedom of the Will*. New Haven, CT: Yale University Press.

Edwards, Jonathan (1746/1971). *Religious Affections* (originally published as *A Treatise Concerning Religions Affections*, in three parts). Grand Rapids, MI: Sovereign Grace Publishers.

Ehrenreich, Barbara (2007). *Dancing in the Streets: A History of Collective Joy*. New York: Holt.

Eisenstadt, Shmuel Noah (1987) (ed.). *Patterns of Modernity*. London: Frances Pinter.

Ekman, Paul (1994). *Emotions Revealed: Understanding Faces and Feelings*. New York: Times Books.

Ekman, Paul, and Richard J. Davidson (1994). *The Nature of Emotion: Fundamental Questions*. Oxford: Oxford University Press.

Elias, Norbert (1939/2000). *The Civilizing Process: Sociogenetic and Psychogenetic Investigations*, rev. edn. Eric Dunning, Johan Goudsblom, and Stephen Mennell (eds). Malden, MA, Oxford, and Victoria, Australia: Blackwell.

Elias, Norbert (1978). *Über den Prozess der Zivilisation, Soziogenese und Psychologischen Untersuchingen*. 2 vols. Frankfurt am Main: Suhrkamp.

Elias, Norbert (1988). 'Violence and Civilization: The State Monopoly of Physical Violence and its Infringement', in John Keane (ed.), *Civil Society and the State: New European Perspectives*. London: Verso, 177–98.

Elias, Norbert, and Eric Dunning (1986). *Quest for Excitement: Sport and Leisure in the Civilizing Process*. Oxford: Blackwell.

Elster, Jon (1996). 'Rationality and Emotions', *Economic Journal*, 406/438: 1386–97.

Etzkorn, Peter (1968) (ed.). *Georg Simmel: The Conflict in Modern Culture and Other Essays*. New York: Teachers College Press.

Evans-Pritchard, Edward E. (1965). *Theories of Primitive Religion*. Oxford: Oxford University Press.

Fauconnier, Mark, and Gilles Turner (2002). *The Way we Think: Conceptual Blending and the Mind's Hidden Complexities*. New York: Basic Books.

References

Fairclough, Norman (2003). *Analyzing Discourse: Textual Analysis for Social Research*. London: Routledge.

Featherstone, Mike (2007). *Consumer Culture and Postmodernism*. Los Angeles, CA: Sage.

Fernandez, Damian (2000). *Cuba and the Politics of Passion*. Austin, TX: University of Texas.

Finkelstein, Joanne (1980). 'Considerations for a Sociology of the Emotions', in Norman Denzin (ed.), *Studies in Symbolic Interaction*. Greenwich, CT: JAI Press, iii. 111–21.

Flam, Helena (2002). *Soziologie der Emotionen*. Konstanz: UVK Verlagsgesellschaft.

Foucault, Michel (1979a). *The History of Sexuality*, i. London: Penguin.

Foucault, Michel (1979b). *Discipline and Punish: The Birth of the Prison*. Harmondsworth: Penguin.

Foucault, Michel (1980). *Power/Knowledge: Selected Interviews and Other Writings, 1972–1977*. New York: Pantheon.

Foucault, Michel (1982). 'The Subject and Power', afterword in Hubert L. Dreyfus and Paul Rabinow, *Michel Foucault: Beyond Structuralism and Hermeneutics*. Brighton: Harvester.

Franks, David D., and E. Doyle McCarthy (1989) (eds). *The Sociology of Emotions: Original Essays and Research Papers*. Greenwich, CT: JAI Press.

Furedi, Frank (2003). *Therapy Culture: Cultivating Vulnerability in an Uncertain Age*. London: Routledge.

Galbraith, John Kenneth (1970). *The Affluent Society*. Harmondsworth: Penguin.

Galbraith, John Kenneth (1983). *The Anatomy of Power*. Boston, MA: Houghton Mifflin.

Garfinkel, Harold (1956). 'Conditions of Successful Degradation Ceremonies', *American Journal of Sociology*, 61/5: 420–4.

Geertz, Clifford (1971). 'Religion as a Cultural System', in Michael Banton (ed.), *Anthropological Approaches to the Study of Religion*. London: Tavistock Publications, 1–43.

Geertz, Clifford (1973). *The Interpretation of Cultures*. New York: Basic Books.

Gehlen, Arnold (1980). *Man in the Age of Technology*. New York: Columbia University Press.

Gell, Alfred (1998). *Art and Agency: A New Anthropological Theory*. Oxford: Oxford University Press.

Gendlin, Eugene T. (1997). *Experiencing and the Creation of Meaning: A Philosophical and Psychological Approach to the Subjective*. Evanston, IL: Northwestern University Press.

Gennep, Arnold van (1908/1960). *The Rites of Passage*. London.

Gergen, Kenneth (2000). *The Saturated Self: Dilemmas of Identity in Contemporary Life*. New York: Basic Books.

Gerhards, J. (1994). 'George Simmel's Contribution to a Theory of Emotions', in David Frisby (ed.), *Georg Simmel: Critical Assessments*. 3 vols. London: Routledge.

Giddens, Anthony (1979). *Central Problems in Social Theory: Action, Structure and Contradiction in Social Analysis*. Basingstoke: Macmillan.

Giddens, Anthony (1987). *Social Theory and Modern Sociology*. Cambridge, Polity Press).

Giddens, Anthony (1990). *The Consequences of Modernity*. Cambridge: Polity Press.

Giddens, Anthony (1991). *Modernity and Self-Identity: Self and Society in the Late Modern Age*. Stanford, CA: Stanford University Press.

Giddens, Anthony (1976/1993). *New Rules of Sociological Method*. Cambridge: Polity Press.

Gilbert, Paul (1991). *Depression: The Evolution of Powerlessness*. New York: Guildford Press.

Ginzburg, Carlo (1991). *Ecstasies: Deciphering the Witches' Sabbath*. New York: Pantheon Books.

Goffman, Erving (1961). *Encounters: Two Studies in the Sociology of Interaction*. Indianapolis, IN: Bobbs-Merrill.

Goffman, Erving (1967). 'The Nature of Deference and Demeanour', in *Interaction Ritual: Essays on Face-to-Face Behaviour*. New York: Anchor Books.

Goffman, Erving (1971). *The Presentation of Self in Everyday Life*. Harmondsworth: Penguin Books.

Goodwin, Jeff, James M. Jasper, and Francesca Polletta (2001) (eds.). *Passionate Politics: Emotions and Social Movements*. Chicago, IL: University of Chicago Press.

Goodwin, Jeff, James M. Jasper, and Francesca Polletta (2007). 'Emotional Dimensions of Social Movements', in David A. Snow, Sarah A. Soule, and Hanspeter Kriesi (eds), *The Blackwell Companion to Social Movements*. Malden, MA, and Oxford: Blackwell, 413–32.

Goleman, Daniel (1997). *Emotional Intelligence. Why it Can Matter more than IQ*. New York: Bantam.

Gordon, Steven L. (1990). 'Social Structural Effects on Emotions', in Theodore Kemper (ed.), *Research Agendas in the Sociology of Emotions*. Albany, NY: SUNY, 145–79.

Greenberg, Jay R., and Stephen A. Mitchell (1983). *Object Relations in Psychoanalytic Theory*. Cambridge, MA: Harvard University Press.

Griffiths, Paul E. (1997). *What Emotions Really Are: The Problem of Psychological Categories*. Chicago, IL, and London: University of Chicago Press.

Grima, Benedicte (1992). *The Performance of Emotion: The Misfortunes which have Befallen Me*. Austin, TX: University of Texas Press.

Gubrium, Jaber, and James Holstein (1997). *The New Language of Qualitative Method*. Oxford: Oxford University Press.

References

Gurwitch, Georges (1962). *Dialectique et sociologie*. Paris: Flammarion.

Habermas, Jürgen (1981). *Theorie des kommunikativen Handelns*. Frankfurt am Main: Suhrkamp.

Halbwachs, Maurice (1992). *On Collective Memory*, (ed.), trans. and with an introduction by Lewis A. Coser. Chicago, IL, and London: University of Chicago Press.

Hall, John R., Mary J. Neitz, and Marshall Battani (2003). *Sociology on Culture*. London: Routledge.

Hall, Stanley (1904). *Adolescence*, ii. New York: Appleton.

Hammond, Michael (1983). 'The Sociology of Emotions and the History of Social Differentiation', in Randall Collins (ed.), *Social Theory*. San Francisco, CA: Jossey-Bass, 90–119.

Hammond, Michael (1990). 'Affective Maximalization: A New Macro Theory in the Sociology of Emotions', in Theodore Kemper (ed.), *Research Agendas in the Sociology of Emotions*. New York: SUNY Press, 58–84.

Hammond, Michael (2004). 'The Enhancement Imperative and Group Dynamics in the Emergence of Religion and Ascriptive Inequality', in Jonathan H. Turner (ed.), *Theory and Research on Human Emotions*. Elsevier: Amsterdam, 167–88.

Hansen, Chadwik (1969). *Witchcraft at Salem*. New York: Mentor Book.

Haraway, Donna (1991). *Simians, Cyborgs and Women: The Reinvention of Nature*. London: Free Association Books.

Hardman, Charlotte (2000). *Other Worlds: Notions of Self and Emotion among the Lohorung Rai*. Oxford and New York: Berg.

Harré, Rom (ed.) (1986). *The Social Construction of the Emotions*. Oxford: Blackwell.

Harré, Rom, and W. Gerrod Parrott (1996) (eds). *The Emotions: Social, Cultural and Biological Dimensions*. London and Thousand Oaks, CA: Sage.

Hatfield, Elaine, John T. Cacioppo, and Richard L. Rapson (1994). *Emotional Contagion*. Cambridge: Cambridge University Press.

Heelas, Paul (1996). 'Emotion Talk across Cultures', in Rom Harré and Gerrard W. Parrott (eds), *The Emotions: Cultural and Biological Dimensions*. London, Thousand Oaks, CA, and New Delhi: Sage, 171–99.

Heelas, Paul, and Linda Woodhead (2005). *The Spiritual Revolution: Why Religion is Giving Way to Spirituality*. Oxford: Blackwell.

Heelas, Paul, Scott Lash, and Paul Morris (1996) (eds). *Detraditionalization: Critical Reflections on Authority and Identity at a Time of Uncertainty*. Oxford: Blackwell.

Hefner, Robert (1993) (ed.). *Conversion to Christianity: Historical and Anthropological Perspectives on a Great Transformation*. Berkeley and Los Angeles, CA: University of California Press.

Heise, David R. (1979). *Understanding Events: Affect and the Construction of Social Action*. New York: Cambridge University Press.

Heise, David R. (1986). 'Modelling Symbolic Interaction', in Siegwart Lindenberg et al (eds.), *Approaches to Social Theory*. New York: Russell Sage Foundation, 291–309.

References

Heise, David R., and Cassandra Calhan (1995). 'Emotion Norms in Interpersonal Events', *Social Psychology Quarterly*, 58/4: 223–40.

Henaff, Marcel (1998). *Claude Lévi-Strauss and the Making of Structural Anthropology.* Minneapolis, MN: University of Minnesota Press.

Henney, Jeanette, et al. (1974). *Trance, Healing, and Hallucination: Three Field Studies in Religious Experience.* New York: Wiley.

Hervieu-Léger, Danièle (1993a). *La Religion pour mémoire.* Paris: Cerf.

Hervieu-Léger, Danièle (1993b). 'Present-Day Emotional Revivals: The End of Secularization or the End of Religion?' in William Swatos (ed.), *A Future for Religion?* Newbury Park, CA: Sage, 129–48

Hervieu-Lèger, Danièle (1999). *Le Pélerin et le converti.* Paris: Flammarion.

Hervieu-Léger, Danièle (2000). *Religion as a Chain of Memory.* Cambridge: Polity.

Hill, Christopher (1980). *The World Turned Upside Down.* Harmondsworth: Penguin Books.

Hochschild, Arlie R. (1979). 'Emotion Work: Feeling Rules and Social Structure', *American Journal of Sociology*, 85: 551–75.

Hochschild, Arlie R. (1983). *The Managed Heart: Commercialization of Human Feeling.* Berkeley and Los Angeles, CA: University of California Press.

Hochschild, Arlie (1989). *The Second Shift: Working Parents and the Revolution at Home.* New York: Viking.

Hochschild, Arlie R. (1997). *The Time Bind: When Work Becomes Home and Home Becomes Work.* New York: Metropolitan Books.

Hochschild, Arlie (1998). 'The Sociology of Emotion as a Way of Seeing', in Gillian Bendelow and Simon J. Williams (eds.), *Emotions in Social Life: Critical Themes and Contemporary Issues.* London and New York: Routledge, 3–16.

Hochschild, Arlie (2003). *The Commercialization of Intimate Life: Notes from Home and Work.* Berkeley and Los Angeles, CA: University of California Press.

Holm, Nils (1982). *Religious Ecstasy.* Stockholm: Almqvist and Wiksell.

Homans, George (1961). *Social Behaviour: Its Elementary Form.* London: Routledge and Kegan Paul.

Hooks, Bell (2003). *We Real Cool: Black Men and Masculinity.* London: Routledge.

Hopkins, Gerard Manley (1959). *Journals and Papers*, Humphrey House (ed.). London and New York: Oxford University Press.

Horney, Karen (1937). *The Neurotic Personality of our Time.* London: Kegan Paul.

Hoskins, Janet (1998). *Biographical Objects: How Things tell the Stories of People's Lives.* London: Routledge.

Hügel, Friedrich von (1909). *The Mystical Element of Religion as Studied in Saint Catherine of Genoa and her Friends.* 2 vols. London: Dent.

Hügel, Friedrich von (1926). *Essays and Addresses on the Philosophy of Religion.* Second Series. London: Dent.

Huizinga, Johan (1924/1955). *The Waning of the Middle Ages: A Study of the Forms of Life, Thought and Art in France and the Netherlands in the Fourteenth and Fifteenth Centuries.* Harmondsworth: Penguin.

Humphrey, Caroline (2002). 'Rituals of Death as a Context for Understanding Personal Property in Socialist Mongolia', *Journal of the Royal Anthropological Institution*, 8/1: 65–87.

Hunt, Tristam (2002). *The English Civil War*. London: Weidenfeld & Nicolson.

Illouz, Eva (2007). *Cold Intimacies: The Making of Emotional Capitalism*. Cambridge: Polity Press.

Inglehart, Ronald (1990). *Culture Shift in Advanced Industrial Society*. Princeton, NJ: Princeton University Press.

Ivakhiv, Adrian (2001). *Reclaiming Sacred Ground: Pilgrims and Politics at Glastonbury and Sedona*. Bloomington, IN: Indiana University Press.

Izard, Carroll E. (1977). *Human Emotions*. New York: Plenum Press.

Jackson, Stanley W. (1986). *Melancholia and Depression: From Hippocratic Times to Modern Times*. New Haven, CT: Yale University Press.

Jaggar, Alison (1989). 'Love and Knowledge: Emotion in Feminist Epistemology', *Inquiry*, 32/2: 151–76.

Jakobsen, Merete (1999). *Shamanism*. New York: Berghahn.

James, William (1884). 'What is an Emotion?', *Mind*, 19: 188–205.

James, William (1902/1981). *The Varieties of Religious Experience: A Study in Human Nature*. Glasgow: Collins, Fontana.

Jasper, James M. (1998). 'The Emotions of Protest: Affective and Reactive Emotions in and around Social Movements', *Sociological Forum*, 13/3: 397–424.

Johnson, John M., and Joseph A. Kortaba (2002). 'Postmodern Existentialism', in John Kortaba and John M. Johnson (eds.), *Postmodern Existential Sociology*. Walnut Creek, CA: Alta Mira, 3–14.

Johnson, Mark (1987). *The Body in the Mind: The Bodily Basis of Meaning, Imagination and Reason*. Chicago, IL: Chicago University Press.

Johnson, Mark (2007). *The Meaning of the Body: Aesthetics of Human Understanding*. Chicago, IL, and London: Chicago University Press.

Jones, Robert Alun (2005). *The Secret of the Totem: Religion and Society from McLennan to Freud*. New York: Columbia University Press.

Kamen, Henry (1998). *The Spanish Inquisition: A Historical Revision*. New Haven, CT: Yale University Press.

Kanter, Rosabeth M. (1972). *Commitment and Community: Communes and Utopias in Sociological Perspective*. Cambridge, MA: Harvard University Press.

Kaster, Robert A. (2005). *Emotion, Restraint and Community in Ancient Rome*. Oxford: Oxford University Press.

Kear, Adrian, and Deborah Steinberg (1999) (eds). *The Mourning for Diana: Nation, Culture and the Performance of Grief*. London: Routledge.

Keltner, Dacher, and Jonathan Haidt (1999). 'Social Functions of Emotions at Four Levels of Analysis', *Cognition and Emotion*, 3/5: 505–21.

Kemper, Theodore D. (1978). *A Social Interactional Theory of Emotions*. New York: Wiley.

Kemper, Theodore D. (1981). 'Social Constructionist and Positivist Approaches to the Sociology of Emotions', *American Journal of Sociology*, 87/2: 336–62.

Kemper, Thomas D. (1990) (ed.). *Research Agendas in the Sociology of Emotions*. New York: State University of New York Press.

Kieschnick, John (2008). 'Material Culture', in John Corrigan (ed.), *The Oxford Handbook of Religion and Emotion*. Oxford: Oxford University Press, 223–36.

Kintz, Linda (1997). *Between Jesus and the Market: The Emotions that Matter in Right-Wing America*. Durham, NC, and London: Duke University Press.

Klass, Morton (1995). *Ordered Universes: Approaches to the Anthropology of Religion*. Boulder, CO: Westview Press.

Klassen, Pamela (2008). 'Ritual', in John Corrigan (ed.), *The Oxford Handbook of Religion and Emotion*. Oxford: Oxford University Press, 143–61.

Klein, Melanie (1997). *Envy and Gratitude and Other Works 1946–1963*. London: Vintage Books.

Kleinman, Sherryl, and Martha A. Copp (1993). *Emotions and Fieldwork*. Newbury Park, CA: Sage Publications.

Knott, Kim (2005). *The Location of Religion: A Spatial Analysis*. London: Equinox.

Konstan, David (2005). *Emotions of the Ancient Greeks: Studies in Aristotle and Classical Literature*. Toronto: University of Toronto Press.

Kortaba, Joseph A., and John M. Johnson (2002) (eds.). *Postmodern Existential Sociology*. Walnut Creek, CA: Alta Mira.

Küchler Susanne (2002). *Malanggan: Art, Memory, Sacrifice*. Oxford: Berg.

Küchler, Susanne, and Daniel Miller (2005). *Clothing as Material Culture*. Oxford and New York: Berg.

Kumar, Krishan (1978). *Prophecy and Progress: The Sociology of Industrial and Post-Industrial Society*. London: Allen Lane.

Kwon, Heonik (2007). 'The Dollarization of Vietnamese Ghost Money', *Journal of the Royal Anthropological Institute*, 13/1: 73–90.

Laing, Ronald D. (1965). *The Divided Self: An Existential Study in Sanity and Madness*. Harmondsworth: Penguin.

Lakoff, George, and Mark Johnson (1980). *Metaphors We Live By*. Chicago, IL: University of Chicago Press.

Lakoff, George, and Mark Johnson (1999). *Philosophy in the Flesh: The Embodied Mind and its Challenge to Western Thought*. New York: Basic Books.

Lakoff, George, and Mark Johnson (2003). *Metaphors we Live by*. With a new Afterword. Chicago, IL, and London: University of Chicago Press.

Lakoff, George, and Raphael Núñez (2000). *Where Mathematics Comes From: How the Embodied Mind Brings Mathematics into Being*. New York: Basic Books.

Lambek, Michael (1981). *Human Spirits: A Cultural Account of Trance in Mayotte*. Cambridge and New York: Cambridge University Press.

Lambek, Michael (2002) (ed.). *A Reader in the Anthropology of Religion*. Malden, MA, Oxford, and Victoria, Australia: Blackwell.

References

Landweer, Hilge, and Ursula Renz (2008) (eds.). *Klassische Emotionsteorien*. Berlin: De Gruyter.

Lane, Christel (1981). *The Rites of Rulers: Ritual in Industrial Society: The Soviet Case*. Cambridge: Cambridge University Press.

Langford, Wendy (2002). *Revolutions of the Heart*. London: Routledge.

Lanternari, Vittorio (1963). *The Religions of the Oppressed: A Study of Modern Messianic Cults*. London: MacGibbon and Kee.

Lash, Nicholas (1988). *Easter in Ordinary: Reflections on Human Experience and the Knowledge of God*. London: SCM Press.

Lash, Scott (1990). *Sociology of Postmodernism*. London: Routledge.

Lash, Scott, and Celia Lury (2007). *Global Culture Industry: The Mediation of Things*. Cambridge: Polity Press.

Lasswell, H. D., and A. Kaplan (1950). *Power and Society*. New Haven, CT: Yale University Press.

Latour, Bruno (2005). *Assembling the Social: An Introduction to Actor-Network-Theory*. Oxford: Oxford University Press.

Law, John, and John Hassard (1999) (eds). *Actor Network Theory and After*. Boston, MA: Blackwell.

Layder, Derek (1998). *Sociological Practice: Linking Theory and Social Research*. London: Sage.

Lazarus, Richard S. (1982). 'Thoughts on the Relations between Emotion and Cognition', *American Psychologist*, 37: 1019–24.

Lazarus, Richard S. (1991). *Emotion and Adaptation*. Oxford: Oxford University Press.

Leach, Edmund (1958). 'Magical Hair', *Journal of the Royal Anthropological Institute*, 88/2: 147–64.

LeBon, Gustave (1896). *The Crowd: A Study of the Popular Mind*. Atlanta, GA: Cherokee.

LeDoux, Joseph (2002). *Synaptic Self: How our Brains Become Who We Are*. Harmondsworth: Penguin.

LeDoux, Joseph (2004). *The Emotional Brain: The Mysterious Underpinnings of Emotional Life*. London: Phoenix.

Lee, David, and Howard Newby (1983). *The Problem of Sociology*. London: Routledge.

Levine, Donald (1971). *Georg Simmel on Individuality and Social Forms*. Chicago, IL: Chicago University Press.

Lévi-Strauss, Claude (1963/1974). *Structural Anthropology*. New York: Basic Books.

Lévi-Strauss, Claude (2002). 'A Jivaro Version of *Totem and Taboo*', in Michael Lambek (ed.), *A Reader in the Anthropology of Religion*. Malden, MA, Oxford, and Victoria, Australia: Blackwell, 210–20.

Lewis, Ioan M. (1989). *Ecstatic Religion: An Anthropological Study of Spirit Possession and Shamanism*. London: Routledge.

Lienhardt, Godfrey (1961). *Divinity and Experience: The Religion of the Dinka.* Oxford: Oxford University Press.

Lindholm, Charles (1990). *Charisma.* Oxford: Blackwell.

Lipsky, Richard (1981). *How We Play the Game: Why Sports Dominate American Life.* Boston, MA: Beacon.

Llobera, Josep R. (1994). *The God of Modernity: The Development of Nationalism in Western Europe.* Oxford: Berg Publishers.

Lockridge, Kenneth A. (1998). *On the Sources of Patriarchal Rage: The Commonplace Books of William Byrd and Thomas Jefferson and the Gendering of Power in the Eighteenth Century.* New York and London: New York University Press.

Longley, Clifford (2002). *Chosen People: The Big Idea that Shapes England and America.* London: Hodder and Stoughton.

Lovejoy, David S. (1985). *Religious Enthusiasm in the New World: Heresy to Revolution.* Cambridge, MA: Harvard University Press.

Luckmann, Thomas (1967). *The Invisible Religion: The Problem of Religion in Modern Society.* New York: Macmillan.

Luhrmann, Tanya (1989). *Persuasion in the Witch's Craft: Ritual Magic and Witchcraft in Present-Day England.* Oxford: Basil Blackwell.

Luhrmann, Tanya M. (2004). 'Metakinesis: How God Becomes Intimate in Contemporary US Christianity', *American Anthropologist*, 106/3: 518–28.

Lukacs, George (1923). *Geschichte und Klassenbewusstsein.* Berlin: Malik.

Lukes, Steven (1974). *Power: A Radical View.* London and New York: Macmillan.

Lukes, Steven (2006). *Individualism.* Essex: ECPR.

Lupton, Deborah (1998). *The Emotional Self.* London: Sage.

Lutz, Catherine A. (1986). 'Emotion, Thought and Estrangement: Emotion as a Cultural Category', *Cultural Anthropology*, 1/3: 287–309.

Lutz, Catherine A. (1988). *Unnatural Emotions: Everyday Sentiments on a Micronesian Atoll and their Challenge to Western Theory.* Chicago, IL, and London: University of Chicago Press.

Lutz, Catherine A., and Geoffrey White (1986). 'The Anthropology of Emotions', *Annual Review of Anthropology*, 15: 405–36.

Lynd, Helen (1958). *On Shame and the Search for Identity.* New York: Harcourt Brace Jovanovich.

Lyon, David (2000). *Jesus in Disneyland: Religion in Postmodern Times.* Cambridge: Polity Press.

Lyon, Margot L. (1995). 'Missing Emotion: The Limitations of Cultural Construction in the Study of Emotion', *Cultural Anthropology*, 10/2: 244–63.

Lyotard, Jean-François (1979). *La Condition postmoderne: Rapport sur le savoir.* Paris: Éditions de Minuit.

McCarthy, John D. and Mayer N. Zald (1977). 'Resource Mobilization and Social Movements: A Partial Theory', *American Journal of Sociology*, 82: 1212–41.

McCracken, Grant (1987). 'Clothing as Language: An Object Lesson in the Study of the Expressive Properties of Material Culture', in Barrie Reynolds and Margaret A. Stott (eds), *Material Anthropology: Contemporary Approaches to Material Culture*. New York: University Press of America, 103–28.

McCracken, Grant David (1988). *Culture and Consumption: New Approaches to the Symbolic Character of Consumer Goods and Activities*. Bloomington, IN: Indiana University Press.

McDaniel, June (2008). 'Hinduism', in John Corrigan (ed.), *The Oxford Handbook of Religion and Emotion*. Oxford: Oxford University Press, 51–72.

McDannell, Colleen (1995). *Material Christianity: Religion and Popular Culture in America*. New Haven: Yale University Press.

McGuire, Meredith B. (2008). *Lived Religion, Faith and Practice in Everyday Life*. Oxford: Oxford University Press.

McKay, Charles (1841). *Extraordinary Popular Delusions and the Madness of Crowds*. London: Richard Bentley.

McLeod, Hugh (2007). *The Religious Crisis of the 1960s*. Oxford: Oxford University Press.

MacMullen, Ramsey (2003). *Feelings in History, Ancient and Modern*. Claremont, CA: Regina Books.

Mahoney, Jack (1989). *The Making of Moral Theology: A Study of the Roman Catholic Tradition*. Oxford: Oxford University Press.

Mann, Michael (1986). *The Sources of Social Power*. 2 vols. Cambridge and New York: Cambridge University Press.

Marcus, George (2002). *The Sentimental Citizen: Emotion in Democratic Politics*. Pennsylvania, PA: Penn State Press.

Marett, Robert R. (1914). *The Threshold of Religion*, 2nd edn. Oxford: Clarendon Press.

Marsh, Clive (1998). *Explorations in Theology and Film: Movies and Meaning*. Oxford, and Malden, MA: Blackwell.

Marx, Karl (1964). *The Economic and Philosophic Manuscripts of 1844*, (ed.) Dirk Struik. New York: International Publisher.

Marx, Karl (1887/1974). *Capital: A Critical Analysis of Capitalist Production*. Moscow: Progress Publishers.

Marx, Karl (1977). *Karl Marx: Selected Writings*, (ed.) David McLellan. Oxford: Oxford University Press.

Marx, Karl, and Frederick Engels (1848/1969). *The Communist Manifesto*, Marx/Engels Selected Works, vol. 1. Moscow: Progress Publishers.

Matravers, Derek (1998). *Art and Emotion*. Oxford: Clarendon Press.

Mauss, Marcel (1902/2006). *A General Theory of Magic*. London and New York: Routledge.

Mauss, Marcel (1979). *Sociology and Psychology: Essays*, trans. Ben Brewster. London and Boston: Routledge and Kegan Paul.

Mead, George Herbert (1934). *Mind, Self and Society*. Chicago, IL: University of Chicago Press.

Mellor, Philip, and Chris Shilling (1997). *Re-forming the Body: Religion, Community and Modernity*. London: Sage.

Melucci, Alberto (1996). *Challenging Codes*. Cambridge: Cambridge University Press.

Merleau-Ponty, Maurice (1955). *Les Aventures de la dialectique*. Paris: Gallimard.

Merleau-Ponty, Maurice (1962). *Phenomenology of Perception*. London: Routledge.

Merleau-Ponty, Maurice (1964). *Sense and Non-sense*. Evanston, IL: Northwestern University Press.

Merleau-Ponty, Maurice (1968). *The Visible and the Invisible*. Evanston, IL: Northwestern University Press.

Merleau-Ponty, Maurice (1973). *Adventures of the Dialectic*. Evanston, IL: Northwestern University Press.

Mestrovic, Stjepan G. (1997). *Postemotional Society*. London: Sage.

Meyendorff, John (1974/1979). *Byzantine Theology: Historical Trends and Doctrinal Themes*. New York: Fordham University Press.

Meyer, Birgit (2006). 'Religious Sensations: Why Media, Aesthetics and Power Matter in the Study of Contemporary Religion'. Inaugural Lecture, Free University. Amsterdam.

Micklethwait, John, and Adrian Woolridge (2009). *God is Back: How the Global Rise of Faith is Changing the World*. London: Allen Lane.

Middlemiss Lé Mon, Martha (2009). *The In-between Church: A Study of the Church of England's Role in Society through the Prism of Welfare*. Uppsala: Uppsala Universitet.

Miller, Daniel (1998) (ed.). *Material Cultures: Why Some Things Matter*. Chicago, IL: University of Chicago Press.

Miller, Jon (2002). *Missionary Zeal and Institutional Control: Organizational Contradictions in the Basel Mission on the Gold Coast, 1828–1917*. London: Routledge/Curzon Press.

Miller, Perry (1949/2005). *Jonathan Edwards*. Lincoln, NB: University of Nebraska Press.

Miller, William Ian (1993). *Humiliation and other Essays on Honor, Social Discomfort, and Violence*. Ithaca, NY: Cornell University Press.

Mills, C. Wright (1970). *The Sociological Imagination*. Harmondsworth: Penguin.

Milton, Kay, and Maruska Svasek (2005). *Mixed Emotions: Anthropological Studies of Feeling*. Oxford: Berg.

Mol, Hans (1976). *Identity and the Sacred: A Sketch for a New Social-Scientific Theory of Religion*. Oxford: Blackwell.

Monberg, Torben (1966). *The Religion of Bellona Island: A Study in the Place of Beliefs and Rites in the Social Life of Pre-Christian Bellona*. Copenhagen: National Museum of Denmark.

Moore, Barrington (1978). *Injustice: The Social Bases of Obedience and Revolt*. London: Macmillan.

Morgan, David (1998). *Visual Piety: A History and Theory of Popular Religious Images*. Berkeley and Los Angeles, CA: University of California Press.

References

Morgan, David (2005). *The Sacred Gaze: Religious Visual Culture in Theory and Practice*. Berkeley and Los Angeles, CA: University of California Press.

Morgan, Edmund S. (1966). *The Puritan Family*. New York: Harper & Row.

Morris, Brian (2006). *Religion and Anthropology: A Critical Introduction*. Cambridge: Cambridge University Press.

Mueggler, Eric (2001). *The Age of Wild Ghosts: Memory, Violence and Place in Southwest China*. Berkeley, Los Angeles, CA and London: California Press.

Mullan, Bob (1983). *Life as Laughter: Following Bhagwan Shree Rajneesh*. London: Routledge & Kegan Paul.

Neville, Robert Cummings (1996). *The Truth of Broken Symbols*. Albany, NY: State University of New York.

Nielsen, Klaus B. (2003). *Kinesisk Filosofi*. Aarhus: Aarhus Universitetsforlag.

Nouwen, Henri (2000). *Behold the Beauty of the Lord*. Notre Dame, IN: Ave Maria Press.

Nussbaum, Martha (2003a). *Upheavals of Thought: The Intelligence of Emotions*. Cambridge: Cambridge University Press.

Nussbaum, Martha (2003b). 'Emotions as Judgements of Value and Importance', in Robert C. Solomon (ed.), *What is an Emotion? Classic and Contemporary Readings*. 2nd edn. New York and Oxford: Oxford University Press, 271–83.

Oatley, Keith (1992). *Best Laid Schemes: The Psychology of Emotion*. Cambridge: Cambridge University Press.

Oatley, Keith, Dacher Keltner, and Jennifer M. Jenkins (2006). *Understanding Emotions*, 2nd edn. Malden, MA, Oxford, and Victoria: Blackwell.

O'Beirne, Maria (2004). 'Religion in England and Wales: Findings from the 2001 Home Office Citizenship Survey.' Home Office Resesearch Study 274.

Obeyesekere, Gananath (1978). 'The Firewalkers of Kataragama: The Rise of *bhakti* Religiosity in Buddhist Sri Lanka', *Journal of Asian Studies*, 37/3: 457–76.

Obeyesekere, Gananath (1981). *Medusa's Hair: An Essay on Personal Symbols and Religious Experience*. Chicago, IL, and London: University of Chicago Press.

Obeyesekere, Gananath (1990). *The Work of Culture: Symbolic Transformation in Psychoanalysis and Anthropology*. Chicago, IL: University of Chicago Press.

O'Donovan, Oliver (1980). *The Problem of Self-Love in Saint Augustine*. New Haven, CT: Yale University Press.

Olbricht, Thomas H., and Jerry L. Sumney (2001) (eds). *Paul and Pathos*. Atlanta, GA: Society of Biblical Literature.

Olsen, Marvin (1970) (ed.). *Power in Societies*. New York: Macmillan.

Orsi, Robert A. (2005). *Between Heaven and Earth: The Religious Worlds People Make and the Scholars who Study Them*. Princeton, NJ, and Oxford: Princeton University Press.

Ortner, Sherry B. (2002). 'On Key Symbols', in Michael Lambek (ed.), *A Reader in the Anthropology of Religion*. Malden, MA, Oxford, and Victoria, Australia: Blackwell, 158–67.

Otto, Rudolf (1917/1923). *The Idea of the Holy*, trans. John W. Harvey. London: Humphrey Milford and Oxford University Press.

Overland, Gwyneth (1998). 'The Role of Funeral Rites in Healing the Wounds of War among Cambodian Holocaust Survivors.' paper presented to the 20th Nordic Sociological Congress, Bergen, 17–19 June.

Packard, Vance (1957). *The Hidden Persuaders*. London: Longmans Green.

Palmer, Susan Jean (1994). *Moon Sisters, Krishna Mothers, Rajneesh Lovers: Women's Roles in New Religions*. New York: Syracuse.

Park, Chang-Won (2009). 'The Movement of Copying the Bible in South Korea: An Embodiment of Christian and Confucian Spiritualities', *Journal of Contemporary Religion*, 24/2: 205–17.

Parkinson, Brian, Agneta H. Fischer, and Antony S. R. Manstead (2005). *Emotion in Social Relations: Cultural, Group, and Interpersonal Processes*. New York and Hove: Psychology Press.

Parsons, Talcott (1977). *The Evolution of Societies*. Englewood Cliff, NJ: Prentice-Hall.

Parsons, Talcott (1978). *Action Theory and the Human Condition*. New York: Free Press.

Peirce, Charles S. (1998). *The Essential Peirce*, ii. Bloomington, IN: Indiana University Press.

Pickering, William S. F. (1984). *Durkheim's Sociology of Religion*. London: Routledge & Kegan Paul.

Pickering, William S. F. (1994) (ed.). *Durkheim on Religion*. Atlanta, GA: Scholars Press.

Pierce, Jennifer L. (1995). *Gender Trials: Emotional Lives in Contemporary Law Firms*. Berkeley and Los Angeles, CA, and London: University of California Press.

Poggi, Gianfranco (2001). *Forms of Power*. Cambridge: Polity.

Plutchik, Robert (1980). *Emotion: A Psychoevolutionary Synthesis*. New York: Harper and Row.

Pratt, James B. (1920). *The Religious Consciousness: A Psychological Study*. New York: Macmillan.

Prown, Jules D. (1993). 'Mind in Matter: An Introduction to Material Culture Theory and Method', in Robert B. St George (ed.), *Material Life in America, 1600–1860*. Washington: Smithsonian Institute Press, 17–37.

Raboteau, Albert J. (1978). *Slave Religion: The 'Invisible Institution' in the Antebellum South*. New York: Oxford University Press.

Ragin, Charles C. (2000). *Fuzzy–Set Social Science*. Chicago, IL, and London: University of Chicago Press.

Rambo, Lewis (1993). *Understanding Religious Conversion*. New Haven, CT: Yale University Press.

Rappaport, Roy (1999). *Ritual and Religion in the Making of Humanity*. Cambridge: Cambridge University Press.

Rasmussen, Knud (2002). *Myter og Sagn fra Grønland*. København: Sesam.

References

Reader, Ian, and George Tanabe, Jr (1998). *Practically Religious: Worldly Benefits and the Common Religion of Japan*. Honolulu: University of Hawaii Press.

Recht, Roland (2008). *Believing and Seeing: The Art of Gothic Cathedrals*. Chicago, IL: University of Chicago Press.

Reddy, William M. (2001). *The Navigation of Feeling: A Framework for the History of Emotions*. Cambridge: Cambridge University Press.

Repstad, Pål (2008). 'From Sin to a Gift from God: Constructions of Change in Conservative Christian Organizations', *Journal of Contemporary Religion*, 23/1: 17–31.

Reynolds, Barrie, and Margaret A. Stott (1987) (eds). *Material Anthropology: Contemporary Approaches to Material Culture*. New York: University Press of America.

Richards, Jeffrey, Scott Wilson, and Linda Woodhead (1999) (eds.). *Diana: The Making of a Media Saint*. London: I. B. Tauris.

Riesman, David (1950/1965). *The Lonely Crowd: A Study of the Changing American Character*. With Nathan Glazer and Reuel Denney. Abridged edn. with new preface. New Haven, CT, and London: Yale University Press.

Riis, Ole (1987). 'Sociological Approaches to the Danish Revivals', *Temenos*, 23: 93–107.

Riis, Ole (1998). 'Religion Re-Emerging: The Role of Religion in Legitimating Integration and Power in Modern Societies', *International Sociology*, 13/2: 249–72.

Riis, Ole (2001). *Metoder på tværs*. Copenhagen: DJØF Forlag.

Riis, Ole (2003). 'Sociologi som dialektisk samfundsbevidsthed', in M. Hviid Jacobsen (ed.). *Sociologiske Visioner*. Aarhus: Systime Academic, 84–103.

Riis, Ole (2005). *Samfundsvidenskab i Praksis*. Copenhagen: Hans Reitzels Forlag.

Riis, Ole (2007). 'Religious Pluralism in a Local and Global Perspective: Images of the Prophet Mohammed Seen in a Danish and a Global Perspective', in Peter Beyer and Lori Beaman (eds), *Religion, Globalization and Culture*. Leiden: Brill, 431–53.

Riis, Ole (2009). 'Methodology in the Sociology of Religion', in Peter Clarke (ed.), *The Oxford Handbook of the Sociology of Religion*. Oxford: Oxford University Press, 229–43.

Ritzer, George (2000). *The McDonaldization of Society*. Thousand Oaks, CA: Pine.

Roberts, Keith A. (1990). *Religion in Sociological Perspective*. Belmont, CA: Wadsworth.

Robson, Colin (2002). *Real World Research: A Resource for Social Scientists and Practitioner-Researchers*. Oxford and Malden, MA: Blackwell.

Roper, Lyndal (1994). *Oedipus and the Devil: Witchcraft, Sexuality and Religion in Early Modern Europe*. London: Routledge.

Rosaldo, Michelle (1980). *Knowledge and Passion: Ilongot Notions of Self and Social Life*. Cambridge and New York: Cambridge University Press.

Rosaldo, Renato (1989). 'Grief and a Headhunter's Rage', in Renato Rosaldo, *Culture and Truth: The Remaking of Social Analysis*. Boston, MA: Beacon Press, 1–21.

Rosaldo, Renato (1993). *Culture and Truth: The Remaking of Social Analysis*, 2nd edn. Boston, MA: Beacon Press.

Rosenberg, Morris (1990). 'Reflexivity and Emotions', *Social Psychology Quarterly*, 53/1: 3–12.

Rosenwein, Barbara H. (2006). *Emotional Communities in the Early Middle Ages*. Ithaca, NY, and London: Cornell University Press.

Rountree, Kathryn (2004). *Embracing the Witch and the Goddess: Feminist Ritual-Makers in New Zealand*. London: Routledge.

Rubin, Julius H. (2000). *The Other Side of Joy: Religious Melancholy among the Bruderhof*. Oxford: Oxford University Press.

Ruel, Malcolm (1982). 'Christians as Believers', in John Davis (ed.), *Religious Organization and Religious Experience*. London: Academic Press, 9–31.

Salomonsen, Jone (2001). *Enchanted Feminism: Ritual Constructions of Gender, Agency and Divinity among the Reclaiming Witches of San Francisco*. London: Routledge.

Sandel, Michael (1984). 'The Procedural Republic and the Unencumbered Self', *Political Theory*, 12/1: 81–96.

Sartre, Jean-Paul (1948). *The Emotions: Outline of a Theory*. New York: Philosophical Theory.

Sartre, Jean-Paul (1960). *Critique de la raison dialectique*. Paris: Éditions Gallimard.

Savage, Jon (2004). 'Researching Emotion: The Need for Coherence between Focus, Theory and Methodology', *Nursing Inquiry*, 11/1: 25–34.

Sayer, Andrew (1992). *Method in Social Science: A Realist Approach*. London: Routledge.

Sayer, Andrew (2004). 'Seeking the Geographies of Power', *Economy and Society*, 33/2: 255–70.

Scheff, Thomas (1994). *Bloody Revenge: Emotions, Nationalism and War*. Boulder, CO: Westview Press.

Scheler, Max (1912/1966). *Ressentiment*. New York: Free Press.

Scherer, Klaus R. (1984). 'On the Nature and Function of Emotion: A Component Process Approach', in Klaus R. Scherer and Paul Ekman (eds.), *Approaches to Emotion*. Hillsdale, NJ: Lawrence Erlbaum Associates, 293–317.

Schiffer, Michael Brian (1999). *The Material Life of Human Beings: Artifacts, Behavior and Communication*. London: Routledge.

Schwartz, Susan L. (2008). *Rasa: Performing the Divine in India*. New York: Columbia Press.

Scott, John (2001). *Power*. Cambridge: Polity.

Seale, Clive (1999). *The Quality of Qualitative Research*. London: Sage.

Shanks, Michael (1992). *Experiencing the Past*. London: Routledge.

Shilling, Chris (1997). 'Embodiment, Emotions, and the Sensation of Society', *Sociological Review*, 45/2: 195–219.

Shilling, Chris (2002). 'The Two Traditions in the Sociology of Emotions', in Jack Barbalet (ed.), *Emotions and Sociology*. Oxford and Malden, MA: Blackwell Publishing/Sociological Review, 10–32.

References

Shott, Susan (1979). 'Emotion and Social Life: A Symbolic Interactionist Analysis', *American Journal of Sociology*, 84/6: 1317–34.

Simmel, Georg (1911/1968). *Georg Simmel: The Conflict in Modern Culture and Other Essays*, trans. Peter Etzkorn. New York: Teachers College Press.

Simmel, Georg (1908/1971a). 'Group Expansion and the Development of Individuality', in Donald Levine (ed.), *Georg Simmel on Indivuality and Social Forms*. Chicago, IL: University of Chicago Press, 251–93.

Simmel, Georg (1908/1971b). 'How is Society Possible?', in Donald Levine (ed.), *Georg Simmel on Individuality and Social Forms*. Chicago, IL: University of Chicago Press, 6–22.

Simmel, Georg (1908/1971c). 'The Problem of Sociology', in Donald Levine (ed.), *Georg Simmel on Individuality and Social Forms*. Chicago, IL: University of Chicago Press, 23–35.

Simmel, Georg (1917/1976). 'The Crisis of Culture', in Peter A. Lawrence (ed.), *Georg Simmel: Sociologist and European*. Middlesex: Nelson, 253–66.

Simmel, Georg (1907/1990). *The Philosophy of Money*. London: Routledge.

Simmel, Georg (1997). *Essays on Religion*, (ed.) and trans. Horst Jürgen Helle. New Haven, CT, and London: Yale University Press.

Simmel, Georg (1898/1997). 'A Contribution to the Sociology of Religion', in *Essays on Religion*, (ed.) and trans. Horst Jürgen Helle. New Haven, CT, and London: Yale University Press, 101–20.

Simmel, Georg (1904/1997). 'Religion and the Contradictions of Life', in *Essays on Religion*, (ed.) and trans. Horst Jürgen Helle. New Haven, CT, and London: Yale University Press, 36–44.

Simmel Georg (1912/1997). 'Religion', in *Essays on Religion*, (ed.) and trans. Horst Jürgen Helle. New Haven, CT, and London: Yale University Press, 137–214.

Simmel, Georg (1914/1997). 'Rembrant's Religious Art', in *Essays on Religion*, (ed.) and trans. Horst Jürgen Helle. New Haven, CT, and London: Yale University Press, 78–97.

Singer, Milton (1960). 'The Great Tradition of Hinduism in the City of Madras', in Charles Leslie (ed.), *Anthropology of Folk Religion*. New York: Vintage Books, 105–16.

Skeggs, Beverley (1997). *Formations of Class and Gender: Becoming Respectable*. London: Sage.

Smart, Carol (2007). *Personal Life: New Directions in Sociological Thinking*. Cambridge: Polity.

Smart, Ninian (1998). *Dimensions of the Sacred: An Anatomy of the World's Beliefs*. Berkeley and Los Angeles, CA: University of California Press.

Smelser, Neil (1963). *Collective Behaviour*. London: Routledge & Kegan Paul.

Smith, Adam (1776/1998). *An Inquiry into the Nature and Causes of the Wealth of Nations*. Oxford: Oxford University Press.

Smith, Anthony D. (2003). *Chosen Peoples: Sacred Sources of National Identity*. Oxford: Oxford University Press.

Smith, Christian (2005). *Soul Searching: The Religious and Spiritual Lives of Amercian Teenagers*. New York: Oxford University Press.

Smith, Jonathan Z. (1988). *Imagining Religion: From Babylon to Jonestown*. Chicago, IL, and London: University of Chicago Press.

Smith, Mick, Joyce Davidson, Laura Cameron, and Liz Bondi (2009) (eds). *Emotion, Place and Culture*. Aldershot: Ashgate.

Smith, Thomas S. (1992). *Strong Interaction*. Chicago, IL: University of Chicago Press.

Sointu, Eeva, and Linda Woodhead (2008). 'Holistic Spirituality, Gender, and Expressive Selfhood', *Journal for the Scientific Study of Religion*, 47/2: 259–76.

Solomon, Robert (1993). *The Passions: Emotions and the Meaning of Life*. Indianapolis, IN, and Cambridge: Hackett Publishing.

Solomon, Robert C. (2000). 'The Philosophy of Emotions', in Michael Lewis and Jeannette M. Haviland-Jones (eds.), *Handbook of Emotions*. 2nd edn. New York: Guildford Press, 3–15.

Solomon, Robert C. (2003) (ed.). *What is an Emotion?* 2nd edn. Classic and Contemporary Readings. New York and Oxford: Oxford University Press.

Sorabji, Richard (2002). *Emotion and Peace of Mind: From Stoic Agitation to Christian Temptation*. Oxford: Oxford University Press.

Soskice, Janet Martin (1985). *Metaphor and Religious Language*. Oxford: Clarendon Press.

Spickard, James V., et al (2002) (eds.). *Personal Knowledge and Beyond*. New York: New York University Press.

Spillman, Lyn (ed.). *Cultural Sociology*. Malden, MA, and Oxford: Blackwell, 199–220.

Spinoza, Benedict (1677/2001). *Ethics*, trans. W. H. White and rev. A. H. Stirling. Ware: Wordsworth.

Spurlock, John C., and Cynthia A. Magistro (1998). *New and Improved: The Transformation of Women's Emotional Culture*. New York and London: New York University Press.

Stanczak, Gregory C. (2007) (ed.). *Visual Research Methods: Image Society and Representation*. London: Sage.

Starhawk (1979). *The Spiral Dance: A Rebirth of the Ancient Religion of the Great Goddess*. San Francisco, CA: Harper and Row.

Stearns, Carol Z., and Peter H. Stearns (1985). 'Emotionology: Clarifying the History of Emotions and Emotional Standards', *American Historical Review*, 90: 813–36.

Stearns, Carol Z., and Peter H. Stearns (1986). *Anger: The Struggle for Emotional Control in America's History*. Chicago, IL: University of Chicago Press.

Stearns, Peter (1994). *American Cool: Constructing a Twentieth-Century American Style*. New York: New York University Press.

Stearns, Peter, and Jan Lewis (1998) (eds). *An Emotional History of the United States*. New York and London: New York University Press.

References

Steedly, Mary Margaret (1993). *Hanging without a Rope: Narrative Experience in Colonial and Postcolonial Karoland*. Princeton, NJ: Princeton University Press.

Stets, Jan E., and Jonathan H. Turner (2007). *Handbook of the Sociology of Emotions*. New York: Springer.

Stone, Lawrence (1977). *The Family, Sex and Marriage in England 1500–1800*. London: Weidenfeld & Nicolson.

Stringer, Martin (1999). *On the Perception of Worship*. Birmingham: University of Birmingham.

Sturlason, Snorre (1899/2009). *Kongesagaer*. Oslo: Stenersen.

Sullivan, Shirley D. (1995). *Psychological and Ethical Ideas: What the Early Greeks Say*. Leiden and New York: E. J. Brill.

Swidler, Ann (1980). 'Love and Adulthood in American Culture', in Neil J. Smelser and E. H. Erikson (eds.), *Themes of Work and Love in Adulthood*. Cambridge, MA: University of Harvard Press, 120–47.

Swidler, Ann (2003). *Talk of Love: How Culture Matters*. Chicago, IL: University of Chicago Press.

Tambiah, Stanley (2002). 'Form and Meaning of Magical Acts', in Michael Lambek (ed.), *A Reader in the Anthropology of Religion*. Malden, MA, Oxford, and Victoria, Australia: Blackwell, 340–57.

Tashakkori, Abbas, and Charles Teddlie (2003) (eds.). *Handbook of Mixed Methods in the Social and Behavioral Sciences*. Thousand Oaks, CA: Sage.

Tashakkorie, Abbas, and Charle Teddlie (2009). *Foundations of Mixed Methods Research: Integrating Quantitative and Qualitative Approaches in the Social and Behavioral Sciences*. Thousand Oaks, CA: Sage.

Taylor, Charles (1989). *Sources of the Self: The Making of the Modern Identity*. Cambridge: Cambridge University Press.

Taylor, Charles (1991). *The Ethics of Authenticity*. Cambridge, MA: Harvard University Press.

Taylor, Charles (2002). *Varieties of Religion Today*. Cambridge, MA: Harvard University Press.

Thoits, Peggy A. (1989). 'The Sociology of Emotions', *Annual Review of Sociology*, 15: 317–42.

Thompson, Edward P. (1972). *The Making of the English Working Class*. Harmondsworth: Penguin.

Tipton, Steven M. (1982). *Getting Saved from the Sixties*. Berkeley and Los Angeles, CA: University of California Press.

Tiryakian, Edward (1962/1979). *Existentialism and Sociologism: Two Perspectives on the Individual and Society*. Englewood Cliffs, NJ: Prentice-Hall.

Tocqueville, Alexis de (1835, 1840/1988). *Democracy in America*, trans. George Lawrence and (ed.) J. P. Mayer. New York: HarperPerennial.

Trilling, Lionel (1973). *Sincerity and Authenticity*. Cambridge, MA: Harvard University Press.

Turner, Jonathan H. (2007). *Human Emotions*. London: Routledge.

Turner, Jonathan H., and Jan E. Stets (2005). *The Sociology of Emotions*. Cambridge: Cambridge University Press.

Turner, Victor (1967). *The Forest of Symbols: Aspects of Ndembu Ritual*. Ithaca, NY, and London: Cornell University Press.

Vitebsky, Piers (1993). *Dialogues with the Dead: The Discussion of Mortality among the Sora of Eastern India*. Cambridge: Cambridge University Press.

Von Hendy, Andrew (2002). *The Modern Construction of Myth*. Bloomington, IN: Indiana University Press.

Vygotsky, Lev S. (1987). *The Collected Works of L. S. Vygotsky*, i. *Problems of General Psychology*, (eds) R. W. Rieber and A. S. Carton. New York: Plenum Press.

Wagner, Peter (2008). *Modernity as Experience and Interpretation: A New Sociology of Modernity*. Cambridge: Polity.

Wagner-Pacifici, Robin, and Barry Schwartz (2002). 'The Vietnam Veterans Memorial: Commemorating a Difficult Past', in Lyn Spillman (ed.), *Cultural Sociology*. Malden, MA, and Oxford: Blackwell, 199–220.

Walby, Sylvia (2007). 'Systems Theory and Multiple Intersecting Social Inequalities', *Philosophy of the Social Sciences*, 37/4: 449–70.

Walby, Sylvia (2009). *Globalization and Inequalities: Complexity and Contested Modernities*. London: Sage.

Wallis, Robert J. (2003). *Shamans/Neo-Shamans: Ecstasies. Alternative Archaeologies and Contemporary Pagans*. London: Routledge.

Walter, Tony (1999) (ed.). *The Mourning for Diana*. Oxford: Berg.

Walzer, Michael (1965). *The Revolution of the Saints: A Study in the Origins of Radical Politics*. Cambridge, MA: Harvard University Press.

Warner, Pnina (2002). *Imagined Diasporas among Manchester Muslims*. Oxford and Santa Fe, NM: SAR Press.

Watson, Sophie (2006). *City Publics: The (Dis)enchantments of Urban Encounters*. London: Routledge.

Watts, Alan (1973). *In My Own Way: An Autobiography 1915–1965*. London: Jonathan Cape.

Weber, Max (1946). *From Max Weber: Essays in Sociology*, (eds) Hans H. Gerth and C. Wright Mills. New York: Oxford University Press.

Weber, Max (1968). *Economy and Society*. 2 vols. Berkeley and Los Angeles, CA: University of California Press.

Weber, Max (1988). *Gesammelte aufsätze zur Religionssoziologie*. 3 vols. Tübingen: Mohr.

Weber, Max (1904–5/1991). *The Protestant Ethic and the Spirit of Capitalism*. London: Harper Collins.

Weber, Max (1915/1948/1991). 'Religious Rejections of the World and their Directions', in Hans H. Gerth and C. Wright Mills (eds), *From Max Weber: Essays in Sociology*. London: Routledge, 323–62.

References

Weber, Max (1919/1948/1991a). 'Politics as a Vocation', in Hans H. Gerth and C. Wright Mills (eds), *From Max Weber: Essays in Sociology*. London: Routledge, 77–128.

Weber, Max (1919/1948/1991b). 'Science as a Vocation', in Hans H. Gerth and C. Wright Mills (eds), *From Max Weber: Essays in Sociology*. London: Routledge, 129–58.

Westen, Drew (2007). *The Political Brain: The Role of Emotion in Deciding the Fate of the Nation*. New York: Public Affairs.

Whitehouse, Harvey (2000). *Arguments and Icons: Divergent Modes of Religiosity*. Oxford: Oxford University Press.

Whitehouse, Harvey, and James Laidlaw (2004) (eds.). *Ritual and Memory: Toward a Comparative Anthropology of Religion*. Walnut Creek, CA: Alta Mira.

Wilce, James M. (2004). 'Passionate Scholarship: Recent Anthropologies of Emotion', *Reviews in Anthropology*, 33/1: 1–17.

Wild, Stefan (1997) (ed.). *The Quran as Text*. Leiden: Brill.

Williams, Raymond (1977). *Marxism and Literature*. Oxford: Oxford University Press.

Williams, Rhys H. (2007). 'The Cultural Contexts of Collective Action: Constraints, Opportunities, and the Symbolic Life of Social Movements', in David A. Snow, Sarah A. Soule, and Hanspeter Kriesi (eds), *The Blackwell Companion to Social Movements*. Malden, MA, and Oxford: Blackwell, 91–115.

Williams, Simon (2001). *Emotions and Social Theory*. London: Sage.

Winkelman, Michael (1997). 'Altered States of Consciousness and Religious Behavior', in S. D. Glazier (ed.), *Anthropology of Religion*. Westport, CT: Praeger.

Winnicott, Donald W. (1971). *Playing and Reality*. London: Tavistock.

Wittgenstein, Ludwig (2002). 'Remarks on Fraser's *Golden Bough*', in Michael Lambek (ed.), *A Reader in the Anthropology of Religion*. Malden, MA, Oxford, and Victoria, Australia: Blackwell, 85–9.

Wolf, Kurt H. (1950). *The Sociology of Georg Simmel*. Glencoe, IL: Free Press.

Woodhead, Linda (1999). 'Diana and the Religion of the Heart', in Jeffrey Richards, Scott Wilson, and Linda Woodhead (eds), *Diana: The Making of a Media Saint*. London: I. B. Tauris, 119–39.

Woodhead, Linda (2004). *An Introduction to Christianity*. Cambridge: Cambridge University Press.

Woodhead, Linda (2007). 'Gender Differences in Religious Practice and Significance', in James Beckford and N. J. Demerath III (eds), *The Sage Handbook of the Sociology of Religion*. Los Angeles, CA, London, New Delhi, and Singapore: Sage, 550–70.

Woodhead, Linda (2010). 'New Forms of Public Religion: Spirituality in Global Civil Society', in Wim Hofstee and Arie van der Kooij (eds), *Religion, Public or Private?* Leiden: LISOR.

Woodhead, Linda, and Paul Heelas (2000) (eds.). *Religion in Modern Times: An Interpretive Anthology*. Oxford and Malden, MA: Blackwell.

Woolf, Virginia (1984). *A Room of One's Own and Three Guineas*. London: Hogarth Press.

Worsley, Peter (1957). *The Trumpet Shall Sound*. New York: Schocken Books.

Wouters, Cas (1977). 'Informalization and the Civilizing Process', in Peter Gleichmann et al. (eds), *Human Figurations: Essays for Norbert Elias*. Amsterdam: Amsterdams Sociologisch Tijdschrift, 437–55.

Wouters, Cas (1992). 'On Status Competition and Emotional Management: The Study of Emotions as a New Field', in Mike Featherstone (ed.), *Cultural Theory and Cultural Change*. London: Sage, 229–52.

Wrong, David (1967–8). 'Some Problems in Defining Social Power', in John Scott (ed.), *Power*, i. London: Routledge.

Wulff, David M. (1991). *Psychology of Religion*. New York: Wiley.

Wuthnow, Robert (1996). *Sharing the Journey: Support Groups and America's New Quest for a Community*. London: Free Press.

Wuthnow, Robert (1997). *Rethinking Materialism: Perspectives in the Spiritual Dimension of Economic Behavior*. Grand Rapids, MI: Eerdmans.

Young, Iris Marion (2005). *On Female Body Experience: 'Throwing Like a Girl' and Other Essays*. Oxford and New York: Oxford University Press.

Zablocki, Benjamin (1971). *The Joyful Community: An Account of The Bruderhof, a Communal Movement now in its third Generation*. Chicago, IL: University of Chicago Press.

Zagzebski, Linda Trinkaus (1996). *Virtues of the Mind: An Inquiry into the Nature of Virtue and the Ethical Foundations of Knowledge*. Cambridge: Cambridge University Press.

Zagzebski, Linda Trinkaus (2004). *Divine Motivation Theory*. Cambridge: Cambridge University Press.

Zeldin, Theodore (1982). 'Personal History and the History of the Emotions', *Journal of Social History*, 15: 339–48.

Zubrzycki, Geneviève (2006). *The Crosses of Auschwitz: Nationalism and Religion in Post-Communist Poland*. Chicago, IL, and London: University of Chicago Press.

Index

Note: page numbers in *italic* refer to figures.

Index

Index

Index